IN SPITE
— OF —
HEROIN

DANA
CHASE

authorHOUSE®

AuthorHouse™
1663 Liberty Drive
Bloomington, IN 47403
www.authorhouse.com
Phone: 1 (800) 839-8640

Some names and identifying details have been changed to protect the privacy of individuals.

Published by AuthorHouse   10/13/2016

ISBN: 978-1-5246-2803-1 (sc)
ISBN: 978-1-5246-2804-8 (hc)
ISBN: 978-1-5246-2802-4 (e)

Library of Congress Control Number: 2016914635

Print information available on the last page.

Any people depicted in stock imagery provided by Thinkstock are models, and such images are being used for illustrative purposes only. Certain stock imagery © Thinkstock.

This book is printed on acid-free paper.

Can the child within my heart rise above
Can I sail through the changing ocean tides
Can I handle the seasons of my life

Landslide
Stevie Nicks

1

THE LARGE CEMENT ELEPHANT IN the center of the playground's swings, slides, and teeter-totters prompted the name—Elephant Park. The elephant served no recreational purpose other than as a place for kids to climb and perch for a spell. The playground sat amid towering elm, oak, and maple trees, which were spaced around the park much like a large group of people who'd held hands and spread out as much as the circle would allow, then released hands and stepped back a few more feet. The park's official name was Percy Goodwin Park.

I'd learned to play tennis as a young girl in Elephant Park, in River Bend, North Dakota, and for me it would become a sport that would soothe my soul and sustain my body at times in my life when despair nearly drowned me. My best friend as a child, Jane, introduced me to tennis in third grade. With pigtails, tennis dresses, and my wooden Chris Evert racquet, I learned how to hit the ball. Jane was the only girl in her family, with three older and three younger brothers. I was my all-girl family's baby, with three older sisters. In our Catholic universe in River Bend, our family had been considered small.

Elephant Park was located between the two homes I lived in as a child and the two homes where my husband, Brad, and I would raise our identical twin sons, Ryder and Avery. All four houses were within three blocks of Elephant Park.

As Ryder and Avery grew older, I'd occasionally walk our dog, Murphy, a wheaten terrier, past all four of those homes, taking less than an hour for the trip. Often times it was impossible to contain my tears as I recalled how blessed I was for so many years of my life. The tears of late were saturated with anguish. I'd traveled the world as a flight attendant for twenty-three years and lived in several cities other than River Bend for fifteen years, but it was there, within that one-mile radius, that I lived my life as a child and as a mother.

The northside of River Bend was predominantly residential, with single-family homes where pride in ownership was evident. Timber Crest was a cozy subdivision, featuring a wide range of houses from ramblers to million-dollar estates. Brad and I purchased a home in Timber Crest in January 2007. Our twins were fourteen years old when we'd moved the one mile north. It was a peaceful neighborhood with winding streets bearing names of trees—lilac, maple, hickory, and evergreen.

In 1971, when I was in eighth grade, my folks moved us to Willow Road in Timber Crest. It was the home where both my parents passed away in 2008. The brick rambler on Willow Road was three-tenths of a mile from our two-story, flat-roofed home on Acorn Drive.

The backyard of our house on Acorn Drive offered a rare elevated view of the Red River—one of the main reasons we'd bought it. In a region of North Dakota known for its flat farmland, this type of view was the exception, and anyone who sat on our back deck, facing south, appreciated it. The home was full of large windows that allowed sunlight to pass through all day long.

A chain-link fence enclosed our gently sloping lot. Evergreens taller than the house gave us privacy from our neighbors. The land that offered us the river view was part of the veterans' hospital on Elm Street. From our deck, we had a panoramic scene of the winding river, with clusters of trees providing a habitat for deer, raccoon, rabbits, squirrels, and countless species of birds, including owls, woodpeckers, and at least one eagle. On the other side of the river was Minnesota, featuring a solid grove of trees extending along the riverbank and providing a backdrop that changed with the seasons.

The house on Acorn Drive was our second home on the Red River. The first one, at 1601 Elm Street, was purchased by the city and demolished in 2008 after new flood zones were drawn up following the epic 1997 flood.

On June 22, 2012, the sky over my River Bend neighborhood hosted a variety of clouds. There were the dense white cumulonimbus that seemed large and thick enough to conceal a chorus of harp-playing angels. These were seemingly chased by smaller dark clouds—fleeting, ominous, scudding quickly across the horizon and randomly dropping rain in spurts. The baseball field in Elephant Park would get wet, but the tennis courts twenty yards away would stay dry.

None of this mattered to me.

I was in Kansas, far away from the DEA squad making its way to our home in three government vehicles—two cars and one van. Six men with badges and a dog were about to knock on the front door of our house and search our home for drugs. My twenty-year-old son Ryder was home alone, high.

In Overland Park, Kansas, I'd joined my three sisters for a coveted sisters' weekend. At least once a year, we gathered—this year at the home of my sister Jackie. Ann, the oldest, lived seasonally between Denver and Pelican Lake, near Detroit Lakes, Minnesota—fifty five miles from River Bend. Third-born Kelly traveled from Grand Forks, North Dakota, seventy miles north of River Bend. As the youngest, I had an established fan club of three doting sisters. They were eight, seven, and three and a half when I came along.

As the drug squad turned into Timber Crest, I was shopping with my sisters, picking out inexpensive necklaces at Charming Charlie's. Some I would wear; others I would later give away, never having worn them.

When the DEA officers pounded on the front door, I was 625 miles away having peanut butter frozen yogurt with hot fudge at Peach Berry, laughing with my sisters. Hundreds of investigation and surveillance hours had gone into the bust. The squad had volumes of documented evidence that Ryder was dealing—selling painkillers, oxycodone, and other drugs.

"DEA. Open up; we have a search warrant," one officer demanded.

"Okay, okay; don't break the door down, I'll open it," Ryder yelled back after peeking through the blinds.

Ryder was high on oxycodone, but his fear was abruptly sobering him. He knew what was about to happen. After a quick trip to the bathroom to wipe the sweat off his face, he let frantic Murphy out into the backyard, and then opened the front door.

The first officer to enter pinned him forcefully against the wall. "Where is it, Ryder? Just show us where, so we can get this over with. No reason to turn this nice home upside down."

He lifted Ryder up off the hardwood floor.

"Whadda ya mean?"

"Don't be a smart-ass, punk. We know you're trafficking. Make this easy on yourself."

"Look around all you want. I'm not a supplier, just an addict trying to survive."

Two officers stayed with Ryder while four others searched his bedroom, his bathroom, his brother's bedroom, and our main-floor living rooms, but they stayed out of the master bedroom. Murphy went nuts outside, barking and jumping against the sliding glass doors. The canine they brought sniffed our home in search of drugs. An hour later, they left empty-handed.

"You got lucky this time. We will catch you; it's just a matter of time," the officer promised.

Ryder walked to the back of the house and out onto the deck to smoke a cigarette and calm down. Murphy darted into the house to follow the scent of the strange dog that had invaded her turf. Ryder didn't notice the deer with her fawn grazing near the river, the squirrels running along the top of the chain-link fence, the scent of blooming lilac bushes, or the lawn that needed to be mowed. He took a long draw on his cigarette and held the smoke in his lungs. What he did notice is he'd just beat the DEA; they had blown their chance. What could stop him now? He exhaled. About twenty minutes and two cigarettes later, he drove to a friend's house to smoke pot and make plans.

2

MY SISTER JACKIE'S HOME WAS a large two-story in a newer development of Overland Park that required homeowners to pick their house colors and floor plans from previously approved options. The result was a continuity and visual rhythm to the upper-middle-class neighborhood that felt tidy, safe, and arranged.

The three guest bedrooms each had a distinct and understated décor. Mine was black French toile. The walls and linens were white with black piping, with several black-framed scenes of rural France arranged above a three-foot-long black shelf on the wall at the foot of the bed. A narrow vase held five red silk poppies on the shelf, the only contrasting color in the room. Below the décor was a white wooden bench padded with black-and-white gingham, where I stacked my clothes each night instead of putting them back in my suitcase. I had an adjacent bathroom to myself. If it was a hotel room, it would be considered high end.

I felt grounded here mostly because of the intimate relationship the four of us shared, but also because of the insulation, the escape from the circumstances with my sons back in River Bend. My sense of refuge was as much about where I was as where I was not.

Jackie had spoiled us with fabulous meals, wine, and transportation around town and to the Kansas City airport forty-five miles away. We wanted to do something special for her, so I volunteered to organize her pantry. The size of a small walk-in closet, it was out of control. My sisters considered me to be most qualified to lead the charge, since I'd had a cleaning business up until a month before our Kansas reunion.

I had called my business New Day Design, and I'd offered housecleaning, decluttering, and organizing services. I'd sold it to a recent college graduate but had retained two housecleaning clients.

I had become a certified life coach in 2003 and a certified feng shui practitioner in 2008. Both certifications resulted from following my intuition—a profound influence in my life. I offered feng shui and life-coaching services through a second business website, Chase Consulting. Neither life-coaching nor feng shui services were in demand.

The housecleaning service had filled my books and paid the bills. But the physicality of it had taken its toll on my shoulders and elbows. I was reluctant to give up the perks: controlling my schedule, decent money, and work I enjoyed. Yet ultimately my passion to remain on the tennis court trumped owning my own business, and compromised shoulders and elbows did not perform in my sport.

When I'd left for Kansas, I'd taken five days off from my new career in sales at a mattress store in the Dakota Mall in River Bend. My new manager had kindly agreed to the time off since I'd had the trip planned for nearly a year.

Before we began to dismantle Jackie's pantry, I said to her, "Okay, we're gonna throw away everything you don't use. All the expired stuff or anything broken goes. Then we'll clean and organize it. I want you to think about what you're making room for in your life."

"You mean the new kitchen stuff I want?"

She smiled, knowing it was about getting rid of stuff not acquiring more.

I wanted Jackie to be aware that she was working with energy. By decluttering physical space, she would reduce emotional and spiritual "clutter" as well and make room for greater blessings. It's important, according to feng shui, to be mindful of what you're making room for in order to manifest your intentions.

I believe the best way to get what you want is to help someone get what they want. The simple act of helping Jackie would bless me too. I thought about what I was making room for. No question for me: better days, and I wanted our sons to get into school, clean up their lives, and become the young men we'd raised them to be.

I knew they were heavy cigarettes smokers (at one point this alone would have gravely disappointed me) but also that they were smoking pot. They worked full time, late-night graveyard shifts at convenience stores. It was hard to keep track of them because of their nocturnal schedule. They no longer played tennis or golf or anything else they'd grown up enjoying. They'd sleep all day, then at night go to work or disappear with friends. Neither of them was in school, nor did they have any ambition to enroll. Brad and I had monthly conversations with them about starting at one of several local vo-tech colleges. It proved impossible to force them into a commitment.

Ryder had completed rehab for addiction to painkillers fifteen months earlier, while in his senior year of high school. He had come to us seeking help, ready to change, it seemed. Avery was living in a house with friends, but now broke, he was planning to move back home with us.

Yes, I was hoping for better days.

Brad called while we were knee-deep in small appliances, cookware, boxed meals, and canned fruits and vegetables.

"How's it going?" he asked.

"Great, we're digging into Jackie's pantry, going to reorganize it before someone goes missing in there."

My sisters laughed as Jackie shook her head.

"What time do you get home tomorrow?" He sounded concerned.

"Is everything okay?" I asked.

"Yes, all fine here, just wondering about your ETA."

Estimated time of arrival, we talked in flight attendant lingo. I'd resigned from Northwest Airlines in 2007 after twenty-three years, but Brad was still flying and in his twenty-eighth year as a flight attendant.

"Should be to River Bend by four thirty if I don't get bumped," I told him.

I flew standby for free since Brad was still an airline employee. My trip home would be two legs, a connection in Minneapolis and on to River Bend.

"Sounds good; call me when you land, and I'll leave for the airport. I'll check the loads and let you know if it's an issue."

I later realized Brad knew about the attempted DEA bust but wasn't going to ruin my last day with my sisters by telling me over the phone.

7

Because my sisters no longer lived in River Bend, our conversations were intermittent. Ann and I spoke most weeks. Jackie and Kelly, I only spoke to once a month or less. I felt equally close to all of them, though. They would do anything for me, and the time with them in Kansas was a blessed reprieve. I was weary from years of dealing with our sons' debacles.

Their misguided trail included traffic accidents, numerous tickets, and a "minor in possession charge" for both boys their junior year. Avery had dropped out of high school when his girlfriend became pregnant (she miscarried nine days later). He completed his GED a couple of months later.

Ryder had a diploma from River Bend High, class of 2011. There was no commencement ceremony or graduation party, since Ryder earned his diploma despite horrible attendance, a D average, plenty of attitude, and the grace of a vice principal. Neither of their advancements seemed worthy of graduation announcements or celebration. There was no prom or senior tennis team banquet; no college applications were sent. There were plenty more mishaps, too numerous to list. None of the milestones we assumed would be a part of their high school years had unfolded.

We sisters spent our last night in Kansas in Jackie's backyard, gathered in cozy outdoor furniture with a large deck umbrella defining our circle. There was also a full-size picnic table, and an often-used chef's grill within the laid cobblestone underfoot. The patio was nestled between their house and a four-tiered garden of shrubs, trees, and flowers that provided privacy from neighboring homes. White Christmas lights were strung along the garden trees, and several spotlights illuminated various arrangements of blooming flowers. A hot, humid Kansas day had led to a warm evening with the sound of distant thunder rumbling. We were all fatigued from the declutter project that had taken five hours to complete.

"Good effort, gals; thanks for participating in the pantry purge," I said as I rocked in my deck chair.

Jackie held up her wine glass, and we all leaned in as our wine glasses met.

"Yes, let's toast. Here's to sisters. Love you guys, so grateful for our time together. Thanks for all your help; the pantry is amazing. I feel so much better!" Jackie beamed.

"Do I really have to go home? Maybe you and Tim can adopt me."

I was grinning at Jackie. My sisters and I had covered the topic of my boys' problems plenty during the trip. I would allow only brief conversations about it before I'd change the subject. I didn't want it to be about me, about them; that's what I needed a break from.

"We'd love that, a live-in declutter pro. Where do I sign?" Jackie chuckled.

"It's going to get better, Dana. You and Brad have laid the foundation; the boys will come around," Ann encouraged.

"You know how I am, how I don't worry about much?" I queried.

"Yes, that's true; you're so unlike most mothers that way," Kelly said.

"Well, I'm starting to wonder if I'm an eternal optimist or the queen of denial. If I worried about every little thing with those two, I couldn't function. But I wonder if my optimism has blinded me. Maybe I trust to a fault?"

"You've got great instincts, Dana; your intuition is well-tuned," Jackie said.

"And Brad is a great father. The two of you will get them on track; they're just going through a stage a lot of kids go through," Kelly added.

"Honestly, I think the fact that I smoked pot at their age has had me less concerned than most parents. I grew out of it and got on with my life; I keep assuming they will too. At least they hold down jobs. They have a good work ethic. There's something to be said for that."

There it was—my tightrope saunter between optimism and denial.

"The boys' work ethic deserves to be acknowledged. Their generation has an extreme sense of entitlement. My friend who teaches high school talks about it all the time; her students want everything handed to them," Kelly said.

Jackie refilled our wine glasses.

"I try and figure out what we should have done differently. There had to have been missed opportunities to—"

Before I could continue, Kelly interrupted.

"That's normal; it's called parenthood. You can beat yourself up over the woulda, coulda, shouldas. Don't do it; it leads to nothing good. And besides, you're a good mom; you're good parents; we've all been witnesses."

It had grown dark, and our faces disappeared in the shadows. I was focused on one of the spotlights revealing a cluster of peach and red geraniums. Despite what my sisters said, I felt guilty. The guilt was not about what I'd done; it was about what I'd failed to do. And I didn't even know for sure what that could be. I just knew my sons were off track, and I was their mother. How could it not be partially my fault?

Guilt was like a disfigurement I'd grown to accept, a dark spot on my soul that I was aware of but didn't allow myself to be consumed by, except for the occasional moments when I'd linger in reflection, when I'd imagine what my life would look like without it.

I saw something moving in the flowers.

"Look at the far spotlight." I pointed. "Is that a snake?" I wasn't sure if it was a hose or a black snake. It was not the small green garden species I'd seen on rare occasion in North Dakota.

"Oh my God, it is! … *Tim!*"

Jackie yelled, and we all moved into the house. Our sisters week had wrapped up, except for the drive to the Kansas City airport early the next morning.

3

I GAZED OUT THE PORTHOLE WINDOW from seat 9F on the DC-9 departing Minneapolis and headed west to River Bend. It was only a fifty-minute flight, and I'd flown the route hundreds of times, both as a commuter and as part of the working flight crew. Once out of the city, the view featured endless miles of farmland early into the brief Minnesota growing season. It was beautiful, serene, and familiar. Fields, vegetation, lakes, rivers, and occasional rural communities rolled along the earth below. It was a place in the world that allowed you to breathe, to pause, leaving you alone with your thoughts, making no demands for your attention. I absorbed the view of farmers' fields that had survived another winter, silently producing whatever had been seeded after the snow had melted months ago.

River Bend sprawled alongside the Red River, the natural border separating North Dakota from Minnesota. It was a perfect day to fly— clear, high visibility, light winds—it seemed as though we'd floated to the ground. Fifteen minutes after landing, Brad arrived to bring me home.

"How was your trip? Did you have a good time?" Brad asked as he loaded my bags into the flatbed of our black Ford Sportrac.

"So awesome; the best." I smiled

"Did you see Lauren and Jason?" he asked, wondering about two of Jackie's grown children who also lived in Overland Park.

"Yep, saw everyone. Jason's wrapping up his residency, and Lauren finished up her master's a couple of months ago. Her baby's due in December."

Jason would soon be a thoracic surgeon, and Lauren was securing her teaching credentials and was pregnant with her third son. I wondered what it might feel like—the privilege of having only to present the facts of your child's pursuits and let the truth do the bragging while you humbly glowed. Instead Brad and I had each mastered a few canned lines, carefully chosen, concise and generic, to conceal the concern and disappointment we'd both felt when someone asked us, "How are the boys doing?"

"They prefer work over school … holding off on school until they're sure of what they'd like to pursue … off track a bit, but finding their way back … they've got a great work ethic …"

We'd once felt kindhearted validation from everyone: pushing a stroller with identical twin boys, adorable and perfect. Onlookers would smile, tilt their heads, and make a quiet, adoring purr. I was humbled to be the recipient of that unsolicited positive vibe from people wherever we went. Knowing some parents pushed a child who had serious struggles physically or mentally made me feel blessed and grateful.

I continued as Brad looked ahead as we drove home.

"We had a lot of laughs. Did some shopping, walking, mostly hanging out talking. But it was so hot we had to get the walks in before eleven, or it was miserable. But it was great on her patio at night—no mosquitoes, warm, lots of fireflies, and wine." I sighed.

It felt good to be home, now with more fond memories with my sisters.

"Glad to hear it was fun for you, a nice break."

The drive home from the airport was only four miles. It was cooler in River Bend, but still a warm summer day was winding down, with a gorgeous pink sunset leaking out between passive clouds. In a little over two weeks, it would be the Fourth of July. The five days I'd spent in Kansas would turn out to be nearly half of my total days off from working that entire summer, between my sales job and housecleaning for my two remaining clients.

Once we were home, Brad broke the news to me while we were standing in the kitchen.

"I hate to unload this on you, but I've got some bad news," he began grimly.

I felt my body constrict in an established pattern as I braced for upsetting news. I leaned into the granite countertop. My stomach tightened, drawing in against my ribcage; my throat swelled. Swallowing seemed to occur in slow motion. I alternated between holding my breath and taking extended purposeful breaths to make up for the missed oxygen. My face stretched wide as my teeth clenched, my ears pinched back. There seemed to be no end to the trouble and disappointment strangling our hopes. I said nothing, allowing Brad to continue.

"The DEA and US Marshalls busted into the house looking for drugs. It seems Ryder has been trafficking out of our house," Brad explained calmly, prepared to absorb my shock and my attempts to process the news.

I was astonished.

Dealing? The DEA? Seriously, is this happening?

"What the hell? Were you home?"

My heart took off racing, sprinting three blocks ahead of my atrophied limbs.

"No, I was golfing; Ryder was the only one here. They scared him pretty bad, but they didn't find anything. It was about six or seven officers and a dog, and they searched the whole house."

"Are you kidding me? I can't imagine how many man-hours went into setting that up … they must have been watching him a long time … they just don't pull that off on a whim … he must be in deep if they justified that many cops … I hope they scared the shit out of him."

Brad allowed me to ramble; I was pacing in a state of disbelief though in familiar emotional terrain. Despair was trekking throughout my body, trying to settle in.

"They hoisted him by the shoulders, threw him up against a wall."

Brad's voice was stoic, no animation or disgust.

"What were they looking for? Was he selling pot, I assume?"

"No. Oxycodone, actually."

We moved outside to the deck that wrapped around the length of our house. Outdoors I could release some of my anguish and allow nature to absorb it. The beautiful summer evening was lost on us. The river was higher than usual after a wet June. Sitting in a pair of red Adirondack chairs that had been a housewarming gift from my parents, we could see the river flowing north. Neighbors sitting on their decks were savoring this early stage of summer. Trees flaunted their achievement; every leaf had finally emerged from dormancy. It smelled fresh, the scent from days of rain mixed with lilac, geraniums, and cut grass. Evening birds were singing, celebrating the bounty of nature. This was a treasured time of year to North Dakotans after the lengthy harsh winter. Summer is euphoric, the season of celebration.

But not in our home that night.

I thought of the rehab Ryder had undergone the year before and realized it'd been useless.

"Dealing ... my God, that is so low, so dirty, Ryder ... how can this be real? Oxycodone? He must be desperate if he chose to deal."

I was still rambling trying to digest the harsh details.

Brad stared at the river, allowing me to rant. He'd had days to process the situation.

Usually I was the one giving Brad the bad news after he'd returned from a trip. I'd have to relay to him what they'd done while he was gone. Often I left out details to buffer the impact. I was used to being the grounded parent, the one who'd already processed the news while dealing the blow to Brad.

"We have to get him back into treatment, don't you think?" I asked.

"Absolutely; this is out of hand. A guy only deals when he's supporting a habit," Brad replied, while walking a couple yards to a flowerbed in the center of our backyard. He stooped down and began pulling weeds.

"Where is he now?"

"Sleeping; he works at eleven tonight. I'm sure he'll wake up twenty minutes before he has to leave and run out of here. We'll sit him down tomorrow and sort through it. Talk about options," Brad said.

"He's been given a huge break. What are the odds of them making a bust and leaving empty-handed? They've got to be pissed off to go through all that time and expense with no arrest. Maybe this is the wake-up call that will set him straight."

"Who knows; he's such a dumbfuck. I'm fed up," Brad said.

"They've got to get something positive going on in their lives. With both of them working graveyard shifts, who knows what the hell they're doing?"

"Selling drugs apparently," I said.

I was shredding my cuticles until they bled.

"They have to get into school, get a plan. This is bullshit," Brad said. His anger was surfacing. The pile of weeds was mounting.

It was natural for us to speak of "them" instead of singling one out. That's the way it was for us, raising twins who were so similar.

"But treatment's got to come first; if he doesn't get clean, nothing good will follow," I said.

"Yes, treatment's the next step. It won't be easy; he's such a stubborn ass."

"Do you think we should send him back to Prairieview?"

We knew that whatever we did, Ryder had to get out of River Bend and into an intensive, maybe residential, group. Clearly the in-and-out of a local program hadn't done much good. We knew the next treatment attempt wouldn't be cheap.

"But he's got to be onboard," I told Brad. "If we force him, he'll just go through the motions. Can we even force him at this point? He's twenty years old."

I was devastated. I rolled up a Kleenex from my pocket and twisted it around my thumb to stop the bleeding cuticle. I wished I could leave for a tennis court and smack the ball around. It had been over a week since I'd played, and I had an edge going.

"I'll contact Hazelden and see what it costs, and what insurance will cover. It's worth checking into."

Brad grabbed the pile of limp weeds to throw away.

It was getting dark. Mosquitoes were coming out. I wanted to watch the moonrise, but the bugs were too nasty. In two days it would be summer solstice, and July third was the next full moon. Those were my next two powerful dates to perform a feng shui blessing in my home. There was so much grief and sadness in our sun-drenched home. Negative energy lingered: fear, contempt, and anger from the DEA invasion, drugs consumed, and at what rate? Toxic and dense, my home felt strangely dark, as though someone had painted the walls black. How was this hell unfolding in our beautiful family, in this peaceful river view retreat? We'd given our son the world, every opportunity. How the hell did our lives take this turn?

I didn't even want to see Ryder yet. I had to allow reality to soak in. Who has the DEA bust into their home, certain of an arrest? Our family in docile River Bend, the parents who had showered our kids with all we knew to be good and true. We raised them with family, baseball, tennis, golf, PTA, volunteering for the book fair, one parent always home, walks, read books every bedtime, anytime. Bought them a puppy for Christmas when they were ten because they wanted her so badly, for so long. Loved them, held them, rocked them to sleep every night, kissed, hugged, played every day, nothing but constant love and security. We gave them all that parents could give. Why us? Why our children? What did we do wrong? What opportunities did we miss to get this right?

I went to bed and didn't fight the tears, pulled under by waves of grief. I was choking on vague regret. In this place of despair, all hope and happiness vanished. Nothing from my once blessed life could offset the darkness closing in. From this point forward, life would be about coping, getting through the horror. No longer could I wake in the morning looking forward to the day unfolding.

It was the first time in my life that I was grateful that life is finite. Knowing my son was wanted for dealing drugs, I was so ashamed. There must have been something I missed along the way, an opportunity to save him from this fate. It was my fault; I'm his mother; I should have seen it coming, should have known enough to stop it, somehow, in some way. My intuition had failed me, or I failed my intuition. I didn't want to be consoled; I deserved this pain; this failure was on me. For the last six years I'd been home every day, every night, while Brad was flying over half of every month.

I was the parent in charge, and I screwed this up, and it was too late to do it all over. Oh my God in heaven, how can we right this ship? I could have never imagined what lay ahead.

MORNING CAME. FOR A CHARITABLE moment, I lingered in that serene, semiconscious state where reality remained mercifully undetected. From this slumber, my innate self emerged, draped in optimism. This is where I longed to live permanently—suspended from the truth, where the lighthearted woman I once was nested and cradled in her dreams. She only had those few moments to breathe each morning, until the harsh details of her life clenched its hands around her throat.

I'd stayed in bed and silently recited the Hail Mary, with one modification. Instead of, "Pray for us sinners now and at the hour of our death, amen." I'd changed it to "Pray for us now and forever, amen." I didn't consider myself to be a sinner, and I had more urgent concerns than my final hour of death.

I recalled how, as a young girl, at the end of the school day, students were assigned first, second or third bus. There were three departure times for the single bus that served Holy Angels, our Catholic grade school. A student would skip down the hallway ringing a big brass bell with a black wooden handle, prompting teachers to excuse the "first bus" students. Sister Teresa, in my third-grade classroom, would bellow, "First bus people, say your three Hail Marys." First bus students would jump up beside their desks and recite, as quickly as adolescent lips could rapid-fire, three shredded Hail Marys and run to the bus that took them home. Second and third bus people would have to wait their turns.

The God I came to know as an adult was much different from the one I was raised to fear by nuns, priests, and Christian brothers throughout my twelve years of Catholic school. Because of my lack of alignment with a God of wrath and judgment and the Catholic Church's beliefs in general, we'd chosen to raise our sons *sans* organized religion. Were we being punished? I did not believe in that God. I wondered which prayers, if any, my sons had memorized and if Sunday school in a Lutheran Church might have made a difference, kept them from trying drugs.

I sat up in bed. Our master bedroom was painted Greek column—a soft sky blue in daylight, and steel gray in dim light. It was in the southeast corner on our second story. One window faced east, framing a tall evergreen tree. Two windows, six feet square, faced south. Through those windows we enjoyed a sweeping treetop view of the river and surrounding wooded terrain and the creatures it sheltered. The bedroom was large enough to fit three king-size beds with room to spare. An adjacent walk-in closet and master bathroom combined to make this my sanctuary, my tree fort.

My God dwelled in nature. I felt His benevolence gazing at the horizon by day and the celestial magnificence at night and while observing the birds and mammals that roamed, nested, and burrowed below. Any occasion outdoors, communing with nature, was my church. In the birdsong I heard God's joy; in the grazing deer I sensed His strength; in the perpetual flow of river waters His protection calmed me. I felt His omnipresence in the night sky. That June summer morning, I asked Him to carry me and my family to a healing place.

I had just poured myself a cup of coffee when I heard the garage door raising. Moments later, Ryder walked into the kitchen, returning home from work. I hadn't seen him since my arrival from Kansas the evening before.

"Are you okay, Mom?"

He saw the puffiness and dark circles under my eyes from crying myself to sleep the night before.

"No. I'm scared to death. Brad told me what happened while I was gone."

I never referred to Brad as "Dad" unless I said, "Your dad." We were not going to become that couple who addressed one another as "Mom and Dad."

"Yeah, it scared me too, a lot."

"What the hell, Ryder, dealing painkillers?"

"I know, I know, Mom. I don't know what I was thinking. I'm a dumbshit, an idiot."

"I assume you're using again. That's why guys deal, right?"

Brad and I had planned to stage a talk with him, but this conversation unfolded, and I wasn't inclined to pause it. Brad was still asleep.

"I'll admit I got off track for a bit, but that bust was all it took. Scared me straight, Mom. You don't have to worry about that."

"You realize that by busting into our home they were certain they'd catch you? They're not going to stop until they do."

"I'm done, Mom, I swear."

"I, we, think you need to go back into treatment. Clearly you're far off track, Ryder. This is extreme. You need help."

"No, I'm not going back to treatment. You'd just be throwing your money away. I'll leave treatment. They can't force you to stay. Throw me out if you want, but I'm not gonna go back in there!"

"Ryder, why don't you want to get clean? This makes no sense to me. You realize you'll end up dead or in jail?"

I was not an addict, and I understood very little about my son's reality as an addict.

Urged on by the caffeine and my frustration, I could feel my heart racing, my hands shaking. I wanted to grab him by the shoulders and shake him back into the kid we'd raised.

"By selling drugs, you could be responsible for another person's death. You get that? Don't you?"

"I made a dumb mistake. I learned my lesson, Mom; you'll see. I don't need treatment."

Brad woke up. The three of us spent another thirty minutes chasing the topic in circles. We'd agreed to allow the drama to settle and revisit the situation in a week. We'd watch and see if Ryder was indeed scared straight. Hauling him off to treatment when he had no intention of investing any effort wasn't a choice we were inclined to rush into.

These kinds of decisions are never straightforward when it's your child, your family. Absolutes were an exclusive privilege reserved for those on the outside looking in, those who had nothing at stake with the potential outcomes. Our thinking was if we forced Ryder into treatment, and he walked out to live with a using buddy … well, then what?

"Throw him out; let him hit bottom," was the obvious advice from objective onlookers (with nothing at stake). What if bottom is six feet under, then what?

On my fifteen-minute drive to work, my friend Jack called. He was always brief, no small talk.

"Can you play tonight? We need a fourth. Island Park. Eight o'clock with Gary and Mark."

"Yes, thank God. Text me if you're up or down. See you there."

I was referring to which set of tennis courts they would be playing on. There were five in one location of the park and two more that were fifty yards away. Eight o'clock could not come soon enough. I knew the other guys playing; all of us were solid tennis players; it would be a very competitive match.

Jack was one of six brothers from a family of athletes. They grew up in our north River Bend neighborhood, and we went to the same schools and church. Our dads played poker every Friday night, and our moms played bridge once a month, all the years we were growing up. When Brad and I bought our first home in River Bend, it was across the street from Jack, Cathy, and their three children. We became reacquainted, and I converted Jack from racquetball to tennis. Being competitive athletes wasn't all that we had in common. My parents and Jack's had all passed away inside of ten months in 2008.

Jack hated to get beat by a woman, most especially me. But he'd rather lose with a male partner against me than take me as his partner. Made no sense, but that was Jack, part Archie Bunker, part caveman. But mostly he was all heart and felt like a crass older brother to me. Jack always called the teams when I joined the guys, which amused me. Tonight the four of us were evenly skilled players; any combination would make a great match. It was Mark and me against Jack and Gary.

We were on the courts that were built on the site of the original Island Park public swimming pool. The pool had been filled in with concrete, and a grandstand of cement bleachers remained on the west side of the courts, shading us from the setting sun. A group of theater types were reciting Shakespeare in a few rows of the bleachers. On the east side of the tennis court fence were two half courts for basketball games. Both were in use, with guys playing loud music. Skateboarders streaked back and forth, forcing us to tune them out or be completely distracted by the inconsistent sound of skidding wheels and bodies crashing. It was like playing next to a train wreck, but we knew what we were getting into when we chose to play under the lights at night in Island Park.

It was a humid evening, still in the low eighties when the match began. I was already sweating from the ten-minute warm-up. I blocked out the mess at home and focused on the ball, the point, the next shot coming to me. *Gimme the ball!* Here on a tennis court I felt my strength, a purely physical zone that served my body and soul. I played aggressively, hitting ground strokes and serves as hard as I could while still controlling the path of the ball. Power and control, only on the tennis court could I experience that euphoric combination of emotions. The rest of life was a grueling challenge of letting go while feeling powerless over the choices my sons were making and their consequences.

I got high from tennis. I left Island Park that night pacified: I'd played great, and we'd won the match. All the sweat that poured off left me feeling much like a good cry does, purged and calm.

Once home I turned on coverage from Wimbledon, hoping to catch Andy Roddick's early round match. He was my longtime favorite. I knew he didn't have a lot of years left playing, and I dreaded his departure from the game, though years away I'd assumed. When Andy was doing well in a tournament, I was completely engaged, and I would move everything off my planner and watch his matches whenever possible. I was in luck that night. Andy's match was beginning.

I felt so grateful for tennis. It pushed my body, reduced stress, lifted my spirits, and offered me the distraction for which I was desperate. Being an athlete fueled my self-esteem and provided me with an element of my personality that felt empowered, albeit a small and waning part of myself. I pictured the day that I'd have my sons back. We would be on a tennis court, healthy, having fun, laughing, competing, and, most importantly, alive and healthy.

That had been my hope, my dream.

MY DAD PASSED AWAY AUGUST 20, 2008. The day before he died he was in his bedroom confined to a hospital bed provided by hospice. His dignity had been compromised, but his integrity prevailed. His wish to die at home would be fulfilled. I sat next to him for my last conversation with him on earth. On the wall above his head was a framed picture that had been there as long as I can remember. It depicted Jesus wearing a crown of thorns; his chest was cut open, his heart was shedding droplets of blood, and his open palms bore raw crucifixion wounds.

Death was approaching methodically to claim my father. Papa was ashen, thin, and helpless; his soul's ascension into heaven had begun. His chest rattled as though he was breathing underwater. The day before he'd seen three angels at the foot of his bed. But he wasn't frightened by them; perhaps they were his three brothers who had preceded him in death.

"Where are the boys?" Papa whispered. I read his lips to help me understand his withered inquiry.

"At home; they'll be over in a little bit." Ryder and Avery were sixteen years old.

I reached for his hands and caressed them in both of mine—the hands that had protected me, provided for me, calmed me, and applauded me my entire life.

"Avery's been working washing dishes at Bailey's. Ryder's going to apply there too." Small talk was mutually soothing and manageable.

He grimaced, though I knew it to be a smile. His eyes were milky, hazy; the eyes that had lit up every time he'd seen me enter a room.

"They're good boys most of the time," I said, fighting to breathe beneath an avalanche of heartache and imminent grief. I wanted so badly to have him back, whole and healthy. I wanted so desperately to be able to let him go.

"All the time." He whispered adamantly. It was the last thing he said to me.

He died the next morning, August 20, at four fifteen.

My mom and sisters were sleeping in our parents' home on Willow Road, my sister Kelly in the same bedroom as my dad when he died. I was sleeping at home, a one-minute bike ride away. Kelly was a certified nursing assistant and worked part time in a nursing home. She'd taken an extended leave of absence to live with and take care of my parents. Kelly was willing and capable of tending to my folks in every regard. The hospice team admired her organization and tracking system of their medical and care-giving needs. Her compassion had no limits.

Shortly after my dad died, he gave us signs that he was still near, that his death was not the end of our relationship with him. Somehow he knew the signals wouldn't be missed by his daughters. The signs came to us within forty-eight hours of his death.

The first came to Craig, Ann's husband. He woke abruptly from a sound sleep at Pelican Lake, Minnesota, sixty miles away. He described hearing someone say in a clear voice, "Moon has passed." Moon was my dad's nickname. Craig noticed it was 4:17 a.m., two minutes after my dad's official time of death.

The next sign came to me. I'd been aspiring to speak at the prayer service, to share memories of my dad but was concerned I would break down. The evening after my dad died, Brad and I went out for dinner. I intended to share some memories with Brad so I brought a notebook to make notes of what I wanted to include when I spoke at the service. I'd planned to compile my notes and type them out so that my best friend Erin could finish sharing for me at the prayer service if my emotions overcame me.

At dinner I recalled a memory that I shared with Brad for the first time. When I was a kid, my dad had a recliner positioned in the family room in a way that whenever you entered or left the room, you passed by him. He'd always put out his hand for us to pat as we passed by him, his gentle way of connecting. I described it to Brad as a type of high five. My dad had been doing it long before the term had even been coined. Recalling that gesture with Brad was the first time I'd thought of, or referred to it as a high five. But in my notes I wrote "high five" as a reminder to include that memory. Later, when we left the restaurant, a different car, a red sports car, had parked next to us. The license plate read HIGH FIVE. I was astonished and comforted to know Papa's spirit was near me.

A couple of days later, I left with my sisters for the prayer service. Brad and the boys followed later. Brad saw the familiar red car approaching in the rearview mirror. He said to the boys, "Watch that red car coming up; the license plate is HIGH FIVE. I'll tell you more about it later." Sure enough, it passed him and led nearly the entire route to the funeral home.

The third sign occurred in Kansas. The day before Jackie's daughter Lauren left for River Bend to attend the services, she had an unlikely visitor. She'd gotten into her van in the garage to leave for work. The van was uncharacteristically dirty, with lots of smudges and smears. *Weird*, she thought as she backed out of the driveway. As she looked closer, she realized they were paw prints, and the next moment a possum landed on her lap. Without thinking, she instinctively flipped it out the open window and drove away, very shook up, to say the least. That was the story that every cousin heard as family members arrived in River Bend for the funeral.

I told Erin about the possum incident, and she said, "Let's look it up in *Animal Speaks,*" a book that interprets messages from animals. According to the book, the message a possum sighting conveys is … "Appears to be dead but is not." I believed my dad was letting us know that although he was no longer with us, he most certainly was not dead to us.

To appreciate the next sign you must know that my dad's nickname was Moon and had been since he was a baby. That's what everyone had called him his entire life. The sign came to my sister Kelly and her daughter Shannon. They were getting ready for the drive from Grand Forks to River Bend with Shannon's little boy, Hunter. Kelly was rearranging the back seat in her Suburban to accommodate Hunter's car seat and found an old newspaper from May 31, 2008. It was folded in half, then half again. A front-page story headline read HONEYMOON IN HEAVEN. The newspaper had been folded in a way that left out "HONEY," and the abbreviated headline read: MOON IN HEAVEN.

My mom followed Dad to heaven fourteen weeks later, on November 16, 2008. Between their deaths was their sixtieth wedding anniversary on September 14. It would be the only anniversary they'd spend apart.

While I faced my despair over Ryder and Avery's addiction struggles, I believed my parents were watching over my boys from heaven. As a mother, I'd felt so helpless, so incapable of influencing them after they'd turned sixteen, but I believed that God and my parents were protecting them. My certainty that my parents were still connected to us helped me to trust that the situation would get better, or if the worst happened, that my parents would help me through it.

I also drew strength from another death that same summer my dad passed away. Jana, my dear friend since high school, lost her oldest son in a tragic accident. Landon was twenty-two years old and was wearing a helmet when he died from injuries incurred from a twelve-foot fall while mountain biking. He had just graduated from college and had moved out to Montana to enjoy the great outdoors and begin his professional life. He was an adventurous spirit, and a beautiful young man. Landon was also a cancer survivor. He'd embraced life fully after his three-year battle with leukemia that had begun when he was ten years old. His enduring passion and joy were contagious.

His funeral was one of the most profound spiritual experiences I've ever had. It was truly a celebration of his life. I was inspired by Jana's courage, and by how gracefully she dealt with such a shocking and devastating loss. Two days after I learned of Landon's death, I was inspired to write a prayer. Maybe Landon whispered it to me to give to his mom?

Dear God,

Show me how to lift Landon to heaven, and release him as he ascends into your arms.

Tell me how to trust your will so that grief doesn't consume every waking moment.

Help me to believe life on earth will have meaning with Landon away in heaven.

Promise me I will know him in spirit, and feel his presence.

Show me a way out of the deep, vast sea of grief that bears no light.

Tell me he's the blessed one that you called back to love by your side.

Help me to believe the tidal wave of love for Landon will carry me through until I can begin to understand.

Promise me he is surrounded by loved ones gone before,

… and that when it's my time, I will hold his face in my hands and be whole again.

Amen.

Jana continues to survive Landon's death with grief and gratitude, and I've drawn upon her example of strength more times that I can recall. I believe that if Jana can survive Landon's death, I can survive whatever fate holds for our family.

By the grace of God, inspired by Jana's bravery, and with my parents' eternal love and guidance, "Whatever happens, I will handle it" became my mantra that summer of 2012, as the situation with Ryder continually escalated—or perhaps more accurately, disintegrated.

6

July is the rowdy month in North Dakota—the carefree, reckless, middle child in the family of summer months. June was transitional. From the last days of school into the summer lifestyle, June sputtered along trying to define itself and establish a rhythm. Early August would present the challenge of trying to savor the ride with one foot on the brake, knowing at month's end the cherished season would be over.

Glorious July is emancipation in motion for thirty-one unbridled days. Life's activities ranged beyond the confinement of the indoors that winter had dictated. Extended daylight and balmy nights were seductive. Humidity and heat partnered after sunset to sabotage prudence and self-care. Most everyone played harder, sleep less, drank more, and abandoned self-discipline. All the cumulative damage would be reconciled in the cold certainty of the coming winter.

Every night there was a destination buzzing for those in search of bustle. Weekends presented the challenge to choose among road trips, concerts, lake dates, sporting events, fairs, or backyard gatherings. Fourth of July week was the peak of summer, of freedom. River Bend was relatively deserted on the Fourth of July, with everyone off to Minnesota lake country fifty miles east or beyond.

My life was contained: work, play tennis, watch tennis, and deal with parental challenges. There were very few people I spent time with that summer. Seclusion made my life seem more manageable. One of the few I talked with was my best friend, Erin. She came over for a walk through my neighborhood the first day of July. Murphy led the way on her leash, excited for the exercise.

"How's work going? You've been there over a month now, right?" Erin began.

"Good overall; it's a great distraction. There's so much to learn: the beds, the computer system, the selling technique. I wish I could fast-forward to being polished."

"How's it working in the mall?"

"Better than I thought, actually. It's such a beautiful mall. Forty hours a week is intense, though, not much time left over for anything else."

Erin was divorced with three beautiful sons. We met and became friends in 1999. Since childhood she'd struggled through just about every hardship there was. She'd left a marriage that'd concluded with her ex eventually marrying a neighbor. It is impossible to briefly articulate what she'd been through and how she managed to survive emotionally. Her courage could fill a stadium. Our mutual support had established a sacred bond.

We both perceived the world the same way, believing that we're all souls trying to transcend the challenges of being human, and utilize our gifts to contribute to others. It was habit for us to examine our lives and our choices, and to aspire to live from a place of love, gratitude, and possibility instead of fear and scarcity. Erin knew most everything about my life; our sons had grown up together. Even so, I couldn't tell her or anyone about the DEA searching our home. I was so ashamed, so afraid for my son's tremulous path. The less anyone knew, the less they'd worry, and the less real it would feel to me. By not speaking of it, maybe I could contain it, fold it up, and put it away somewhere dark and out of reach, and hope it would dissolve from neglect.

I caught up on her new career in real estate, her sons, and their plans for the Fourth.

"How are the boys doing?" she asked.

"Same, working nights, I don't see them much."

Murphy was tugging hard on the leash, trying to break loose to chase a squirrel. I had to stop and center myself to hold my ground or be pulled over by her single-minded efforts.

"Are you going to Ann and Craig's for the Fourth?"

She gracefully moved on from the topic of my boys. She knew me well enough to know if I wanted to talk about them I would.

"No, I wish. I'm working. Everyone's scheduled. What a waste; nobody goes to the mall on the Fourth. Brad's gone, on a six-day trip. The boys work too."

My sister Ann's lake home was an hour away with an open invitation all summer.

"How do you like your coworkers?"

I told her about Keith, the high-level, spirited manager—Linda, a woman my age, who had a ridiculous sense of humor that I appreciated.

We arrived at Elephant Park and found a bench in the shade where we could see the tennis courts. Erin had grown up playing tennis too, but had given it up. Murphy settled down, content to sniff about in the four-foot radius her leash allowed.

"The full moon's on the third, I'm gonna do a space clearing," I said.

"What do you usually do for that?"

Erin and I had traveled together to California in 2008 to become certified feng shui practitioners. She knew what a space clearing was; she just wanted to know the details of my plan.

"I make sure everyone's gone for at least half an hour. If I think I'm going to be interrupted, it's too distracting."

"Do you journal your intentions first, like you do before a blessing?" she wondered.

"Yes, just a sentence or two for each life area."

I was referring to the nine life areas represented in our homes that feng shui impacts: family, wealth, health, helpful people, children, knowledge, reputation, career, and marriage.

"I like using my bell; sound penetrates every inch of the space. It wouldn't hurt to burn incense too, but I hate the smell of it."

I kept one eye on a doubles match, four men I didn't know, but often saw playing there. I wished I was out there slamming the ball around.

I continued.

"Then I just go through every room in the house ringing my bell, that brass one, with the mallet. I bang the *baa-jee-bas* out of it in the boy's bedrooms."

We laughed.

On the walk home, Murphy was compliant with the pace we'd set. She'd had her fill of chasing and sniffing.

On the Fourth, mall traffic was sparse, as expected. I sought to make the best of it and made up a game for the four of us to play. The corporation referred to the entrance to the retail store as the "Opportunity Zone." Policy stated that when an employee was "up" (his or her turn to greet and help a customer), that person would circulate within this zone engaging shoppers.

So we played "Opportunity Zone Bingo." We brainstormed a list of potential characteristics in mall shoppers and scenarios and created four different bingo cards. If one of us witnessed something from the list during his or her "up," the employee could mark it off his or her card. Some of the scenarios were common, while others were more obscure. They included:

Guy wearing socks with sandals

Biker dude with massive key chain dangling from his front to hip pocket

Hairy dude wearing a tank top

Toddler having a meltdown

Someone spilling his or her Orange Julius

Anyone with a flag on his or her clothing

A flag tattoo

Guy wearing a Canadian Tuxedo (denim jeans and denim vest over T-shirt)

Father in charge of kids on mall sofa with kids out of control

Teenagers making out

By three that afternoon I'd won; my bingo card was blacked out. The mall closed at six, and none of us had shown or sold a bed. But we had a lot of laughs and made the best of a day we would have all preferred to be lakeside with friends and family.

It was already one of the hottest summers in decades. Those blessed to have a lake home were enjoying one awesome season. I only managed to get to my sister's lake home for one brief afternoon that entire summer. I dearly missed our long walks on Gosslee Road, happy hours reclining on the deck gazing at the lake, and pontoon rides to the sandbar followed by wine and laughter in the hot tub.

I vowed next summer would be different.

7

Twenty years, where'd they go?
Twenty years, I just don't know.
Sometimes I sit and wonder where they've gone.

—"Like A Rock," Bob Seger

THE BOYS' TWENTIETH BIRTHDAY WAS approaching, on July 18, 2012. Their early birthdays filled our home with extended family, and our first River Bend home on Elm Street North was built to handle ruckus. The basement, mostly a large rec room, was eighteen hundred square feet. It was big and open, allowing small bodies to exhaust large muscle groups. I wallpapered the white brick block walls with bright jungle scenes. A traditional brick fireplace took up an eight-foot wall with a bench where we stacked toys and games.

The first time we'd seen the backyard with the Realtor, the boys were ten months old, and I'd said to Brad, "This is a Tom Sawyer, Huck Finn backyard." We knew it was our next home. It featured a hundred yards of gently sloping green lawn, and dozens of mature trees, including a towering willow tree a few yards out from the kitchen window that stood watch over the view down to the slow-moving Red River. Our lot ended with a deep grove of trees and brush, beyond which was a twenty foot drop to the water. There were adventures to be had in every season—sledding down the snowy slope in winter, tag football in the fall, and a world of pretend all summer. An old tire swing was hanging from a majestic oak tree in a clearing near the river, where the boys launched many adventures.

As parents of twins, we felt it was important for them to have experiences as individuals. In kindergarten, we'd separated Avery and Ryder into different classrooms, and by their choice, they never shared a homeroom thereafter. Consequently, between the two of them, they knew every kid in their grade at Washington Elementary. We celebrated their childhood birthdays on Elm Street North with mobs of boys running free in the heart of summer.

Twenty years old. Trying to put my head around it made me incredibly sad. I simply could not make sense of who they were at this point in their lives. How was it possible that our sons had detoured so far from our intentions, our efforts, our example, their upbringing? What had we done so terribly wrong? It was impossible to leave the topic of our sons' sordid direction unexamined, but doing so left Brad and me bewildered and haunted. Ryder and Avery had become people we had nothing in common with except DNA, name, and address. Surely, we'd hoped, they would mature, grow out of it, and become the boys we'd known and raised.

Avery had recently moved back home after living in a house with friends for six months, so both boys were home again. Their bedrooms were always trashed, and they did nothing to help out around the house or yard. They came to us only if they needed help with a car, or some other favor. They had no hobbies; they'd given up tennis, golf, and going to baseball games of the Eagles, the local AAA team. Neither of them had plans to get back into school. Brad and I were fed up with both of them.

Conversations about drug treatment continued to float around, never landing long enough to take effect. The talks would always end with Ryder's spin and our decision to table the issue. Ryder didn't appear to be using so far as we could tell with our limited exposure to him, and searches of his bedroom produced nothing. So we delayed taking action, such as an intervention. He said he'd move out if we didn't want him living with us. Without planning ahead, we knew he'd just run out of money living on his own, then what choices would he make?

We wanted them back in school by fall semester. It was difficult to get the four of us together to sort through any of it. Both boys still worked overnight and slept days. I worked forty hours at the mall, then another eight hours cleaning houses. Brad was flying to Asia seventeen days a month. One weekend a month he was also on call as a radiology tech at

St. Luke's Hospital in Kellogg, sixty miles west of River Bend, and that meant he stayed overnight. In all, he slept away from home about eighteen nights a month. When he was home, he was jetlagged, sleep deprived, or both, from being on call 24/7 at the hospital.

It was time for an ultimatum.

We'd told the boys that if they weren't attending school by fall, we would slowly cut them off. We'd stop paying for their phones and car insurance and expect them to move out of our home by November. They needed to begin to save money for the move. Or they could attend school, live at home, and we'd hold true to our promise of academic funding, where they would have to be responsible enough to take out student loans, which we would pay off if they graduated. We believed that would deter them from bouncing in and out of school, wasting our money and their efforts. We believed it to be reasonable and mutually fair. But they continued to drag their feet and refrained from enrolling anywhere.

On their twentieth birthday, we managed to gather together long enough to go out for breakfast. Brad and I agreed no lecture, no agenda. They chose The Skillet, a local diner. They were both tired from working all night, hair disheveled, oversized T-shirts and baggy shorts riding low, and baseball caps pulled below their eyebrows. A subdued birthday, to say the least.

I'd bought them each a heart-shaped token I'd found in the men's jewelry case at TJ Maxx. In the center was I love U (love was represented by a black heart). This was overlaid by an arrow. The pewter tokens were about the size of my palm, with an engraved line creating four sections with the words FOREVER, INFINITY, MORE, ALWAYS. Spin the arrow and see which sentiment it landed on. I love you … more, always, forever, infinity. *Indeed.* Ryder later hung his from the ceiling fan in his bedroom. Avery's went on his keychain.

A week later, about eleven p.m. I was watching TV in bed, still wired from playing tennis under the lights. Ryder had been downstairs watching TV; no one else was home. I couldn't sleep and thought I'd just go downstairs and tell him that I loved him. I wanted to connect; he'd seemed morose earlier.

He was no longer on the sofa in the living room. Something didn't feel right. I felt compelled to find him, unsure if he was still in the house. A light was on in the basement. Why would he go down there to watch TV when he had the plasma TV to himself in the living room? I wondered. Quietly I descended the carpeted stairs. He was alone, with a loaded syringe. He didn't hear me approaching. I looked into his startled, frightened, desperate eyes. Those beautiful almond-shaped, blue-gray eyes belonged to a heroin addict.

My son, our son, dear God in heaven.

Ryder pleaded with me.

"Mom, I'll quit; I can quit. Don't tell Dad. If you don't tell Dad, I'll go in the morning to treatment. Please don't tell Dad, Mom, please!"

I gathered up all the debris of his usage and hid it to throw away later. I told him to go to his bedroom and stay there. We would talk more about it in the morning. I cannot honestly recall why I didn't rush Ryder into treatment right then, other than fear. Rehab and immediate treatment that night might seem like the obvious decision now, but nothing was apparent to me in the bludgeoning haze of maternal shock and grief.

Brad was due home the following afternoon after being on call all weekend at the hospital. He'd have one night at home, then leave for a five-day Asian trip. I had to find a way to take care of everyone. How do I tell Brad and expect him to carry on, go to work, get enough sleep to function as our rock, our provider? If Brad had missed work for every family crisis over those years, we wouldn't have had a roof over our heads. I decided not to tell him about it until he returned from his upcoming trip.

I sat in my bedroom and focused on breathing. I was trying to calm down, to find strength. I tried to quiet my fear, hoping to hear God's voice. Before I had the courage to tell the truth to anyone else, I had to allow it to burn like acid through the thick layers of denial I'd built up to protect myself from this grisly reality.

One drip at a time, into my bloodstream, like chemotherapy, cautiously, I allowed only what my emotions and body could handle in each moment. Calculated amounts of poison were dissolving my assumptions and annihilating my illusion that this tragedy would never happen to our child, to our family.

I began to cry and continued to sob until my body had purged the darkest elements of my despair. Then I lay in bed in that softly elevated retrieval post tears. I sensed that life was more than the horrific scene I'd just survived. My son would not live or die as a drug addict. Was it my eternal optimism, self-preservation, or was it God whispering to my soul?

8

I WAS SET TO PLAY TENNIS at nine the morning after I'd discovered my son was someone who injected heroin into his veins.

It was a typically peaceful Monday morning in Island Park. Like River Bend's version of Central Park, it began where downtown River Bend ended. On the park's northeast side sat a YMCA and the River Bend-Mayport Community Theater. A large public swimming pool had been built on the site of the old River Bend Arena, where I'd taken skating lesson as a young girl. The city had retained the original front entrance wall of the arena that stood along the north end of the pool complex. An old-fashioned raised gazebo sat in the center of the park. It was wood, painted white, and was the site of many fair-weather weddings and summer concerts. A playground, practice soccer field, and green space occupied the rest of the park. Intersecting sidewalks allowed passage in and around the entire park.

Across the street to the east was Prairieview, the rehabilitation facility where Ryder was treated for addiction to painkillers his senior year of high school in 2011. Formally St. Paul's Hospital, it was also the building from which Moon and Colleen Chase brought home their fourth daughter, Dana Lynn.

Other than the eight women playing tennis that morning, there were occasional dog owners walking their joyful pets, and mothers pushing strollers. The courts we played on would have partial shade for the first forty-five minutes, and then full-on sun for the second half of the match. On that day in late July it was already seventy-eight degrees, humid, calm, and the sun was rising hot.

I'd arrived at eight fifty with one intention: to focus on the ball. The fuzzy yellow orb would be my mantra as I aspired to block every fear-drenched thought from my mind. I would be present in the sacred space that I considered a tennis court to be. Pushing my body physically helped me push reality aside. Armed with my Babbalot racquet, I was not a mother of a heroin user, an aspiring salesperson, or a wife; I was an athlete, a passionate tennis player. How blessed and grateful I was for this incredible sport that allowed me to escape my life and enjoy the aspect of myself that I loved best. For this brief hour and a half, I would come into a quiet, personal experience of power and control that felt completely void in the rest of my life. My life did not depend on playing tennis, but the quality of my life most certainly did.

It was the type of day that the physicality of competition was magnified by the heat. I played out of my mind, rarely missed a shot. I poached aggressively, and drove backhands down the line before my opponents even considered moving their racquet. I hit aces that kicked out so sharply the returner fanned, missing my serve by a foot. *Gimme the ball!* My partner and our opponents praised the high level of game I'd brought that day.

My tank top, wristbands, and hair were completely drenched with sweat. I felt delivered. These women were my tennis comrades. I didn't socialize with them much outside of playing tennis, just an occasional holiday mixer or milestone birthday celebration. They knew almost nothing about the hell I was going through.

We moved into the shade afterward to cool down before going our separate ways.

"You were on fire today," one of my opponents said. "We couldn't get anything past you."

"Yeah, thanks; it felt great." I wiped off my face, still wet and blushed from the heat and exercise.

In a few weeks several of their children would be going away to college.

"When does Abby leave for school? She's a junior now at Michigan State, right?"

"No, actually, this is her year abroad; she leaves for Madrid in two weeks."

"How about Lexi?"

"Yes, she's going a little early … I hope her new roommates work out … big change from the sorority house. She starts an internship … needs to adjust to that commute."

"Good for her; what an exciting opportunity."

"Thanks, I'm so proud of her!"

I managed to smile; I was truly happy for my friends. How blessed they were to have the luxury of fretting over how their kid's roommates would work out. God, I wish I had the lavishness of those types of "normal" concerns about my children.

No one asked about my kids. They knew not to bring it up unless I did. They were aware I'd been struggling over the years with my kids, but I didn't give details, and they respected my privacy. I wanted to keep my personal struggles separate from my tennis world in every regard. And I was ashamed. In the past, my comments were always vague.

"They're off course right now … hopefully back in school soon."

Well, yes, of course they'll get on course, after all we're such a good family; we've laid such a solid foundation, of course; yes, just a matter of time …

Once Brad returned home five days later I told him about Ryder, the syringe, the horrible scene I'd encountered. It was my turn to be the grounded parent, as he absorbed the blow. I asked him to not mention anything to Ryder until we had a plan in place, pretend not to know what had happened yet. Let's get the treatment lined up, plan the intervention, and proceed with professionals in place.

Later that night, Ryder called me at work. He was frantic.

"I'm calling the cops. I'm gonna turn myself in Mom. They want me, so I'm going to 'fess up to everything."

"What? Ryder, what's going on? Where are you?"

"You told Dad, didn't you? He called me a fucking druggie, a lowlife addict. I am, Mom; I'm a loser. I deserve to go to jail."

"Ryder, hold on. Where are you?"

"At work, I'm calling a friend for a ride. I'm not coming home."

"I'll pick you up at nine thirty. Just stay there. Wait for me. I'll be there in twenty minutes. Will you do that?"

"Don't know. Maybe I'll be here, maybe not."

I was alone at work. I called Brad.

"What did you say to Ryder? He's hysterical."

"I called him out. I'm sick of this shit."

I asked you not to say anything until we had a plan."

"I've had it. I'm done with his bullshit."

I had to close at work, which meant some computer functions, paperwork, e-mails to district managers. I couldn't get the computer operations in the correct order. I kept failing, disallowed to proceed to the next step. I'd only closed solo a few times. I had a complete meltdown and ended up calling Keith, crying, barely able to speak. He reassured me and said to lock up and take care of my family; he'd figure it out in the morning.

I drove the quarter mile to the Dakota Inn, where Ryder was. It was dark, hot, and the wind was blowing over thirty miles an hour. Plastic grocery store bags whipped around like miniature parachutes. A crow, visable in the light of the parking light was struggling to fly, at a near standstill, suspended with its wings fully expanded but not flapping, at the mercy of the gusting wind. Ryder was in the parking lot pacing, chain-smoking, anxious, angry at me, at Brad, at who knows what.

I coaxed him into the car and got him home.

The three of us finally settled down and began to talk through what needed to happen next. Ryder was willing to get some type of help, but he wanted to be a part of the decision. He didn't want us forcing him into a treatment facility. He wanted to find out more about an option: Suboxone, a drug prescribed by only a few psychiatrists in the state of North Dakota. One of them had an office less than a mile from our home. Suboxone helped addicts by reducing withdrawal symptoms and minimizing cravings because it contained a low level of opiates. It also negated a high from opiates when taken as prescribed.

Two weeks later, we were able to meet with Dr. Mitchell to begin a treatment plan for Ryder that included Suboxone and weekly counseling sessions. It was essential, she said, that a parent administers the prescription. I would be giving it to Ryder at the same time daily and ensure that it was absorbed under his tongue. Brad and I hoped this was the beginning of a full recovery for Ryder.

We were still capable of unjustified hope.

I had come to experience despair as a blanket I woke covered with every morning. I had two choices: I could drag it around all day, insulating me from joy, weighing me down, or I could choose to leave it at the foot of my bed and remain available to the blessings each day might offer. I had come to view my plight as despair management. Just as some people deal with chronic physical pain, I had to manage chronic emotional pain. If my life was going to be balanced, it was up to me. I was unwilling to become a victim of my child's addiction and its consequences. It was up to me, every day, to make the choice not to measure the quality of my life by that scale.

At work, I did my best to check my problems at the door and devote my full attention to improving. I was committed to being professional, and I appreciated the opportunity and the distraction. Worrying all day at work was not an option in which I allowed myself to indulge. The recent closing-shift meltdown had been the rare, brief exception.

A week after that meltdown, an older couple entered the store, and it was my "up." The woman was in a wheelchair, pale, with a scarf covering her bald head. Her demeanor was gentle and kind. I had the sense she was trying not to let her illness define her. Her husband pushed her wheelchair. They too, were managing despair, I presumed. They shared with me that she was terminally ill. At one point, they interrupted our conversation for an abrupt departure to the bathroom to relieve her nausea. Thirty minutes later, they returned to finish the purchase. They required a bed that would be comfortable for her during her final months, and one that suited him as a widower. I felt compassion for the couple, and I recalled how intricate the last months with my parents had been. But my prominent thought was how lucky she was. She was close to leaving her earthly suffering behind and entering heaven's gate.

9

THE BOYS WERE TEN MONTHS old when Brad and I moved to River Bend in 1993. Both of us were flight attendants, and we flew opposite schedules so a parent was always home with the boys. They did not spend a single hour in a day-care facility. When I flew, Brad was home with the boys, and he was with them solo around the clock. Avery and Ryder had more time with their dad by age five than most boys do their entire lives.

We didn't have much time together as a couple. Nor did we ever establish the lifestyle of a five-day workweek with weekends off. Spending time with other couples was nonexistent. Our time together was as a couple or as a family. We had a rhythm that was mutually comfortable, and our commitment to raising our sons was our first priority.

Brad and I were married in 1990. We were both very independent and self-secure. Our relationship was low maintenance; neither one of us required much in the way of attention from the other. We trusted one another completely. I cannot recall one conversation or issue in all of our years of marriage that involved jealousy.

Brad had been flying mostly international since 2010. E-mail was the only contact we had while he was away. The fact that I trusted my husband completely is testimony both to his character and to his integrity. Brad is extremely attractive. Not only because he's handsome and has a great build, but also because of his understated way, his humility, his kindness, and the respect he extends to everyone he encounters. I knew he could hook up every time he was on a trip. After all, at the end of his workday, he checks into a hotel with a group of women. I actually asked him years ago about that. "Obviously you could be getting laid anytime you want. What keeps you from making that choice?" He answered candidly. "I made the choice when we were married; I could play that game or not. It's not for me; it's not who I am."

Our boys grew up with the security that a solid marriage offers a child. Brad has been an exceptional model as a father and as a man. Every decision we've made was dictated by how it would impact Ryder and Avery. If we believed it would have a negative impact on them, we made a different choice.

All of my sisters remained happily married to their husbands, as were Brad's siblings. Our boys were raised within a large extended family of highly educated, successful individuals, and everyone got along.

I will admit this rock-solid foundation is in part why I was lulled into believing that drug addiction would never happen to our children. I truly believed we were above it. I thought if we raised our sons the way we'd been raised, the way I saw my sisters raise their kids, that Ryder and Avery would turn out just like all of us. They have nine older cousins on my side, including two nurses, a thoracic surgeon, a master's in education, a master's in guidance and counseling, a business executive, a wealth adviser, an entrepreneur, and a geoscientist. Why on earth would I be concerned that my children were at risk of becoming addicts?

That was naïve, and I'm guilty of false assumptions and complacency by allowing myself to be blinded to the severity of the situation as it unfolded with my sons. I'd kept thinking it would be a phase that they'd snap out of by way of their nature and all the standards by which they'd been raised.

In August of 2012 I began to isolate myself from others more than ever. It became a pattern of coping that I fell into without consciously choosing it. I mostly processed my anguish on my own. That was how I dealt with my personal horror. Speaking with others about Ryder's heroin use, about the DEA searching our home was impossible for me at this point. Our reality was too frightening. If I told others, the truth would escape, spread out, and gain momentum, and it would be harder for me to contain it, manage it, and clean it up.

I knew the women who loved me would worry if I gave them details. I didn't want a worry circle, and I didn't want to take anyone else down with fear. Keeping others updated required energy, and it took all the energy I had to cope with the situation. Factoring in others' opinions and advice complicated my emotions. I didn't want to explain or justify how we handled the challenging task of trying to influence our children in a new direction. For the most part, Brad and I agreed on how to handle each situation as it occurred.

Before I went to work, I compartmentalized my worries. I was gregarious, engaging bed shoppers and connecting with coworkers. Once I was home, I dealt with my fears alone. My choice to cope privately would prevail. I trusted myself to find my way with all of it; I didn't know how I would, but I believed in my instinct to survive and to handle whatever happened.

I was able to sleep at night only because I'd been on a prescription for sleep since the boys were three. In 1995, I'd suffered for months with insomnia. I'd been to a sleep disorder clinic and had tried several prescriptions. The one that finally worked was amitriptyline. Being able to sleep every night was essential for my survival by day, and there would have been no way for me to sleep unless medicated.

I didn't drink alcohol to calm my fears. I might have a beer or glass of wine a couple times a month, but not to try and feel better because it didn't help. It just made me sad, and complicated my sleep, and it aged me. I consider myself a fairly vain woman still, and the morning after any amount of alcohol consumption made my eyes puffy and my skin dehydrated. So I chose to deal with it all straight-on sober. Even though my sons were dragging me through hell, I was determined not to look like it. I believed one day we'd come out of our struggles, and I didn't want permanent battle scars of the rapid aging kind. I was committed to self-care physically and emotionally.

Since the attempted bust, Ryder was getting pulled over all the time for any reason the cops could come up with: failure to use a turning signal, rolling through a stop sign, no seatbelt; they knew his car and were determined to catch him at some point with enough reason to arrest him. They had a lot of money and time invested in his pursuit.

I never reported anything to Brad while he was on a trip. He would just lose sleep worrying, and that job is difficult enough on a full night's sleep. Once he came home, I'd fill him in on some of what went on, but usually not everything because I wanted to save him the anguish and disappointment. I also didn't want the anger and arguments it led to between him and the boys. I grew up in a home where my parents never raised their voices. The boys knew I left out some details occasionally in my reports to Brad, and they played me because of it.

As the weeks went by under Dr. Mitchell's care, Ryder emerged from his dark, elusive demeanor. She primarily held him accountable to take the Suboxone as prescribed, with me administering the daily dosages. It was understood that if he violated her rules, the opportunity and prescription would be terminated. Ryder remained cooperative, and appeared to be motivated to wean himself off Suboxone eventually and clean up his life.

Late August he applied for full-time work at several upscale hotels in River Bend for the night audit position, which is what he'd been doing part time at the Dakota Inn. He ended up with three offers and chose an upscale hotel in downtown River Bend.

I was so proud of him, and hopeful that he was on the right path. The team at his new job treated him well, and it was remarkable that he'd found his way to such an excellent opportunity. Finally, we were making progress. We hoped he'd start taking some classes too, since he could study at work.

He'd been hired on August 20, the fourth anniversary of my dad's death—a positive omen, I'd believed. That day I'd been running errands, thinking about my dad, missing him terribly. He'd felt about golf the way I did about tennis. When I was a kid, whenever we drove by a golf course, my dad would say, "Lucky ducks."

On the way home that day, I drove along Elm Street North. It parallels El Zagel Golf Course to the west, a par three course that'd been near our first home. On the right is the Red River. As I drove along this stretch of road, I was recalling "lucky ducks" when I saw a car that approached traveling south had the license plate PALS. My dad had always greeted me saying, "Hi, pal." Somewhere, somehow, he was watching over us; my mom was too. Moments like that one occurred now and again and nurtured my hope. If the worst was to happen, I believed that there was a heaven and that my parents were there to welcome us when it was our time. I would lean into that belief hundreds of times in the years to come.

It had been one of the hottest summers on record. By August, there were no signs of mosquitoes; the hot, dry summer had killed them off and turned lawns yellow. I never recall a summer when the air conditioning was on nearly every day. It was a lot like winter in that you're only comfortable indoors. I went between the mall and home, and then cleaned two large homes on my days off. Tennis had dropped off to only once a week. I simply had no time or energy to play more often.

Murphy had developed a bad limp, and I missed our long walks. I'd been the only no vote when the decision was made to add a dog to the family back when the boys were ten years old. Nevertheless, Murphy was my baby. She followed me throughout the house; I was the one that took care of her, which I'd known would be the case. But I was grateful for her companionship, as I was seeing less and less of friends. Dogs are known to absorb the stress that humans emit. No wonder she was limping.

All summer I had been diligent with skin care. I'm a skin-care freak, and I also have a master esthetician license. I spent many evenings watching tennis and slapping treatment masks on and off my face. On August 29, I was home with goo on my face watching the US Open. I loved watching this tournament. It was one of the four majors (Grand Slam) tournaments in professional tennis, and the only grand slam held in the United States. Settling in to watch hours of matches was my perfect evening. Then a buzz began; there was going to be coverage of a press conference. Andy Roddick had requested it … "stand by," announcers had said.

I knew what was coming; I could feel my stomach tightening, turning sour; I felt a dry lump in my throat. I'd suspected he was going to announce his retirement at the end of 2012. Instead he boldly decided this tournament would be his last. All those years of watching him compete, emotionally invested in the outcome of his matches, would end with his next loss. I broke down and sobbed, mushy facial mask dripping off my face. I know the breakdown had just a little to do with Andy's news. But once I was triggered to cry, my brain downloaded everything else that was breaking my heart. When he did finally lose in the second week of the tournament, I cried again; it was torture to hear his final speech.

On August 31, 2012 there was a blue moon, the second full moon of the month. The summer was officially over, and I prayed the change of season would be a gateway to positive changes for our family. I'd done my monthly full moon feng shui blessing in our home. Then I moved outside to sit in a teak rocking chair on the back deck to view the blue moon rising. Gently rocking, I focused on my breathing, trying to inhale the healing rays of the moon illuminating our backyard, our life. Absorbing the lunar energy and staring at the stars made me feel connected to my parents and to God. Gazing at the enormity of the universe strengthened my belief that something greater than myself was in charge, and that there was a purpose for our journey that I couldn't possibly conceive of yet.

But destiny was a wicked, cold-blooded beast lurking in the shadows, capable of mauling me to death. Maybe if I just stayed still, quiet and hopeful, it would leave me alone. Maybe not.

10

I'VE DEDUCTED THAT I ACQUIRED my love and respect for nature from my maternal grandmother.

My grandparents spent winters in Del Ray Beach, Florida, and summered at Breezy Point, then a mere resort village near Brainard, Minnesota, three hours east of River Bend. Growing up, we'd travel to spend long weekends with them several times every summer. Mae Lawrence, my grandmother, was a mellow, sweet, nurturing woman. She and my grandfather Patrick were married sixty-five years. Both were avid, accomplished golfers. I have fond memories of lying in the grass searching after four-leaf clovers with her. She'd take me to areas she'd scouted for blueberries, and we'd pick them by the bucketful. "Waste not, want not" was one of her often repeated musings. I attribute my value of resourcefulness to her influence. I'd felt we were kindred souls. My personality was much more like Mae's than my mother's.

August had concluded with a blue moon, such a potent, commanding exit to the month and the summer. I was grateful for twelve months, twelve opportunities a year to close a chapter and begin anew. The cycles of nature soothed me.

Autumn, it seemed to me, was the season of surrender. Nature surrenders her bounty with weeks of fall harvest. In the Red River Valley, we're surrounded by farmland in every direction. It's impossible for the harvest to go unnoticed—the fleet of trucks hauling sugar beets around the clock, Apples for Sale signs along county roads, and pumpkins and gourds stacked outside of the grocery stores.

Living in North Dakota demands that by late autumn one must yield to the inevitable arrival of winter. I'd lived with four distinct seasons my entire life, and their lessons resonated in my soul. The message of surrender I'd intuited from autumn dwelled deep in my bones. It would be the most significant of Mother Nature's lessons for me to translate into my life and choices, to enable me to cope. The most powerful thing we can do is surrender. That is a profound truth that is a challenging paradox to believe, and to live. As humans we seek control of outcomes, but that's a fallacy in many situations.

It was another fall semester that my sons were not in school, and we were disappointed. I began to question why we remained in River Bend. It was becoming a town full of grief landmarks for me. The trouble with the boys began after my parents' deaths. It seemed as though I'd lost all four of them in 2008. I missed my parents; none of my family lived in River Bend anymore. Every place I went, there was something to remind me of our happy years raising the boys, of my folks, and of the disappointment with how our lives had been since they'd died.

All those years in River Bend had required Brad to fly back and forth to the Minneapolis base to commute to work. It added a lot of stress, and we'd aspired to move back to Minneapolis one day. I started to wonder if that day wasn't fast approaching. I brought it up to Brad as we sat on the Adirondack chairs on our deck, the evening still warm enough to relax in shorts and T-shirts.

"Another fall semester and the boys are still not back in school. I gotta wonder, why are we still in River Bend? Maybe we need to pull the safety net and move back to Minneapolis," I said.

"I don't know; they still rely on us for so much."

"That's my point; maybe they need to grow up. River Bend's got nothing to offer them or us. We can find a psychiatrist to prescribe Suboxone for Ryder in Minneapolis."

I could see in the distance a flock of geese flying in V formation along the bend of the river, honking. Minutes later, they were close enough to hear the wind they stirred with the flapping of their wings. They didn't rely on logic to know when to migrate. They navigated on pure instinct, sans intellect to sabotage destiny.

"I'm not gonna lie, I hate the commute. I would like nothing better than to get out of River Bend."

"If we start getting the house ready now, maybe get it on the market late this year, we could be in Minneapolis by spring."

Brad gave it some thought. He never jumps into a decision.

For me there were reminders of the horrible last years of high school everywhere. Avery's girlfriend had become pregnant; he dropped out of high school, and she ended up with a miscarriage. By then it was too late to resume high school. Ryder's senior year, escalating drug use, then treatment, left him barely earning a diploma—the complete lack of anything we hoped and dreamed about for their future. My heart would sink whenever I'd drive by a marquee at their high school that announced the students of the week. I wondered what that must be like, the simple joy of your child thriving.

We decided to meet with my friend Erin, a Realtor, and find out more about the market and the value of our home. The initial steps of preparation could certainly begin without a firm commitment.

Everything you own requires energy to store it, clean it, maintain it, insure it, organize it, and on and on. All of that requires energy and it's depleting. When we have too much stuff it can block us from receiving greater blessings. I absolutely believe this, yet I still hung on to far more stuff than we needed.

Part of my challenge with purging is that I struggle to throw something away if I believe it could be of use to someone else. So I have to find a home for everything. Waste not, want not. I began by clearing out and purging all sorts of excess we no longer needed. Much of it I'd acquired from my parents. Furniture, household items, china, that sort of stuff that I'd never used, or unpacked, I was now ready to let go of it.

Feng shui taught me that less is more, yet I wasn't living that wisdom. But with the prospect of leaving River Bend, I ambitiously aspired to downsize all the stuff that no longer served a purpose. I grouped like items together and donated them to appropriate charities. With every load to Goodwill, I felt lighter, and the house was opening up. I was making room for change. I wondered what blessings might be manifested by the release.

Curiosity is akin to hope. I innately sought to cultivate every nuance of hope in order to survive emotionally. Judgement, fear, and assumptions were battling to conquer my spirit. I would continue to fight them off as though my life depended on it. The key would be to view my plight as my soul perceived it. If I had relied on the human perspective I surely would have been slayed and lost the battle early on.

11

SEPTEMBER FOR THE MOST PART was manageable. Ryder was doing well at his new job; the appointments with Dr. Mitchell were beneficial, and he was taking responsibility to better himself. Every day I removed the Suboxone from its hiding place and gave Ryder the prescribed dosage to place beneath his tongue. I believed he was committed to his recovery and to a new positive direction.

I especially looked forward to the full moon that month, which would appear the evening of my nephew's wedding in Chicago, where we planned to be. The reception was planned for the fourteenth floor of a downtown Chicago building offering a panoramic view of the rising moon. The bride and groom were graduates of Notre Dame with a beautiful future setting up for them. I so looked forward to my sons being with my family to remind them of the solid, blessed pack to which they belonged. This would be a bonus weekend with my sisters, and a glorious celebration with my extended family.

We had planned as we always had to fly standby, free fare, courtesy of Brad's employee benefits. September is traditionally an easy time of year to pass ride without the threat of getting bumped, but not that weekend. All the flights were oversold, and we never got to the wedding. I was sick about it for all the obvious reasons.

A couple of weeks later, one of Ryder's peers, a young woman who had been a heroin user, mistakenly injected air from a partially empty syringe into a vein in her arm and died. I had no idea who the girl was. Ryder planned on going to the funeral in Fergus Falls, a seventy-minute drive. As much as I understood his reasons for going, I did not want him to go. I worried about him driving his small, fragile Honda Del Sol on the interstate. It wouldn't survive getting hit by a bicycle, let alone a large semi. And the car was notorious, with every cop in the region knowing about the failed DEA bust in June and who drove it.

Cops wanted to catch Ryder somehow, someway, and the fewer times he drove, the fewer chances of something bad happening. I also didn't want him putting himself amongst addicts attending the funeral, and all the temptation and triggers that would present. I told him my reservations, but it had no effect. He went anyway.

Later that evening, once he'd returned to River Bend, he picked up his girlfriend. She requested they stop so she could use the restroom while he waited in the car. She'd spent a while inside, and once she rejoined Ryder, and they left, the suspicious station attendant searched the bathroom and found a discarded spoon with residue. He reported it to the police.

Ryder claimed he had no idea she had contraband. He could tell she had a buzz, but he'd just picked her up from a party. He had not used for over a month. Two cops pulled him over and approached the car.

"How's it going, Ryder?" They were on a first name basis. "You've got expired tabs." One officer with a flashlight was low-key. A second squad car arrived driven by a sergeant.

He shined his flashlight into the car. She was becoming paranoid for good reason.

"Okay if we take a look in the car, Ryder?"

"No. Why do you have to search my car for expired tabs?"

"You both need to step out of the car immediately," the sergeant demanded. He'd seen the footage from a security camera in the service station and knew Ryder's companion was the one who left the spoon in the bathroom.

Ryder was led to the officer's squad car and she was put into the sergeant's squad car while he searched the car and her purse.

"If I'm not being detained, I'd like to be let go," Ryder said after a couple of minutes of waiting.

"So long as he doesn't find a severed head or body parts, you'll be free to go shortly." The officer clearly felt this was going to be a routine search.

The sergeant found a pipe under the front seat. In the purse he found needles and heroin.

"Ryder has nothing to do with this; he didn't know I had this on me. It's not his fault. Leave him out of it," she told the police. She felt panicked and guilty for involving Ryder.

The sergeant came over and stated fiercely: "This just turned from a routine traffic stop into a narcotics investigation. You're both going to jail."

The cops actually high-fived one another and would later be credited for apprehending Ryder.

Ryder spent the weekend in jail, a huge setback for him. In jail, he dwelled on his bad luck, concluding that he'd been clean for over a month and still wound up in jail. Might as well be using.

Court procedures said that he could bond out for $5,000 no strings, or pay $500 and submit to regular drug testing until his hearing. Brad and I went into full-spin damage control, hiring his attorney, Kurt Williams, to once again defend him. Kurt had represented Ryder his senior year of high school after Ryder had been charged with theft. Ryder and a friend had pawned a ring belonging to the friend's stepmother, and she filed charges against Ryder. We'd learned of Kurt Williams through a friend, and learned only later that he had a reputation of being one of the best defense attorneys in the state.

There was no question who we'd hire to defend him this time.

We paid the $500 fee and brought Ryder home that Monday. Our tentative plans to list the house and move back to Minneapolis were extinguished with that arrest. The looming fears we'd had since Ryder's narrow escape in June from the DEA bust had now become a reality. The best-case scenario would have him restricted to living in Cass County for at least one year after sentencing. We would need to stay around.

The case Kurt was building for him would hopefully lead to a sentence called "drug court." If successful, a drug court verdict would require Ryder to submit to random drug testing, to report regularly to a probation officer, and to complete thirty days at a treatment facility. But there would be no jail time. If he stayed clean and compliant for one year, his felony possession charges would be dropped. The hearing would not be until January, so we had three months to wait, to wonder, to try not to worry about Ryder's future as a potential felon, along with the perpetual concern that he would slip back into addiction.

It was late October and past peak for the autumn colors. I'd noticed over the years that the trees release their leaves in a consistent succession annually. The same trees that go bare early do so every year. And the same is true for the trees that hang on until the last brutal wind in November to let go. It's difficult in the best of times to avoid a heavy heart when the only remaining foliage is the dormant lawn and the evergreen trees and shrubs. The landscape is stripped of color. It was as though Mother Nature had grown weary and fatigued. She washed her face, shed adornments, and retired for the approaching winter.

Wild turkey and deer were now visible in the grove of bare trees along the Minnesota river bank in the distant view beyond our backyard. The branches of the evergreen tree outside our bedroom window were littered with chunks of apples the squirrels were hoarding. The songbirds quieted, the geese migrating south honked their good-byes, and it was all very chilling to my spirit. The nets came off of the outdoor tennis courts, bringing a blunt reminder that winter was lurking. There really was no way to prepare for winter emotionally; we're simply forced to resign ourselves because it's part of life in North Dakota. I was grateful that at least I had a sport I could play twelve months out of the year. Every week of the winter I had at least one match to look forward to, and I enjoyed playing in a climate-controlled environment.

Halloween approached, and I'd never been a fan. To me, it's a very foreboding, sinister holiday. My birthday is November 6, and for most years in my life it had provided a bright day in a dim month. My mom died November 16, 2008, ten days after my birthday, and ever since, the first two weeks in November had become a fortnight of sorrow. This time of year was layered with reminders of loss and mortality—my aging body, and the harsher conditions and shorter days that came with the compulsory detachment from nature.

My mom had been a young-at-heart grandma until the day she died. She had adored my sons, spoiled them, and provided unconditional maternal support my entire life. She'd been frail from COPD symptoms when my dad passed away, but we'd never anticipated that we would lose her so soon after him—fourteen short weeks. During that time, Ann, Kelly and I divided the week into caretaking shifts while Kelly traveled from Grand Forks to stay with mom on weekends. Ann and I alternated weekday nights and slept over. We hired caregivers for the weekdays, and hospice volunteers and nurses filled in the gaps. Jackie felt awful for not living close enough to help, though we understood the situation for what it was.

The Sunday my mom passed away, she'd been content alone in her bedroom resting most of the day. The hospice nurse had been by, and Kelly asked her if mom seemed okay. The nurse felt that she was declining but that death wasn't imminent. Kelly was hesitant to return to Grand Forks when I relieved her at 5:00 p.m.

Once Kelly, left my mom grew increasingly despondent, and by eight forty-five I called Kelly about my concerns. She told me to call the hospice nurse and have her come back and check on mom again. The same nurse returned, and she was astonished at how quickly mom was failing. The nurse looked at me and said it would be soon, and recommended I call the priest.

Kelly got right back into her car and began the seventy-five-minute trip back to River Bend, hoping to be with our mother for possibly the last time. I lay in the bed embracing my mom's tiny, fragile body, my head nestled next to hers. She weighed only about ninety pounds by that time. COPD had demanded every ounce of her energy, every calorie just simply to breathe, to exist.

"I love you, Mama. It's okay; you'll be okay," I whispered. "I'm here; I love you."

Her breathing was rattled, as though her lungs were filled with fluid. I recognized that sound. I don't think she was in pain. She was staring up at the ceiling, transfixed, reaching with one arm, as though an angel was taking her by the hand to carry her home. Mom was transitioning to the next world as I held her close. This beautiful, precious woman, who loved and was loved so dearly, was in her final moments of life on earth. She had brought me into the world, and now I had to release her to the afterlife. I believed my dad was near, taking care of both of us.

The young priest was praying for her until I looked up at him and said, "She's gone." I only knew it was her last breath when no more were forthcoming. She'd wanted to die privately; I believe she wanted only me there because I'd always been tougher around the edges, in her opinion. I suspect Mom thought it would be too difficult for Kelly because of her tender, caring heart. Kelly had definitely taken my dad's death the hardest of us daughters. Mom's most dreaded scenario was to die with her family surrounding her. She said as much when she'd read in obituaries, "died surrounded by family."

"That poor soul," she'd joke. "Who wants a bunch of relatives around you watching you die? God, that sounds awful! You girls better not stand around looking at me when I'm on the way out."

Kelly arrived forty-five minutes after my mom died. She spent the night in their home on Willow Road, and I went home. In the morning, I got up to get back over there as soon as possible, and I let Murphy out and gazed out the backyard. It was calm, and light snowflakes fell softly as the sun rose in a clear sky. I don't know where the snow came from as it silently floated in slow motion to the ground. The sun reflected off of each flake in an iridescent shimmer. I intuited that it was "confetti" from my dad and all of our loved ones in heaven celebrating Colleen Cronin Chase's homecoming. When I drove the one-minute route back to Willow Road, a song came on the radio with Romeo and Juliet in the lyrics. More signs from above.

Our parents were together again.

My mom had a very playful, mischievous nature all of her life. Occasionally, when one of us asked her what time it was, she'd say, "Ten to."

We'd reply, "Ten to what?"

"Tend to your own business," she'd respond with a wink and a smile.

At 9:50 p.m. she'd taken her last breath. I realized later, when I was asked by the funeral director for her time of death, that it had been "ten to" ... 10:00 p.m. I believe she was smiling at that, and that my dad was in on it. She wanted us to tend to our own business now that she had moved on to heaven. Both of my parents died in their home with loved ones near. That meant the world to me and my sisters, because we'd known that was surely their desire.

It had been four years since they'd passed away. Because of my unrelenting grief during the year following their deaths, I hadn't tuned into the boys' grief keenly enough. My parents were like a second set of parents to my kids, only more patient and indulgent than Brad and I. I realize now that losing their grandparents at the age of sixteen, and the subsequent pain it brought, had been the beginning of their dark journey toward addiction.

They were grief stricken with only their teenage perspective to navigate through it. Our boys at that age were pulling away intrinsically, creating emotional distance, and they weren't willing to talk about it with me.

At that time, Avery and Ryder had just gotten their driver's licenses and were gaining control of where they went and with whom they hung out. I was losing them quicker than I could've ever imagined. But I also believed, with my parents on the other side, that my boys had two committed guardian souls to guide and protect them. Benevolent protection indeed, is the only explanation as to how we survived their descent into the hell of heroin addiction and the consequences that lay ahead.

12

I N LATE NOVEMBER, AVERY INFORMED us he was moving to Mayport, Minnesota, just across the river. He'd only been back home living with us for five months. As much as he'd enjoyed the relief from paying rent, he said he just felt the need to be on his own. The excuse he gave me was that we didn't allow girls to spend the night, and he didn't want to be bound to our house rules.

He and a friend, Kyle, rented a home. They worked together at a Holiday gas station and convenience store. We weren't surprised, nor were we happy about it. He still wasn't in school and would soon be spending every dime on living expenses. It was not a formula for getting ahead in life.

Ryder had become increasingly elusive. He was making it more difficult for me to ensure he was taking Suboxone on schedule. He'd want to wait because it made him sick, or it kept him from sleeping, or he didn't need it that day, or some other excuse. What he was doing was playing me, but I didn't know it. He was back to using painkillers and, of course, didn't want Suboxone in his system, or the opiates would make him violently ill. So he'd pace it so he could use on occasion, but needed the Suboxone on the days he wasn't using. That game went on for a while. Brad would come home from trips and get impatient with me because I didn't have the dosage hammered down to a set daily routine. It was so much easier said than done. How long do I try and roust him, argue with him, when I've got to leave for work, and he's asleep from working all night?

In early December, Ryder told me he planned to stay at Avery's house most of the time.

"You mean you're moving out?" I asked.

"Well, yeah, kinda."

"Have you asked Kurt about this? Are you able to live in Minnesota with your charges?"

"For now it's okay. I won't be there all the time."

"How do you think you can even afford it?"

"Kyle's paying rent too. They're not gonna charge me very much for rent. I'm going to want to see Avery anyway; it's the only way I'll be able to spend time with him."

"What about Suboxone? You're not taking that with you. The understanding is I give you one day's dose at a time. Dr. Mitchell doesn't want you to have charge of it. That's the agreement."

"I think I should be able to take responsibility for it. I've been doing good, Mom; I'm not using. I take it how I'm supposed to."

"There are so many reasons you should not be moving out now, Ryder; none of it makes sense for your situation, legal and otherwise."

"Mom, I don't want to talk about it. I know it just makes you mad; never mind."

All of our conversations concluded that way. Once I spoke my mind and offered a contrary opinion, the discussion was over. As bad of an idea as I knew it was to have them moving out when neither of them could clearly afford it, I was also fed up with trying to reason with them. The brief weeks of harmony and calm we'd had early fall had dissolved back into the tension that prevails when addiction has one foot inside the door.

Over the years, Brad had attempted logical, mentoring conversations about managing money with them: the importance of saving, having a nest egg before moving, and what it actually cost to live. They'd considered these conversations to be demeaning "lectures about money" from Dad, and they took none of his advice. They avoided those conversations as much as possible; they avoided Brad as much as possible. Now that Ryder was moving out, I felt ambivalent. A part of me just wanted them gone; out of sight meant less work and frustration for me. The other part of me wanted them underfoot in the hopes that I could be a positive influence.

I started to imagine living in our home without the boys. It promised a clean house empty of chaos. But in reality, they were in no position to better themselves, and the move, it seemed, would only set them further back. Even though Ryder said he wouldn't be living at Avery's all the time,

I knew that was just his way of buffering it so I didn't go on about what a bad decision that was, given his situation in every regard.

Our house wasn't huge, about three thousand square feet, but the reality was that Brad was gone over half the month. I didn't mind being alone, but I didn't want the house to feel so empty all the time. Our beautiful home was meant to be shared. I also didn't want Murphy to be alone all day, and I didn't want to feel like I'd have to race home to take care of her as soon as I finished work.

I was so often in the middle between the boys and Brad, because they were fearful of his wrath. Me, they just seemed to step all over. We knew the boys saw us as good cop/bad cop. Brad and I agreed that it wasn't a bad thing. Although they took advantage of my trust and optimism, I at least had a relationship with them. I believed the only way to have an influence on them was to have a relationship with them and keep the line of communication open. I was still trying to find my way as their mother, forever hoping to get them on the right path. I never wanted them to feel alienated or harshly judged by me. I believed that anything I did to make them feel loved and supported was a positive maternal choice. Tough love was foreign to me and counterintuitive.

I decided to let Brad sleep for twelve hours after a trip before telling him of Ryder's plans.

"Ryder is moving out with Avery."

Brad's face was crossed with a look of disgusted resignation mixed with anger.

"Are you serious?"

"He made it sound like he wouldn't be there all the time, but obviously he won't be here much," I said.

"How's he going to stay clean if he's living there? They're so f'n stupid. Did he ask Kurt about it?"

"He claims he did, and that it's not a legal issue. I don't know how we work this in with his Suboxone. You know how they only give two-word answers, and then cut the conversation short when I don't respond favorably. It was one of those conversations. He won't hear anything I have to say, so I didn't say much."

"They're both going to end up broke, in debt, using, and desperate. Stupid and stubborn is not a good combination, and they're both, in a big way."

Brad attempted to talk to them about it. They simply would not listen to any perspective that was contrary to whatever agenda they were pursuing. We were sure Avery was still smoking pot. It seemed Brad and I were not going to be able to derail their plan to move out. We would have to once again sit on the sidelines and wait for the inevitable downfall from their stubborn, misguided decision. It wasn't a question of if this would end badly. It was a matter of how bad will the damage be and when? They had no appreciation for how much of their lives we bankrolled: health and car insurance, cell phone, groceries, attorney fees, treatment, and on and on. Another unspoken "I told you so" scenario was setting up.

Ryder was planning to create enough distance to disappear, unnoticed, for a weekend in Minneapolis to use heroin one last time before his hearing in January. He knew this game of Suboxone and occasional use couldn't go on forever; he decided one last hurrah with it, then he'd be done with heroin. Done at least until his legal situation was settled and behind him.

I learned a year later what happened. Ryder finally told me over the course of several conversations, revealing only as much information as I could stomach at a time. I believe he broke up the story because it was so horrific.

He went to Minneapolis, bought some heroin, and then checked into a hotel room with several addicts. Ryder made the mistake of dosing himself with the amount he was capable of using when his tolerance was high. The moment the needle hits his vein, he knew he'd made a terrible mistake, but it was too late.

"Fuck, he's blue. He took a hotshot!" one of the addicts gasped.

"He's not breathing, he flopped!"

"Grab the dope and his phone and get the fuck out!" said another.

With that, they all fled in fear of incriminating themselves. A random guest of the hotel, a woman, overheard the commotion and called 911. One of the addicts returned; his conscience wouldn't allow him to abandon Ryder. He performed rescue breathing until the paramedics arrived. The EMTs credited him for saving Ryder's life.

They couldn't get him to breathe on his own, so they took him by ambulance to the ER at a nearby hospital. The team there hooked him up to Narcan for heroin overdose and oxygen. Ryder stopped breathing and was resuscitated sixteen times, *sixteen times*. The ER team considered having him transported to the Mayo Clinic in Rochester, seventy miles away, in hopes of saving his life.

Meanwhile a hospital chaplain came to Ryder's side, held his hand, and prayed. Ryder was unaware of how long the chaplain was there praying for him, hours for sure. When Ryder awoke, he was no longer hooked up to Narcan or oxygen. Somehow he had stabilized. The attending physician told Ryder:

"I've never seen someone survive what you have. It's a miracle you're alive, and the fact that you haven't sustained permanent brain damage, well, I cannot explain it medically. Clearly someone wants you alive."

13

F AITH IN GOD AND MY belief in the afterlife were central to my ability
  to cope. I believed my parents had been guiding and protecting us
since their deaths. My Christian roots remained intact, but my stem most
resembled Buddhism; the blossoms of my faith were eclectic and enriched
by my connection with Mother Nature. I felt profoundly aligned with the
Dalai Lama's statement: "My religion is simple. My religion is kindness."

I believe my intuition is the voice of my soul, and my soul is the
essence of me that came from God. The whispers of intuition were God's
voice guiding me; my intuition was a compass I relied on to navigate
through both dark times and opportunity. My perspective on life is best
captured by Pierre Teilhard de Chardin, the French philosopher and Jesuit
priest: "'We are not human beings having a spiritual experience. We are
spiritual beings having a human experience." Since early adulthood I'd
aspired to live life, to make decisions, to be guided more from my soul and
less from my humanness. I aspired to transcend the influences of ego, fear,
and the inner pessimistic voice that dwells within all of us.

From my life, I'd learned that by following my intuition I was led
to the lessons and experiences that would fulfill my purposes in life, my
destiny. Living intuitively did not ensure a shortcut to ongoing fulfillment
free of jeopardy and pain. But I believed it did ensure I was living in
alignment with my soul.

My experience with intuition began in my late teens. I'd get intuitive
"hits" and make decisions, often spontaneous, based on my interpretation
of the cues. I refined my connection with intuition over the years. As a
result, I can look back on my life and acknowledge that I've been a risk
taker, a free spirit. I've felt secure in decisions, many life altering, that logic

wouldn't advocate. I've been willing to "fail" knowing that the wisdom I'd gained and my evolution were the purpose and reward. I've left everything on the court in this game of life.

Since 2008, feng shui had become an additional resource, enabling me to live intentionally, to align with my soul's destiny and to attract providence. By practicing feng shui principles, I maintained an uplifting, supportive environment. Our home inspired and elevated me.

You might question my convictions by asking, "How on earth, with all my prayers, with my parents watching over us, with my compelling intuition, and with the feng shui I'd practiced—how in the world did our sons end up descending into the hell of addiction?"

Fair question, and I'd asked it myself. The answer that resonated was that we're never privileged to know what would have happened if not for prayer, divine benevolence, intuition, and feng shui. Quite possibly without each our family—my sons—would have been far worse off. And second, our story was not over; addiction had us under siege, but it was still the beginning chapters of our sons' lives, and the middle chapters of mine and Brad's. It was premature to judge the long-term result of God's plan for us, and our collective destiny. So I kept on praying, to God and to my parents; I kept on practicing feng shui, and I completely trusted my intuition.

In feng shui, the principles of yin and yang—opposite energies that attract each other—are a significant facet. You include them when striving to improve and balance the energy in a home or office to achieve a positive flow of energy (chi). A balance of both is optimum to facilitate positive chi flow and to create harmony. In addition to the chi of a room or home, there is also personal chi to address, to enhance.

Yin energy is quiet, resting, inward, and dark. Yang is loud, active, outward, and bright. My personal energy (chi) had been unbalanced, predominantly yin as a result of the struggles with Avery and Ryder, most especially since the DEA broke into our home the previous June. I had withdrawn from friends and family. My sense of humor, my playful nature, had been hushed. I preferred to process my emotions alone, to suffer silently, though not in self-pity.

At work, I was engaged and extroverted, but it was contrary to how I felt. I transcended my despair because I was a professional, and my employer deserved to have the person I'd presented in the interview. Not to mention I needed to earn as much money as possible, and selling more beds meant more income. I appreciated the positive distraction the career offered me.

In North Dakota winter is a season predominated by yin energy. Darkness prevailed with daylight shrinking. The cold climate forced a varied degree of social isolation depending on one's lifestyle. Winter, I felt, was more about the absence of life than what was present. Except for the deer grazing in the wooded patches along the river, all was quiet. Creatures hibernated, birds were silent, the earth was buried under snow, the trees were bare, and the river was frozen. My connection with nature became distant, more observation than interaction.

With the 2012 holiday season approaching, Brad was gone on a six-day Asian trip. Before he left, I'd said to him:

"I'd like to find someone to move in. The house feels so empty with the boys gone. Murphy is lonesome all day alone."

"What did you have in mind?"

"I'm not sure, maybe a college student, a graduate student who's outgrown partying."

"That's okay with me. You'll think of something; you always do," Brad affirmed.

With the boys moved out and Brad flying a lot in the beginning of December, it would be up to me to decorate for Christmas. I had no idea about the ER visit in Minneapolis and how close we'd come to losing Ryder weeks before. Maybe I felt it on some level because I was especially heavy of heart. Once down from the rafters in the garage, the artificial Christmas tree we'd had for many years went up sporadically. The two large cardboard boxes with the limbs, truck and treetop, and several more containers with trimmings, stockings, and ornaments, cluttered the living room for several days. I assembled it partially, but the treetop remained boxed for several more days. I strung some lights, but only one color was working out of four.

I struggled to bring myself to unpack the ornaments. Nearly all of them were collected from the boys' childhood. There were silver bells commemorating baby's first Christmas, one each with his name and 1992 engraved. Another was an acrylic snowflake; in the middle was a photograph I'd cut to fit the circle. It was of the boys asleep, wearing baseball caps, cuddled next to one another, when they were almost two years old. There were dozens of homemade ornaments the boys proudly brought home from elementary school each December. Wreath designs created from their green finger-painted handprints on a handkerchief. The sight of the keepsake ornaments laid out on the carpet brought me to my knees. The echoes of endearing memories splintered my spirit into lonely fragments of despair. I cried silently, my shoulders heaving, tears flowing. Alone, I tried to muster the energy to arrange the shredded pieces of my heart, on that tree.

I recalled one of our blessed Christmases with my entire family when the boys were five years old. Ryder and Avery were still shy. They would cling to my legs, for the first half an hour after we'd arrived anywhere. That Christmas Eve the boys were playing on the floor in the center of our large asymmetrical circle of love, all twenty-one of us, talking, eating, and joking. The boys had a turn to open a gift, a Fisher Price pirate ship with all the figures and props to go with it. They immediately escaped into a shared spontaneous pirate escapade without deliberation, pure imagination. We all hushed and took in the magic of Christmas, of twins, of family. They continued their adventure unaware of the captive audience for over ten minutes. No one in my family will ever forget that precious scene.

In the quiet, empty home, post tears, I could hear my inner voice, my intuition. I felt a clear unequivocal directive … "Call the Freeze, and see if they need a host family for a hockey player."

It was as though someone had called and spoken to me over the phone, telling me to do this without reservation or hesitation. Although I didn't technically hear a voice, it was more a knowing, a sensing of the message. It was intuition. I knew better than to dismiss the unfounded and unlikely notion. The only thing I knew about The Freeze was that they existed.

The idea seemed unlikely to me because Brad was not a hockey fan. He was unimpressed with what he perceived as redneck coaching by a handful of the hockey parents the year we allowed Ryder to play league hockey. We'd steered our boys clear of it because our flight schedules conflicted with the travel and expenses the hockey lifestyle required.

To pursue my intuition, I knew all I needed to do was to take the next step and see where it led. I went to the Freeze website and learned they were a USHL hockey team. The players were elite athletes aged sixteen to twenty. The younger Freeze players attended South River Bend High

School, and the USHL covered all their hockey and travel expenses. It was not a pay to play league with wannabe players. Ninety percent of them went on to earn hockey scholarships at Division 1 universities. Some were already committed to an NHL team post college.

I'd never been to a Freeze game, nor had I been in the River Bend Arena, where they played. I certainly was not a fan. Why would they need a family to host a player in the middle of their season? Unless the player didn't get along with his family, in which case we weren't interested. If I'd navigated by logic alone, the pursuit of this intuitive hit wouldn't have moved another inch. Yet I believed that I needed to respect my intuition by taking the next step. And as Brad had validated, "I'd think of something."

I searched the website and found a contact, someone named Terry. I wasn't sure if that was a man or a woman, but I left a message … "Are you seeking a host family at this time? If so, what requirements need to be met to be considered for this opportunity?"

I contemplated other options while I waited for a response, believing it would be sensible to get a renter. With all the legal bills coming in to defend Ryder, why not find another income source to help offset the expenses? Perhaps there was a grad student at one of the three local universities looking to live quietly in a residential neighborhood away from all the distractions of campus life—someone who was done with the party scene. I didn't want another SSDD (same sh*! different day) scenario playing out.

The next day I heard from Terry with a phone number to reach her.

"Thank you so much for your interest, Dana. Yes, we do actually need a host family currently."

"Really? I wasn't sure; given this time of year, it seemed unlikely."

"The trade deadline is next week, and we've acquired two new players. We've already placed one, but we still need a home for the other. Jesse's allergic to cats; I hope you don't have any?"

Her voice inflexion hinted to me that she wanted this to be a match.

"We definitely don't have cats; in fact, both my husband and one of our sons are allergic to cats as well. We do have a dog, but she doesn't shed."

"Awesome! The player's name is Jesse Marcus. He came from the Nebraska Knights. He is one of the most delightful young men I've ever met, and I've met plenty over the years! He's a nineteen-year-old African

American. His family lives in North Carolina. How soon might you be available once we complete an eligibility search?"

"Honestly, I have to let my husband know. He's out of town. He's open to the opportunity, but we haven't discussed the details. Let me e-mail him, and I'll get back in touch."

"Perfect; meanwhile, I'll send you an application and some guidelines. I look forward to hearing from you, Dana."

I searched the Nebraska Knights website and found a bio on Jesse. On the screen I gazed at his endearing face. In the photo his expression was neutral, as though he was looking at a clock or a menu, something that required no reaction. I saw a handsome young man with kindness and humility in his eyes, and I felt God's hands holding my heart. I knew bringing him into our lives was going to be a blessing. I felt it.

The tenderness of that moment was paralleled by the rush I feel when I'm on course, when something good is setting up, when I'm riding the wave of my intuition. I felt elated to have a young man, an elite athlete, in our home. I'd often wondered how it was possible that Brad and I didn't have sports crazy kids, given our interest and athletic abilities, and my competitive nature in tennis. I anticipated the pleasure and distraction of going to Jesse's games, being invested in his pursuit of success. It would be a parental experience so contrary from what we'd been enduring for the last three years. I could feel a vibration shift within. Yin receding, yang increasing. The heaviness of dread and concern that had been bearing down on my shoulders was replaced with joyful anticipation. It had been so long since I'd felt excitement about anything. Brad said I'd think of something—I sure did!

I explained the opportunity in an e-mail to Brad but didn't give him Jesse's name. Then I patiently waited for his validation. He was in the middle of a Tokyo and Guam trip. I never paid attention to the time zone differential and knew Brad would check his e-mails once he woke up.

The next morning his response was in my inbox: "I can't believe you'd seriously consider having another nineteen -year-old male move into our home. After all we've been through isn't it time for some relief? The last thing I want is some kid drinking my beer, sneaking girls over, and having to track him down after curfew. I like that you're coming up with ideas, but keep thinking. I don't need the headaches of this one."

Ouch.

That hurt, and I didn't expect it. The trouble was that I'd more or less committed to Terry, and my heart was melting for this young man I hadn't met yet. I felt my intuition was leading me by the collar to this outcome, and I was attached to it already. I steadied myself and responded to his e-mail with one question. I knew what not to do when it came to my husband.

I typed, "Is that your final answer?" and hit send. I knew a well-written rebuttal was not the way to handle this. Becoming defensive, in spite of how badly I wanted this to happen, wouldn't help either. As big of a responsibility and commitment as hosting a player was, I didn't want Brad to feel forced into the idea if he was truly opposed. I was also aware that he knew nothing about the opportunity, that he was reacting based on assumptions and the depleting experiences we were having with our sons.

His next e-mail response was softer, and began, "Well maybe I'm just being an asshole …" He had some questions and concerns he asked me to address with Terry before he would decide. Does he have his own car? Is his gear left at the arena? What's his curfew? What are our grocery/cooking responsibilities? What does his previous family have to say about him? Brad really didn't have serious concerns when it came down to it.

Terry set me up with a suite for the next game to watch Jesse and meet him afterward. He would then be leaving for home on Christmas break, and if it all worked out, he'd move in with us when he returned December 27.

Terry came to the suite and introduced herself between periods.

"Wow, Terry, this is so awesome, thank you!"

"You're welcome, and thank you for becoming a billet family."

Jesse, wearing number 13, impressed me quickly.

"Jesse looks amazing; he's crazy fast!"

"Yes, he's an awesome player, and we're very lucky to get him. He's got a great reputation as a team player and disciplined athlete. He was co-captain of the Knights."

"Seriously? They traded a team captain. What happened?"

"The coach was under a lot of criticism, and I think he wanted to shake it up. He traded the other captain too."

"I'll bet that was hard for Jesse's billet family."

"Yes, it was. They've been a billet family for over ten years to many players. His billet mom decided not to take on another player for now. She's totally devastated by it. She adored Jesse."

"Sounds like I had good timing e-mailing you. Thirteen must be our lucky number!"

"Yes, it was perfect timing, actually. I had another family inquire a couple of hours after you. I'm glad he's going to be with you and your family, Dana. I can tell you'll be an awesome billet mom."

I could feel myself choking up; any compliment to me as a mother tapped into very raw emotions. I held it in. I went on to explain that my sons had recently moved out but may come around occasionally.

The game was a blast to watch. Jesse was clearly a very physical player, which landed him in the penalty box several times. He would fast become a fan favorite. I had flashbacks to my collage years at UND in Grand Forks, going to the Sioux hockey games. There's nothing like live hockey for a spectator; the pace and the energy were electric. This was a distraction I would be thrilled to include for the remainder of the winter. Life had been all work and damage control with the boys. What would it be like to have this awesome young man in our lives? Something within me was beginning to thaw. I felt the strength and shift of yang energy within me restoring balance.

Delightful, unpretentious, and good-natured, Terry and I chatted while waiting for Jesse to wrap up in the locker room. She was proud of her three children, including a daughter who had been voted Ms. Hockey North Dakota her senior year of high school.

Jesse appeared in a wool cap, steel gray vest, and suit pants. His lavender shirt was perfectly pressed. He had quite a presence, very GQ, strong, striking, and all smiles. We chatted for about ten minutes, just the small talk required to become acquainted. Terry and her daughter were included, and they exchanged playful banter. He'd only lived with them a week but already a tremendous comfort level had been established. My heart was cartwheeling!

I couldn't wait to tell Brad what a charming young man he was. I knew Brad would feel the same. Jesse was truly an exceptional young man, playful and outgoing—clearly comfortable and confident in himself without conceit. In one week he'd be living in our home, and I couldn't wait.

The next day the boys were moving some more belongings out. I interrupted them to show them Jesse's bio on the Knight's website and to tell them about the decision. I was confident they couldn't care less.

Ryder was upset.

"What? You're having a Freeze hockey player move into our home? Why?"

"I don't want to live in an empty house; you know how much Brad is gone. I don't like Murphy being home all day alone. And the Freeze needed a home for Jesse, and we have plenty of home to share with him."

Is he going to be able to have friends over?" Avery wasn't making eye contact.

"Of course. Why wouldn't he?"

"Well that's not fair. You forbid us from having friends over, and now a complete stranger moves in and his friends, you've never met, can come over? That's insulting, Mom."

They were trying to leave.

"You know why you guys could no longer have friends over. You've broken every rule we've ever set. You and your friends were doing drugs in our home," I said with pseudo calm. I wanted to knock them upside the head.

"That's humiliating. I'll be completely embarrassed when our friends find out they couldn't come over, but now a Freeze player and his friends can hang out in our home. That really sucks."

I contained myself. There was no way of having a reasonable conversation with them, about anything, it seemed. I wouldn't be able to convince them to see my perspective, and I wasn't going to waste energy trying. It was clear how I needed to play this one to get the outcome I was seeking. I didn't expect them to be pals with Jesse, although that would be great, but I certainly didn't want them to resent him. So I responded.

"That's what bothers you about him living with us? That he can have friends over?"

"Yes," Ryder answered, and Avery nodded.

Nothing else about it bothers you then?"

"Nope, it's your house; we're not gonna be here."

"Well, okay, then, I tell him he's not allowed to have friends over," I said sincerely.

I knew that in a matter of time they would no longer care about it. Once they met Jesse, they would see how unreasonable they were being. But for now, I wanted them to give Jesse a chance and not resent him before they even met him.

"Really?"

"Yes. I don't want you to be resentful that he's here."

That was that. They took whatever they came for and left. They seemed appeased about the situation. I looked forward to the inevitable energy shift in our home with the two of them gone and Jesse moved in. I felt a sense of relief and hope. And I was proud of my ability and approach to win Brad and the boys over to an agenda that I believed would benefit all of us.

The day Jesse was due to move in, I was at work. Brad was home, and as it turned out, the boys were home as well. I felt distracted at work, so curious and nervous. I wanted to be home acting as the liaison, introducing Terry and Jesse to Brad and the boys, smoothing out any awkward moments. Instead Terry arrived from the airport with Jesse and his minimal belongings to meet the rest of our family for the first time. I was stuck in the mall wondering how it was going.

I finally had a chance to call. Brad didn't answer his cell phone, so I tried Ryder.

"How's it going, honey? Is Jesse there yet?"

"He was here, but he had to go to practice. He brought his stuff up to his room and left for the arena."

"So you got a chance to meet him?"

"Yeah, Mom. He's awesome—very cool, really nice guy. I like him! I might be coming home a lot more than I thought; he'd been fun to hang out with."

"What did Brad think?"

"I don't know, but he was smiling the whole time."

14

BRAD AND I NEVER SERIOUSLY considered having more children after the boys were born. Once married, I'd gone off birth control and relied on the rhythm method, which I'd learned about growing up as a Catholic girl. It predicted ovulation by taking your temperature nightly and recording it. By doing so, you'd know when to abstain or to try, depending on the desired outcome. After a year and a half of trying not to conceive, we reversed the rhythm method for the first time, and I conceived. I had the sense that Ryder and Avery had been patiently waiting to come into our lives and that they seized their opportunity the first chance they got.

Once you've had twins, your likelihood of having a second set increases. Brad and I agreed that four children were probably more than we could reasonably handle, so we stopped at two. Our families had no history of twins. I felt so lucky and blessed to have had two healthy babies in one pregnancy. I leaned later that identical twins have nothing to do with genetics; they're just a random miracle with which God graced us.

Nineteen years later, we had a third son. The new year felt like a fresh start with Jesse joining our family; overnight, I became a hockey mom. His presence in our lives was much like moving to a lake home for the summer, a refreshing and exciting change of view that soon blended into delightful status quo. Becoming a host family wasn't something we'd had on the back burner for years until the timing was right. It went from being a notion out of nowhere to reality in a matter of weeks. Oddly, those were the types of decisions that felt the truest to me. I didn't require a methodical forecast to endorse my hunches. Spontaneously responding to my intuition was my comfort zone, my wheelhouse.

Jessee adapted to his new surroundings as easily as sinking into a warm bath. If he was struggling with any aspect of his abrupt departure from the Nebraska Knights, it wasn't apparent to me. It was his nature to be positive and move forward; he was one happy-go-lucky young man. He'd been living away from his parents in North Carolina since accepting an invitation to attend a prep school in Minnesota his freshman year of high school. His passion for hockey, and his desire to play on a college level, were his driving motivations. He considered the trade to the Freeze as an opportunity to play for a team that had a better season record, and he appreciated the new arena, training facilities, coaching staff, teammates, and the raving fan base the Freeze had established.

The River Bend Arena, where the Freeze played their home games, was only five years old and was state of the art. It captured the excitement of a large arena with the bold lighted signage that wrapped around the entire arena flashing advertisements, USHL score updates, and cheers to rally the home crowd. Yet it provided intimate seating with a great view from every seat, and offered private suites that filled the upper deck perimeter. Two big screens mounted high at each end of the rink replayed goals, advertisements, and other distractions between periods.

Minutes before the Freeze would enter the ice, those screens would show a black and white prerecorded pep talk of the coach touting the skill set required to be a hockey player: "You're special athletes." The arena then would go dark except for multiple roaming spotlights. There was a rousing palpable buzz, much like it feels moments before a rock band takes the stage. The fans were on their feet as the home team flew onto the ice, lapping the rink several times before the starting lineup was introduced. One by one the spotlight would follow each of the five starters and the goalie to center ice. They'd come to a quick stop, and shaved ice would spray as each starter took his place. Every game a soloist de jour would sing the national anthem, and the crowd would erupt in applause and hollers. Game on!

I had two season tickets as part of the billet package. About half the time I went alone, arriving just in time for the pregame warm-up. I would work from eleven to six, change clothes at the mall, and go right to the arena. Brad was usually flying on weekends and didn't make it to many games. Jack, my tennis buddy, joined me for about eight games during the season. He knew a lot about hockey and briefed me about the rules and strategy, of which I'd known very little. I befriended a younger couple who had season ticket seats right next to me, and they were thrilled to learn I was Jesse's "mom." All around me at games I often heard admiring comments about Jesse from fans unaware that I was his billet mom.

It had been five years since I'd cheered a son competing in an athletic event. Avery's sophomore year he'd lettered in tennis, but that was the end of high school sports for my boys. Ryder had begun his sophomore year on the tennis team, then quit when one of the team captains berated him. Their tennis team photographs were the last captured memory of them as the sons I had known before addiction dug her nails into their souls. Each photo portrays a fifteen-year-old boy wearing a marine blue team jersey standing next to the net holding a tennis racquet, smiling. I'd imagined their senior tennis season, how good they'd be by then with all the lessons and court time in which we were willing to invest. I'd envisioned the team banquet senior year; I was so sure it would be one of my fondest memories of their high school years. None of it happened, dissolving instead into an expanding puddle of grief.

Becoming a hockey fan and billet mom blessed me with a compelling distraction. It was medicinal. Instead of spending the winter evenings watching vocal competitions and movies on TV, I was at the River Bend Arena invested in the outcome of every shift, every game. I didn't even mind attending games alone; I didn't want to be distracted with conversation. I was there to watch the game, to support Jesse, and I didn't want to miss a moment.

Shortly after Jesse arrived, the Freeze launched a winning streak, generating buzz and momentum within the team and in the community. Jesse was grabbing more than his share of press coverage in the local *River Bend Forum* newspaper. He was featured in newspaper articles three times that January. He had star power. Freeze fans had fervently supported Jesse, an explosive skater who never hesitated to drop his gloves if it came down to a fight. Hockey fans love a fight.

Off the ice and at home, Jesse could not have been more buoyant or gregarious. He and Murphy bonded. The two of them had the house to themselves a great deal of the time. We knew we could trust Jesse completely from day one. What we had was nearly a complete opposite child from our own. After years of hoping people wouldn't ask me about my kids, I suddenly had a "son" who had a rapidly expanding fan base. It was a foreign, uplifting feeling. I was aware that I had nothing to do with his success, and clearly felt no credit was due to me. Gloating was an option, but it didn't suit me. Bringing Jesse into our family had been one of the greatest gifts rendered from intuition. Proof, I believed, that no matter how deep in despair I found myself, my intuition was still available to guide and bless me.

Amid the press Jesse was attracting in January, I also was contacted by the *River Bend Forum* on a completely unrelated matter. Amber Nelson, a reporter, called to ask if I'd be willing to be interviewed for an article on desk organization. She'd found my website by searching feng shui. Our conversation so intrigued her that she wrote the entire article about feng shui featuring me. It took up two pages, including photos of me and our home. Kind of crazy really; out of nowhere, I end up featured in a two-page spread, with a teaser on the front page. I believed it was the influence Jesse cast; as my spirits were raised, so too was the level of opportunity I was attracting. That was the way I saw the world—there was no such thing as coincidence, and all events are somehow related.

My website offered my life coaching and feng shui services. In humility I will say I have a powerful skill set to offer anyone seeking positive transformation. I never aspired to rely on my consulting to pay the bills. I didn't want to ever be in the position to feel pressure to maintain a regular list of clients. That hustle vibe felt contrary to who I was as a life coach and feng shui practitioner. The website was beautiful, with high-resolution photos rotating on the home page partnered with inspiring quotes. I paid a monthly hosting fee, and sometimes I wondered why I even bothered, yet intuitively I believed the website would serve a greater purpose at some point in my life.

I'd decided to schedule a feng shui class to capitalize on the newspaper article. The fact that I was willing to be in the public eye, ever so briefly, was evidence of the shift that was occurring within. I had eight students enroll in a beginning four-week class, and suddenly I was very busy preparing curriculum, teaching classes, working full time, going to hockey games, and keeping the refrigerator stocked for Jesse. Tennis once a week was all I could fit in.

Ryder's court date was approaching. The worst-case scenario would have him incarcerated for a length of time "to be determined," with a felony charge that would remain on his record for seven years—a situation that called for me to hope for the best and let go of the rest. There was every reason to make worry my pastime, but when it came to worry, I was uncharacteristically pragmatic. Worry was a destructive current always within reach that could easily pull me down. It was my choice to either dip in and be swept under, or to keep my legs moving, treading to stay above it. I can't say I never worried, but I had my ways of managing it with my personal spin on life, which was a mixture of positive distractions and denial. Mostly I trusted God's plan and my ability to survive.

I gravitated toward hope as though it was a tulip struggling to bloom in late February. I watered it, kept it in the sunshine, fertilized it, and protected it, trying to give it a chance against all odds to flourish. The slightest gain in Ryder and Avery's progress would have me believe that it would just be this one last hurdle to clear, then on to the life we'd planned. One day, one month, at a time we'd help Ryder get through his sentence so he could learn his lesson, beat addiction, and move on to better days. Without hope, I'd end up falling through the ice, drowning in freezing darkness.

His court date finally arrived in late January. We were relieved to have him accepted into "drug court". As long as he abided by their rules he'd be spared from serving time in jail. If he made it, the felony charges would be reduced to a misdemeanor after one year. He was required to live in Cass County, North Dakota, which meant he had to move back home with us, since Avery's rental was in Minnesota. Ryder was assigned a probation officer and was subject to random drug testing. He was scheduled to enter and complete a thirty-day drug treatment program due to begin in March 2013.

I was happy Ryder was forced to move back in with us for a month before he moved into a treatment facility. I believed having him home with Jesse around would be a positive influence. And despite all their differences, Jesse and Ryder became close. They spent many hours watching NHL games, and switching over to the reality shows during period breaks. They'd laugh and banter about the dysfunction of the misfits communing together on MTV's *Real World*. Their polarized directions seemed to meet in the middle and balance out. Those times with Jesse and Ryder hanging out in our living room were my only glimpses of what homeostasis was relative to nineteen-year-old males.

15

WE QUICKLY GREW TO LOVE Jesse, as any parents who held him under their wings would have. Initially my maternal instinct with Jesse was inadvertent restraint, tempered with joy. I didn't want him to feel that I was an impulsive wannabe hockey mom attempting to bask in his celebrity. I was accustomed to my sons' disengagement from my influence and nurturing. Maybe I was protecting myself from compounded maternal dejection, knowing that his time with us would be brief. My confidence as a mother had been mugged and left for dead before Jesse was even on the radar. I gradually relaxed into the blessing of this new facet of family. I was grateful for Jesse's warm, unpretentious charm, which he extended to everyone.

What coach cuts the fan favorite, the captain, a disciplined contributing player? What mother emotionally bankrupt from her sons' destructive paths trusts her maternal fortitude? I'd met with opposition from Brad and the boys. Yet somehow mine and Jesse's paths intersected at a serendipitous crossroad. He was superlative evidence of my intuition, my connection to the Divine. I was humbled by the tangibility of an unlikely whisper that survived to blossom into the endearing gift that he was to us. Jesse blended with our family as naturally as waves melt into the shoreline. I was in awe of the providence that ordained it.

A typical day for Jesse included a morning workout at the arena with the team, then back on the ice in the afternoon for practice. On game day, he'd leave for the arena around four. I went to all his games in River Bend, but I never invited myself along for the team's postgame pit stop, often at his favorite restaurant near the mall where I worked. I figured if parents were included, he'd mention it. He would be gone for up to five days at a time when they had a road trip.

He adjusted to our home immediately, in part because he was so adaptable and in part because we made an effort to accommodate him. I allowed Jesse his independence within the Freeze rules, but I wasn't sure if I left him on his own more that he wanted. I'd told Terry, the host family organizer, that I worked retail hours, and we didn't have a typical family dinner hour, or typical life, for that matter. I explained that Jesse would be on his own a lot, but I would cook when I could, and I'd keep the refrigerator stocked. She assured me that was all acceptable. The "no friends over" rule I'd negotiated with Ryder and Avery regarding Jesse never went into effect. Jesse had teammates over occasionally, as well as female friends.

One evening I decided to check in with Jesse and make sure he was happy with everything.

"I hope you're comfortable here. I know I'm not around much, and with Brad flying and Ryder's work schedule, you're here alone a lot."

"No, it's all good," he smiled. "I got everything I need."

"I know your billet mom in Nebraska was a stay-at-home mom. I'm sure you got a lot more home cooking."

"Yeah, she was home every day, and she was real active with the team too, but she had the time to do it."

Murphy jumped up on my lap for some comfort.

"Honestly, I'm so used to my boys pushing me away, avoiding me."

I focused on scratching Murphy behind her ears.

"I may have assumed you've wanted the same level of independence. I don't want you to feel that we're not here for you, for whatever you need."

"No, it's cool; we're good. I like it here." He smiled again, and I knew he was sincere.

"Well, please don't wait for me to ask if you want anything; just shoot me a text. Having said that, do you need anything for the road trip?"

"Some more Gummy Bears and string cheese would be great. Thank you."

"Sure thing. I'll have them before you leave tomorrow."

None of us, including Jesse, knew if he would return to the Freeze for his final year of eligibility in the fall of 2013. The decision relied on potential offers from Division 1 colleges. He was playing well, but no offers he couldn't refuse had come calling. I didn't probe. I didn't want Jesse to feel obliged to share every detail about his life.

One of my innate values was maintaining harmony in relationships. I never wanted to be perceived as a bugger by anyone, ever. I've wondered if that was in part to blame for my sons' detour into drugs. Did I default to my comfort zone when I should have gotten up in their faces? Was I trying to maintain harmony when I should have been turning them upside down? Had I trusted too much? Now, having another "son," I was prone to examine my tendencies as a mother. I held myself to blame that my boys had become lost. Maybe I could figure it out and fix it somehow.

By mid-February, the Freeze had several away series coming up and only eight more regular-season home games. The team had a great chance of making it into the playoffs, which would have meant more games. Jesse ended up missing five games with an ACL injury that he acquired during practice. Luckily, it was a bruise and not a tear. But the coach held him out so he'd be at full strength for the playoffs. He also came home from practice one day with stitches in his upper lip from a puck.

"What happened?" I tried not to smother him with concern. His lip was swollen, with raw stitches.

"Ah, well, I just took a puck to the face." He tried to downplay it.

"Did you go to the emergency room?"

"Yeah, and waited forever, so annoying. The doc wanted to send me to a plastic surgeon, but I was sick of waiting around. I said, 'Forget about it … just stitch it up and get me outta here!'" He muffled a laugh, not wanting to strain his stitches.

Around that time, Jesse's mom came from North Carolina for a weekend series. Tamera and I quickly became comfortable with one another. I admired the fact that she and Jesse's father had raised such a remarkable young man, even though he'd left home at fourteen years old. She had my respect before I'd met her. I could tell Jesse had much in common with her. He resembled her, and his lighthearted spirit was very much her personality.

I'd asked her, "It must have been difficult, letting Jesse move so far away from you when he was still so young?"

"Well, of course, but I knew it was the best thing for him. It was an exceptional opportunity, and I knew it was right. The boy is driven!" She laughed in her easy way.

I didn't go into detail about our troubles with Ryder and Avery, but she knew they were struggling to get on track.

"It's so inspiring, the positive influence you've had on Jesse thousands of miles away. Then I look at our situation; our kids have had at least one parent home every day of their lives and can't seem to find their way. Go figure."

"They will; don't you worry. You're good parents; Jesse loves you two. It's all gonna work out."

For her second trip to River Bend in April, she stayed at our home. Tamera was very generous sharing Jesse with us. She'd nudge me at the games when Jesse scored goals: "There's your boy!" And when he'd drop his gloves, she'd bury her face in my shoulder, and we'd laugh about it once the brawl ended without injury.

Jesse's dad came to watch his games several weekends too. His parents had been divorced since Jesse was a little boy, their only child together. On one occasion Jesse, his Dad, and I went out to dinner after a game. His dad was very different from his mom. It was a similar blend of parental influence, much like Brad and me. Michael was more businesslike, a strong and positive paternal influence of love and support. At dinner that night, the female server extended a note to Jesse.

"It's from the girl at the table over there." She nodded toward an attractive blonde who smiled and quickly looked away.

It was a brazen move, and Jesse's dad recoiled a bit at the gesture.

I caught on and said to the server, smiling, "Better give that to me." And I put the note in my purse and winked at Jesse. We laughed. I gave the note to Jesse once we got home. It said "Call me maybe," with her name and number. No doubt it wasn't the first time an attractive fan had made herself available to him. It most certainly wouldn't be the last.

Near the end of February Ryder was scheduled to enter thirty days of treatment at Central Rehab in River Bend. He had stayed clean and was reliable with Suboxone and the sessions with Dr. Mitchell since his overdose in December, of which Brad and I were still unaware. We'd felt the situation was under control, moving in the right direction, and we believed treatment would be an essential part of his recovery. Central Rehab would provide him with dorm housing, and his days would be filled with group sessions and Narcotics Anonymous meetings in-house many nights a week. Regular drug testing would continue. He was dreading it, but it was part of his sentencing, and he had no choice. At least he'd be local, and we'd be able to visit and support him.

I would later come to see these transitions as the threat to sobriety that they were. An addict, looking ahead to confinement of this type, will seek to use before his freedom is restricted. A week before he reported to Central Rehab, Ryder made a quick, clandestine trip to Minneapolis. Avery rode along to see a girl he was dating in St. Paul. That occasion would cast an evil seed that would begin to germinate. Now Ryder's twin brother, who'd sworn to me he would never use anything stronger than pot—he'd flinch at the thought of sticking a needle in his veins—now knew the heroin dealer and where he lived.

16

As PARENTS OF TWINS, BRAD and I pulled single-parent shifts around the clock for up to five days at a time, and the first few years were grueling. Recurring ear infections would sabotage any progress we'd make toward getting the boys to sleep through the night, and it took twenty-two months before I could get uninterrupted sleep. Compared with what I saw my friends with one baby go through, I'd say our job was twice the work on half the sleep—and that is an understatement. I'd joke that I didn't care if they'd chewed tobacco if it would get them to sleep through the night. I had returned to a full- time flying schedule when the boys were three months old and, I won't lie, getting to a hotel room at the end of a workday with no parental demands was a luxury. I missed the boys, but knowing they were with their dad made it easier.

I gained so much respect for Brad. Every diaper, bath, meal, playtime— he got it done. How many fathers have taken that on? Some help from my parents and trips to the YMCA to work out were Brad's only breaks. He didn't have friends stopping by with their toddlers for play dates like I did. Once the boys were asleep, Brad would pick up the house, take care of laundry, mix formulas, and then take some time for himself. When I was home solo, I'd be passed out face down two minutes after the boys were asleep, in a tee shirt full of baby spit up. The house looked like a daycare that got hit by a tornado. We definitely had our own styles of managing baby duty. My sister Kelly used to tell me, "The days go by slow, but the years go by fast." Indeed.

We never had to teach the boys how to share, perhaps because they had shared from the moment of conception: my womb, DNA, nourishment, the sound of my heartbeat. They never competed for attention. If I was holding one, the other would climb up and share my lap, never upset. I'd often cradle both babies in my lap holding two bottles. Most evenings for many years, one of my parents would come over at bedtime and rock one child to sleep, while the at-home parent rocked the other.

Ryder and Avery never tried to capture our attention the way I notice some children would with a "Watch me, Mom ... Look, Mom, look." Maybe it's because they spent all their time with a parent in view. Neither of them had an interest in sucking their thumbs or pacifiers. They didn't seek out a must-have blanket or stuffed animal. They had each other, and that seemed to pacify them. Their personalities were so much alike, truly identical twins. Their love was innately unconditional. In spite of the workload, it was a fascinating and heartwarming relationship to witness.

The word *mine* wasn't in their vocabulary, and I never once heard either say it to his brother or to another child. Once a YMCA child-care director asked me; "Do your sons go to day care full time?"

I thought she was about to tell me something they'd done wrong, a toddler faux pas.

"No, actually, they're home with either Brad or me all the time, other than when Brad drops them here to work out."

"I can tell," she said, "most kids come here, and the first thing they do is grab toys and stand guard. Your boys are different; they share so naturally, not at all possessive. That's wonderful to see, and is very unusual."

The boys always seemed to enjoy having a friend over, and three was a fun number in our home. One would never leave his brother out, and they certainly wouldn't leave out the friend. The majority of our days from toddler to junior high included at least one of their friends in our home. One Sunday morning when they were in second grade, they started in as soon as they woke up about having someone over. Sunday morning obviously isn't an opportune time for a play date, and there were maybe two friends we could call who weren't likely at church with their family.

That morning I finally caved in and said, "Fine, we can try Jake, but if he can't, you guys will just have to wait until afternoon."

Jake's mom, Cora, had been battling cancer. She was a spirited and devoted mother. Jake's dad enjoyed the twins and always appreciated the long afternoons Jake spent at our home playing with our boys during such a devastating ordeal.

That Sunday, Jake was available. When I arrived to pick him up, his dad came out ahead of Jake to thank me. He thought that somehow I'd known that Cora had died the night before and that I'd extended the invitation to help out. I was stunned when he told me, yet so humbled that he entrusted his son to us on such a tender occasion. I was so grateful that we had that precious boy in our care while his mama ascended into heaven. I didn't have to say anything to my sons to ensure that they were especially kind to Jake; they always were.

According to the zodiac, the boys were Cancers, born July 18, and they were definitely homebodies as their zodiac sign portrays. Although we could fly standby for free, we didn't take many vacations. With both of us flying for a living, the last thing we wanted to do was get on an airplane on our days off. "There's no place like home" was a unanimous sentiment among the four of us.

The first fifteen years with our sons blended blessings with the conventional sacrifices most parents make. When the boys began to pull away, I was unsure how much distance was a normal, healthy progression. I'd grown up with only sisters; I didn't have a frame of reference to gauge a teenage boy's maturation. I just continued to believe that the endearing, precious boys we'd known would prevail in spite of the challenges that began to surface once they were in high school.

After all, high school, especially freshman and sophomore years, was notorious for conflicted hearts, awkward transitions, and hormonal distress—all typical dysfunction, nothing to panic about. That's what I told myself as I struggled to let go of the little boys they no longer were.

When Avery and Ryder began high school, my parents' health began to decline rapidly. They were dying. They were the only reason we'd moved to River Bend in the first place. We'd built our lives beneath the shelter of their adoration and support; we loved them so deeply. All those years they'd helped us with the boys, and then the roles had reversed. I was at their home almost daily to care for them, and I battled despair's aggressive encroachment as grief was gaining on me faster than my denial could dissipate it.

The boys were sixteen when my parents died. The loss I felt as a daughter filtered my awareness as a mother. My sons' grief echoed within them, ricocheting among undiagnosed ADD, surging testosterone, and identities anxiously circling, seeking clearance to land. I've surmised that in the turbulence of my grief, the cues were blurred as my sons' lives were taking an irrevocable turn. By the time I figured it out, they'd fallen too far for me to catch them.

Ryder was due to enter treatment. Central Rehab, a chemical-dependency treatment facility that had been offering intensive primary treatment and outpatient care to adults since 1975, was in south River Bend. Ryder dreaded it though he knew he was fortunate to be going to treatment instead of jail.

Ryder's first experience in treatment was at Prairieview his senior year, two and half years after my mom and dad died. It had been a complicated placement because at eighteen he was on the cusp between teen and adult care. Policy had him placed with the teenagers. That time he'd been "dope sick" with prescription painkiller withdrawals. He didn't want my help or comfort and finally asked me not to visit anymore. I think the pain he saw in my eyes only amplified his agony. The level to which I was force to let go continued to escalate. The conflict of wanting to save him while being powerless to do so was torture. And it was just the beginning for Brad and me of many years navigating that conflicted void.

I brought Ryder to Central Rehab to be admitted, and thought that at least this time he wouldn't suffer withdrawals. Although he'd used heroin a week prior (we were unaware of it at the time), it wasn't enough to elicit withdrawal sickness. He was assigned a unit with three men in varied stages of treatment. They shared two bedrooms, a bathroom, living room, and adjacent kitchen. I wished it was a dorm on a college campus somewhere. We were so far from that reality, so far from where I'd always assumed we'd be.

Science was reporting that a male's brain does not reach its full capacity to function until age twenty-six. At nineteen, Ryder and Avery were making life-threatening decisions that would impact the rest of their lives. I recalled the times we'd try to explain that to them. "Just imagine if as ten-year-old's we'd allowed you to get tattoos. How would you feel sporting a Pokeman tattoo now? You'll change so much that what matters now will seem trivial down the road. Don't pay a long-term price for a shortsighted mistake."

It was like telling them not to sweat in a sauna.

Easter morning, I spent a couple of hours with Ryder in a visitation room that had a dining table, sofas, and a TV with a Wii. Ryder taught me how to play tennis on the Wii, and I thought of how long it'd been since we had done anything playful together. It was amusing to trash talk our way through the tennis match. Once we were done goofing off, Ryder leaned into me on the sofa when no one else was around and held my hand. I could feel how much he loved me, and how much he relied on my love and support to bolster him. It was a fleeting interlude that I cherished. Avery came later to visit him. They both preferred to have their time together privately. Later that evening, Jesse and I had Easter dinner at home, just the two of us.

I had also been thinking about my working life and wanted to spread out and cut back, if that makes sense. I'd been working at the mattress store for nine months as its fourth employee—added because business had increased after ten years. But it seemed to me the traffic through the store didn't justify a fourth employee for forty hours a week, and I asked if I could drop to thirty. With an extra day off, I'd have the chance to grow my consulting business, where I had recently added another class I'd designed called "Clutter Coach," a four-week course that offered structure, motivation, and perspective to help students to reduce clutter and reap the benefits. I also had a new life coaching client booking regular appointments.

I told Keith, the manager, that I could work every weekend, every sales event, any vacation or sick day coverage, and any hours they needed, just fewer of them. The other two sales staff supported my offer since they stood to make more money with one less full-time person. Keith asked me to write a letter with my request, and he would submit it to the district manager, who denied it. But I do believe it set change in motion. I'd written my aspirations, and it seems the universe was taking notice. Another intuition intervention was brewing; the outcome was endowed with layers of potential providence. My angels were navigating ahead of me with the hopes that I was still willing to trust, strong enough to follow, and brave enough to risk.

17

IN 2004, WHEN OUR SONS were young and innocent and still being boys, I completed a life coaching program offered by the Coaches Training Institute. The test for certification included a written exam and two life coaching sessions with master coaches acting as my clients. The classes enhanced my knowledge of intuition while I worked with clients, but I still had gained much of my intuition expertise from self-study in the school of life.

I'd coined the term "intuition intervention" to explain times in my life when I'd had life-changing experiences with intuition, and wrote a book about it in 2007, *Intuition A-Z*.

This is what I wrote:

"An Intuition Intervention occurs when an onslaught of intuitive information and experiences sweep through your life, leaving you forever changed. An intervention can last hours, days, weeks, even months. The experience is full of coincidences, synchronistic events, vivid dreams, precognitions, and insights that capture our attention, and collectively support the direction in which our soul is leading. If you flow with the current, you will discover a deeper understanding of what your life is about, and what you're here to contribute."

Days after my request to cut back my hours was denied, I answered the phone at work and found myself talking to Frank Peterson, who worked selling boats in Detroit Lakes, Minnesota, an hour west of River Bend. Frank cut to the chase.

"I'm a big guy, as in fat and out of shape. My wife is a small woman, as in petite and fit. We need a bed that's gonna make us both happy. Can you advise?"

I laughed out loud several times during our conversation. He scheduled an appointment, and a couple of days later I met the Petersons. Stout and animated, Frank reminded me of Fred Flintstone. Replace the leopard print toga with khaki pants and shirt. Julie was lovely and gracious. We connected instantly.

I began the required sales process. Frank had a short attention span, and he rambled off trying the beds as he pleased. Six beds were in the Dakota Mall showroom, and Frank was bouncing from one to the next. I was amused and followed his lead. They were a delightful couple; they made their selection, and we concluded the sale with a handshake.

Frank became serious, crossed his arms, and looked me in the eyes.

"As I told you, I sell boats, been in sales a long time, over thirty years. You're very good at this, Dana. I'm quite impressed. Would you ever consider selling boats for Lakeland Marine?"

"Wow, Frank, that's quite a compliment. Thank you!"

I was totally surprised and immensely flattered.

"And, no, I can't say I have, at least not until now."

I smiled brightly, elated that I'd impressed someone with thirty years of sales experience.

"You could make fifty to sixty thousand a year and have a few months of light duty in the off-season. You'll work your tail off in the summer, but its good money."

"I'd love to hear more—when I'm not at work."

I winked at Frank and Julie.

"Great. Here's my card. Please call. I'd love to tell you more."

"You'll hear from me very soon. Thanks again for your business; my pleasure to meet both of you!"

An intuition intervention had been launched, and it would have a profoundly encompassing impact on my life and family. This random encounter, was set in place by God? My angels? My parents? All of them, perhaps? Whatever, whoever, was setting me up knew precisely where my family's life was heading, and they were ahead of me sowing grace that would sustain me when my life was crumbling.

Still dazed by Frank's offer after they left, I said to my coworker, "That customer just offered me a job selling boats; said I could make sixty thousand a year."

"What? Are you serious?"

He was surprised and perhaps jealous. He'd been selling beds over six years and had never received an offer like that. My next thought was to keep my mouth shut. No need to stir the pot when it was merely speculation.

I also needed to take pause before considering another professional detour. In the five years since I'd resigned from Northwest Airlines, I'd rebooted my career path several times. The first job I took after I resigned was at a day spa, doing facials and up to fifty pedicures a month in the summer. My elbow was predisposed from tennis, and the added strain of massaging faces and feet blew it out. I required elbow surgery to secure a future of playing tennis.

I moved on to the health club industry, recruited by friends who were expanding. The position incorporated my life coaching skills as well as sales and marketing. A year later, the position was eliminated when they closed the second club. That's when I began my cleaning business. Housekeeping took its toll on my shoulder and elbow, and I wasn't going to let my occupation keep me off the tennis court. I sold my business and accepted the offer of selling beds.

Twenty-three years in one career had been followed by five years of professional instability. Brad was never onboard with my decision to resign from Northwest Airlines. He was a numbers guy, and the flight attendant career put up good numbers. I'd wanted to quit for years, but it wasn't until a near tragedy proved to be the beginning of the end of my career as a flight attendant. It happened in 2005, and I believe was the result of specific intentions I'd offered to the universe five days prior.

I was working on a DC-9 that had been having hydraulic problems inbound from Columbus, Ohio, to Minneapolis-St. Paul. We prepared for an emergency landing. Although the landing proved safe, a series of mishaps after landing set up the disaster. Our aircraft lost hydraulic functions, rendering the aircraft unable to steer or brake. The nose of our DC-9 collided with the wing of an A320 Airbus, which also serves as the Airbus's fuel tank. The Airbus was fully loaded, taxiing for takeoff on its way to Albuquerque. I supervised an emergency evacuation that succeeded in getting all passengers off safely. Only the flight attendant next to me on the jump seat and the pilots had minor injuries; the captain and first officer had been trapped in the cockpit in a fuel shower, drenched by six hundred gallons of fuel. Authorities were unable to explain why there was no explosion.

Before that accident, I had been as comfortable on an aircraft as a child playing in a sandbox. I took three months off after the accident, used up my sick leave, and had to return. We relied on my income, and I didn't have a way to replace it. I flew fifteen more months, attended night school to become an esthetician, and finally resigned to work at the day spa.

My current job selling beds offered solid compensation and benefits, and I would also be able to transfer to a Minneapolis store if we decided to move back. Brad was relieved to have me working for a national corporation again. When I met Frank Peterson, I'd only been working at the mall nine months. Quit to sell boats? At a marina an hour away? Well, that would be nuts. What was I thinking? Hmmmmm …

Intuition is often dismissed for one simple reason: assumptions. Intuition gives one hint, one clue at a time. Often we get that first nudge, and its human nature to jump ahead to presumed outcomes. Judgment takes over, and the intuitive direction is derailed, deemed to be too risky or farfetched. To align with intuition, the key is to replace judgment with curiosity and to navigate one step at a time. It's like driving through fog; your vision is limited, and you can go only as far as your visibility prevails. You see where that leads and continue until you find your way. Intuition is the same, one step at a time, access the situation, and proceed, stall, or terminate depending on the signs.

I could have thrown Frank's business card away and been content with the compliment. I could have "heard" my husband's voice—"Are you nuts? You're just hitting your stride. Get real; settle in. Quit chasing possibilities."

Yet I knew if it was meant to be, I would be able to interpret the signals. I trusted that my soul would lead me where I needed to go, and I trusted myself to make the correct decision.

I detached from assumptions and tuned in to any signals that might show up to support the offer or notice if momentum was lacking. I didn't wait long. The next day, Keith was selling beds at the Home Show in Bison Stadium. He had limited time and computer function, so he e-mailed his orders to us at the store, and we processed his sales for him.

Normally I was unaware of the names of coworkers' customers. The first sale I processed for Keith was for Mae Lawrence, my grandmother's name. I was stunned. In that moment I sensed the barrier between the earthly realm and divinity evaporate. It was like floating in a lake on a hot summer day, staring at the sky; weightless yet connected, not of the earth, but on it still. I felt goose bumps—what I refer to as truth chills—all over my body. When it comes to intuition, your body doesn't lie. Involuntary reactions like goose bumps, or unexpected tears, is your body signaling you to pay attention because what you're experiencing is profound.

Mae Lawrence. This sign was unmistakable to me. She represented Minnesota, being at the lake, pontoon rides with my grandfather wearing his captain's hat. Those childhood road trips to Breezy Point passed through Detroit Lakes on Highway 10 East, right past the location where Lakeland Marine was destined to be built years later. I absolutely knew what it meant, and I felt humbled and blessed to be embraced by destiny.

The next day at work, I had Chinese food. My fortune cookie read, "A recent encounter with a stranger will prove fateful." Soon after that, I called Frank Peterson and made plans to stop at the upcoming boat show Lakeland was hosting in River Bend at the Civic Hall, only six miles from our home.

That following Sunday, I drove to the Civic Hall before work. I had the radio on as usual. I came of age in the eighties, and I love rock music. I was definitely not a country music fan. That music, I judged, was for rednecks. However, I was in the habit of keeping one preset channel on a popular country station. Why? Because on the rare occasion when I couldn't find anything I liked on the other five channels, I defaulted to country music. I did it because I'd rather listen to something unfamiliar than a song I didn't like. Months could go by without choosing the country station backup. But that Sunday morning, on the way to the boat show, I switched to 99.9 and heard the song "Pontoon," by Little Big Town, for the first time. Minutes later, when I walked into the Lakeland display, there were no fewer than fifteen pontoons. I got tears in my eyes—more truth chills.

I found Frank, and he introduced me to some of the staff and gave me a brief history of the company. He also said to me, "I told Scott, the owner, all about you. He's not here today. Scott is a great guy, a fair and generous man. He's already concerned about the commute for you; he already cares about you."

Frank smiled, and so did I.

I stayed and chatted for an hour. These guys, all men, were down to earth, welcoming, and I liked how it felt. I fit in. I was very curious about the owner.

The signs kept coming. The next day, Brad was reviewing an investment file, and he needed to answer the password question, so he asked me, "What's your maternal grandmother's name again?" Yup, Mae Lawrence. Later, when I got to work, the paperwork for the bed sale to Mae Lawrence was sitting out on the counter before Keith mailed it. Seriously!! That week, I also updated to a smart phone. The sales person was demonstrating the "Suri" feature. He asked Suri, "Where's the best place to hide a dead body?" (*Very odd question*, I thought to myself). Suri answered, "Detroit Lakes."

All of this may sound wacked, but I'd been at this intuition thing too long to not be curious about all the signs. I also noticed that I hadn't sold a bed since I shook Frank Peterson's hand after he bought his bed. I hit a dry spell that ended up lasting three weeks. Three weeks not one bed; it was unreal. Everyone else was down in sales too, but zero beds? Especially odd because just before I'd met Frank, at the end of February, my numbers for six months had earned me a hike in pay, and I advanced from a sales associate to a sleep professional. The momentum most definitely wasn't at the mattress store.

A couple more e-mail exchanges, and I had an interview scheduled with Scott Harrison, the owner!

18

I F I COULD ATTEND ONLY one more concert in my life, there would be no question who I'd see. After decades of obscurity, Bob Seger was coming to Bison Stadium. Wrapped up in Jesse and the Freeze and the Central Rehab schedule, I hadn't heard about the concert until it was two weeks away. How did I not hear about it sooner? I assumed the Seger concert would be sold out, especially since he was sharing the night with his Michigan kin, Kid Rock. Before I checked into tickets, I called my dear friend Lisa, who owned the health club I'd worked at. She was a committed Kid Rock fan.

"I assume you've got tickets to the Kid Rock concert?" I asked.

"Absolutely, cannot wait. Are you going?"

"That's why I'm calling. It's actually Seger I'm jacked to see. You don't by chance have any tickets up for grabs. I know you usually travel in packs to see Kid Rock."

"You're right; I've got a bunch of pals coming from Iowa. Not sure if I'll have an extra ticket, a slim chance though."

"I don't care if I have to blow a biker in the parking lot to get a ticket. Seger's my man. I can't miss it!"

"Well, I certainly want to spare you that public humiliation." Lisa was howling with laughter. "I'll know more in a week."

"Tell ya what. I'm going to the box office and see if there's a decent seat left. Can I party and ride with you guys, assuming I get a ticket?"

"Of course; that'd be awesome!"

I was so jazzed you'd think I was going to prom with Ashton Kutcher.

I bought a ticket and joined the crowd. My seat was far from my friends, but I didn't care. It was a great view on short notice. I had only one beer before the concert; I didn't want to have to run back and forth to the ladies' room. I was plenty high just being there, and I didn't want to miss one note. It was amazing and exhilarating, and I danced the entire time—best exercise in a year.

I knew every lyric to every single song Bob Seger performed. It was the music I'd listened to when I was my sons' age. I too had been wild, bold, full of myself, pushing my luck. My parents lost plenty of sleep worrying about me as I went after what I wanted regardless of whose heart I broke. Our sons' paths weren't completely foreign to me. But thirty years later, it seemed that evil was a cliff at the end of a dark street I thought I had known by heart.

The concert and the intuition intervention surrounding Lakeland Marine provided me with buoyant interludes of optimism. I chose to believe that whatever forces were guiding me, those influences were also embracing my sons. In spite of that, the gravity of Ryder's situation was ominous and pressing. It was our understanding that one failed drug test or violation of his probation terms meant he would enter jail for the remainder of his sentence and remain a felon for seven years.

Once Ryder entered the legal maze, his future was threatened to be painted from a monochromatic palette. Seven years a felon, until he was nearly thirty years old. How do you envision the future with that deficit? Who hires felons? If you can't get a decent job, why not make gobs of money dealing drugs? It becomes an imploding cycle of failure, and the consequences can spin a promising life into a desperate existence.

I felt as I'd imagine a pilot might feel flying in life-threatening weather conditions. In my favor, I relied on a proven navigation system, my intuition. I had confidence in my aptitude, and I believed I would survive the storm. But no one can control where lightning strikes, if wind shears come crashing down, or if the point of no return arrives. Risk is part of the human condition. If I flew through my life intimidated by fear, I'd never experience the miracles that happen when trust and optimism prevail.

Intuition interventions were restorative and inspiring because they served me with proof that life held more possibility than what was evident from the human perspective. The duality of being a human and a soul; that knowledge, and my efforts to live in alignment with my soul, cultivated the grace that helped me to transcend despair. Each time an intuition intervention occurred in my life, I was certain there'd be more, and that I'd continue to weave blessings together. I would look back on my life and see that the tapestry was flawed yet somehow perfect at the same time. My capacity to interpret paradox kept me sane.

While destiny was coaxing me in a new career direction, the three young men I loved were on paths of their own. Jesse continued to get favorable press coverage: "Tri City tried to outmuscle and bully the clearly more-skilled Freeze. But judging by the fact the only thing Freeze defenseman Jesse Marcus was wiping off after a fight with Storms' Brian Ward was his knuckles, that game plan didn't work."

Jesse was chosen for the "Player Spotlight" one week, where his lighthearted interview with the assistant coach was posted on the Freeze website and also played between periods at the games that weekend. Jesse never attempted to own the tough-guy persona off the ice. His mom was in town that weekend, and Jesse concluded the interview by saying, "A shout-out to anyone who needs a great tutor. My mom's here from North Carolina. She'll Skype, talk over the phone—whatever you need. She's awesome!"

As part of Player Spotlight, the Freeze published an eight-by-ten color photograph of Jesse as a mock magazine cover—*Freeze Illustrated*. After the game, he signed autographs for a long line of adoring fans patiently waiting their turn. The picture of Jesse wearing suit pants, a vest, and a lavender dress shirt with the sleeves rolled up was striking. His expression portrayed a confidant athlete, and he looked stunning.

The cover write-up included a quote from Jesse: "Enjoy life to the fullest." His female fan base was huge.

Meanwhile, Ryder was in Central Rehab surrounded by desperate souls trying to rise above the shackles of addiction. Some patients would find this time around to be the emancipation they sought. For other addicts, treatment was a live chat room that served as a networking opportunity to discover where to get drugs after release.

Avery's world was mostly a mystery to me. He rarely came home and never attended a Freeze game. I could tell by his Facebook posts that he traveled to Minneapolis frequently to see a girl he was dating who was also from River Bend. He told me she was a nice girl, and that she despised drugs. I accepted her friend invite on Facebook. A positive sign, I'd felt. More than once we'd talk about Ryder's situation.

"Don't worry, Mom; I would never do that. I'm learning from Ryder's mistakes," he would tell me.

I'd watch one son from my season-ticket seat in an arena ignited by young males in their prime. Adoring fans cheered as they skated and muscled their way toward a bright future, some destined to be NHL stars. Another son I'd visit at appointed times, sitting on tattered waiting room furniture worn by the parade of addicts and loved ones. Confessions and lies frayed the upholstered piping; the cushions sagged from the weight of cumulative anguish. My third son skimmed beneath my parental radar, murky from fatigue and denial. I loved the three of them so completely.

I got the invitation I'd been waiting for.

Scott, the owner of Lakeland Marine, called my cell phone while I was at work. I excused myself and left the store while my coworker covered for me. Scott and I scheduled an interview at his office in Detroit Lakes. I asked if he'd like me to send my resume. He said it wasn't necessary. No doubt Frank had said good things about me.

The previous month at the store had been slow at work, for everyone. All four of us were required to sign off on a letter from corporate stating that if our numbers didn't improve, that would be grounds for dismissal. Really? The others had been through similar "threats" before, but I was offended that one month off track, and I'm on the chopping block? Or worse, that they had us sign off on a false threat to shake us up. The others assured me it was just a formality. Either way, I considered it to be a shady tactic. But I intuited the threat for what it was, another nod from the universe guiding my decision. I began to detach from a career I'd been excited to cultivate, an opportunity for which I'd been grateful. The emotional shift was moving in one direction, east, down Highway 10.

Scott and I were scheduled to meet in three days. I was thrilled!

When I got home, my excitement crashed when I learned that Ryder was in jail—kicked out of treatment for a failed drug test. What next? He told us he had to wait until another treatment facility in town had an open bed, and he'd start the thirty days over. Seems the rules and consequences weren't as rigid as we thought. More failed drug tests had Ryder spending the next several weeks bouncing between home and jail.

When he was home, there was at least one occasion I was sure he was high. When I asked him, he denied it. "Mom, I'm getting drug tested all the time. I can't use."

But I could see it in his eyes and in the slack of his demeanor.

Where was my beautiful baby boy, my innocent son? There were several tiers to my despair. It wasn't only that Ryder's life might be spent as a drug addict in and out of jail. Or that he would die young from an overdose or, worse, cause someone else's death. Those possibilities were horrific enough. As his mother, I felt another facet of sorrow—the grief of what could have been, should have been. We'd already lost their high school years and the adventures I'd assumed that one day would have filled a graduation photo collage on display for a houseful of well-wishers in our home for a double celebration.

Fear would try and convince me that Ryder's fate was in his brazen, naïve, addicted hands. Faith would tell me that God was in charge and that we would find a way through whatever His plan was and manifest a way to serve others with our journey.

Although we weren't giving up on Ryder, Brad and I were sinking into resignation. Our stress became streamlined because we were no longer making decisions. Ryder's probation officer and attorney were calling the shots. Our energy was no longer spread between distressing about his fate and strategizing how to save him from himself. We'd moved from the sideline to the bleachers.

19

I N MID-APRIL, JESSE'S MOM CAME for the final two games of the regular season. Ryder was home in limbo, waiting to learn which treatment facility he'd be assigned to next. His polite, well-spoken manner couldn't conceal the physical cues of drug use and neglect: unkempt hair, red blemishes that wouldn't heal, scraggly whiskers, and grubby clothes. He was addict thin, and wore his pants off his backside, exposing his plaid boxers. How his pants stayed on was a mystery that provoked my disgust rather than curiosity. I was embarrassed, ashamed actually.

I didn't share details about Ryder's situation with anyone, including Tamera. But his elephant-in-the-room appearance compelled me to speak to her when we were alone.

"I get so frustrated with my boys. We keep trying to persuade them to get back into school." My voice trailed. "I won't lie; I feel very defeated as a mother."

"Well, they all take a different course to find their way. Your boys will come around. You're good parents; just takes time."

"Thanks, Tamera, that's very kind of you. I'm so grateful to have Jesse here; he helps to balance my frustration with joy. You must be so proud of him; you have every reason to be."

"Oh, well, you know, our kids are gonna do what they're gonna do." She smiled and shook her head. "I let Jesse know he better behave when he's living in the generosity of others. He better not give you any trouble."

"Jesse's an angel, a total pleasure to have around," I said with a smile.

"It's a very kind gesture, bringing him into your home, treating him like he's your own. We appreciate it more that we can say. If it wasn't for you folks, this opportunity couldn't happen for us. He's your boy too."

"I will always treasure our time with him." I hesitated before asking, "Do you have any idea if he'll return to the Freeze next fall?"

"His dad's more in charge of that agenda. We'll certainly let you know as soon as the decision is made."

Tamera had an ease about her that was comforting. I appreciated her nonjudgmental attitude. Even though Jesse was so completely awesome, she had no airs about it. I didn't feel obliged to do anything differently with her as our guest. It felt like one of my sisters was spending the weekend with us. Tamera and Jesse spent time together talking and watching TV in our living room while I lounged upstairs in bed watching the Masters golf tournament, which always brought back fond memories of my dad and decades of watching it with him.

River Bend was under a winter weather advisory—blowing snow, low visibility, and slippery roads. Tulips should have been pushing their way to daylight, but instead we had several feet of snow on the ground and conditions just shy of a blizzard. It's only considered a full-blown blizzard in River Bend if the Dakota Mall closes. North Dakota's climate had a way of attempting to teach patience by beating you with a baseball bat. The only redeeming factor was that it kept hockey fans in the mood. Over forty-four hundred fans packed the arena for each game that weekend. For the second consecutive season, the Freeze ranked second in the USHL league in fan attendance.

The weekend series was against Sioux Falls. The Freeze had won seven of their previous nine games and had clinched a playoff berth. Friday night was parents' night, which meant each player would escort his parents and billet parents out to center ice in a pregame ceremony. Tamera and I joined the family members lining up out of sight under the stands. Brad was working a five-day Asia trip, and Jesse's dad was at the game but didn't join us. Terry was in charge of organizing the families to synchronize them to match the line of players on the ice. Parents and siblings had come from as far as California to be with their sons and brothers for this occasion.

I was a mother of a drug addict, here among these fortunate families with boys who had probably been the stars of every team they'd played on growing up—until destiny launched them into the USHL. They had the raw talent, innate drive, and parental support to live their dream. I was in line about to be escorted onto the ice, in front of a packed house, on the arm of this remarkable young man. Jesse had captured the hearts of the Freeze fans in three short months, and an improbable celestial thread connected us. Jesse offered his left arm to Tamera, his steadfast and generous mother. She'd let go of her only child when he was fourteen so he could pursue his future thousands of miles away from North Carolina, at a Minnesota prep school. I secured my right elbow into Jesse's and held on tight.

I joked "If I go down, I'm taking you with me." I could see his bright smile through the face mask of his helmet.

I shuffled and slid along as Jesse steered us to center ice in front of a full house at the River Bend Arena. Who wouldn't want to be me in that moment? I looked across Jesse's chest and smiled at Tamera, each of us only inches from his heart.

I loved Jesse and was honored to have him in our family. I felt blessed that in spite of all the oppression I'd been under, I still managed to stay aligned with my intuition. Jesse was tangible evidence of that. Intuition was the only reason this unlikely match-up manifested. I was proud of myself for claiming every ounce of happiness I could find when curling up and hiding from the world was a compelling temptation every day. This beautiful young man was magnificent proof of my faith in a benevolent force I cannot see or measure. Proof, I felt, that my identity was more than just a mother bearing the weight of sorrow, regret, and grief.

With Jesse on my maternal resume, it felt like God had found a remote angle to validate me as a mother in spite of the failure I felt. Jesse was the type of person I'd assumed our boys would've grown up to be like, and somehow I'd drawn into our family a young man who at this point in time was the opposite of my sons in myriad ways: focused/misguided, peak health/addicts, driven/broken, strong spirit/anemic character, bright/shady—yin and yang.

In spite of the divergence, I believed that all three young men each had a divine destiny to fulfill. Clearly Jesse's path was golden. Yet still, a delicate, resilient, ambiguous corner of my heart believed my sons were equal to the best. I truly believed their souls were leading them, and their journey was far more than the jeopardizing scenes from our current life story.

Motherhood is a brave, ardent island from which our children sail away. We wave from shore on tiptoes in moist, shifting sand, squinting to hold them in view as long as possible. We pray they find friendly seas, breathtaking sunsets, bounty at every port, and on occasion their way back home to share their adventures. Fate promised nothing, yet my heart remained eternally open. The fruits of our efforts and intentions lie dormant. I kept believing that blossoms were imminent. I held possibility as tenderly as I'd once cradled my infant sons.

Brad took a heartfelt interest in Jesse's comfort in our home as well as his progress and success. Jesse and Brad established the strongest bond within our family. It had nothing to do with hockey and everything to do with mutual respect. Brad held the best trips by flying weekends, and for that reason he missed most of the games. The time they spent together was working on Jesse's car, which was unaccustomed to the harsh North Dakota winter, running errands to stock Jesse up for road trips, and at home relaxing.

One of my fondest memories of our time with Jesse was game four of the division playoffs in late April, one of the few games Brad attended. A Freeze victory would mean a fifth and final game in Sioux Falls. The winning team would be crowned the Western Conference champions and secure a berth in the Clark Cup Finals, the Stanley Cup of the USHL. A loss would end the season and have Jesse packed and gone three days later—and for how long we still didn't know, forever?

The Freeze trailed the entire game until the final ninety seconds, when they put in two quick goals to win. The packed arena went nuts. I was jumping, fist pumping, tears flowing. Brad and I shared the beautiful emotions that occur when your child has a pinnacle moment. Parental pride and elation had been as foreign as a Mediterranean breeze.

Before the game, the entire team arrived with their belongings packed for the championship road trip back to Sioux Falls. They left immediately after the victory. If we won game five in South Dakota, then it would be on to Dubuque, Iowa, where the Dubuque Fighting Saints had secured the Eastern Conference crown in a sweep, earning home ice advantage for the first two games of the Clark Cup Finals.

The next night we watched the game against Sioux Falls on Fast Hockey, an obscure network that covered USHL games. The connection was poor, and the reception kept cutting out. I wished we could have seen that game in person.

The *River Bend Forum* reported, "The Freeze twice fought off their quick strike opponent for a 7–4 win that propelled them into the United States Hockey League's Clark Cup Finals ... The Freeze roared back with four unanswered goals that put them up 4–2 after two periods ... Jesse Marcus's second goal of the game put River Bend back on top at the midway point of the period, and Alex Cruz made it 6–4 two minutes later."

The team dog-piled on the opponent's ice; gloves and sticks went flying in celebration of the Western Division championship. We wished that game had been in River Bend so we could have celebrated with Jesse, but the team was already on the road south to Iowa for the national championship.

During the playoffs, Ryder had been sent back to Cass County Jail in River Bend for flunking drug tests. He thought they were holding him until a local treatment facility had an open bed, but we would soon find out that they were actually waiting for a vacancy at Valley Rehab, a state prison/rehabilitation facility in Jamestown, North Dakota, ninety miles west of River Bend. Most of the inmates there were transitioning out of prison back into the real world. The minimum time an inmate was required to spend at Valley Rehab was one hundred days—longer if there were issues of any kind.

Brad and I became acquainted with the visitation schedule and culture of Cass County Jail. I had been there before to bail the boys out for "minors in possession" charges their sophomore year, and again later after Ryder's arrest. I'd never been there to visit an inmate, certainly not my son the inmate. We could visit only at specific times and days of the week. For me, that meant calling between one thirty and two thirty every afternoon, then waiting sometimes forty-five minutes to schedule a half-hour visit. Sometimes I'd have to spend an entire lunch break on hold.

The jail was in the middle of town, several blocks south off of Main Avenue in an industrial park area. The interior walls were brick and cement block. Metal park benches on tiled floor in the waiting area lacked soft edges to absorb the pain. Usually a line of visitors waited to pass through the required metal detector. Once cleared, we were given a badge color-coded to indicate the visiting area in exchange for our driver's license. Until it was our turn to take the elevator, we waited in a lobby that served as a corral for the lingering crowd of haggard mothers, mucus-drenched toddlers, begrudging fathers, and gloomy girlfriends with random tattoos and piercings scattered among them.

Everyone had his or her individual method of avoiding eye contact. There were also people coming through the line who were required to take a breathalyzer test by a certain time in the evening. They appeared to have consulted the same stylist as Ryder. One officer was assigned to replace the disposable tube between blows and read the instant result. I'm not sure what happened if they flunked.

A lone TV was mounted near the ceiling, a bulky box with a twenty-eight-inch screen. One evening a program featured a vampire pouncing on a victim, blood everywhere—as if the environment wasn't hostile enough. How did we get here? How did it ever come to this? I felt like we'd gone to a football game and were forced to sit in the opposing team's hostile cheering section, awkwardly attempting to appear invisible.

We would then take the elevator to the second floor, where a long hall led to six different-colored doors, about one every twenty yards. Corresponding color tiles at the threshold of a matching door indicated you had arrived at the proper visitation area. It seemed like a malicious Stephen King version of Parker Brothers' Candyland board game.

Brad and I had been upset with the barrage of Ryder's recent lies. He'd claimed to have no idea why Central Rehab had sent him packing. We'd also opened a letter addressed to Ryder from an attorney we didn't know and didn't hire. Apparently Ryder had been pulled over for a traffic violation, and they'd found a needle. It must have been when he went to Minneapolis for the binge before moving in with Avery. Brad and I agreed on the way to jail that we'd no longer tolerate his BS.

We weren't in the mood for sympathy.

We took our seats in one of three designated conversation areas lined up against the glass with a narrow shelf at desk height. A six-inch partition separated the view between the cubicles. Each visitor was provided with a phone receiver allowing a conversation with his or her incarcerated loved one. Ryder appeared dressed in an orange sweatshirt, stained and frayed at the cuffs. His pants were matching orange scrubs. He sat down across from us.

I took a deep breath and exhaled slowly through my lips. A fog of nausea expanded in my forehead, throat, and solar plexus. My guarded, neglected fears had found a way to survive in spite of the spirited battle I'd waged with weapons of denial and hope. We'd failed to save our son from incarceration, from himself. He'd taken one step deeper into a sand pit. I felt that too many more, and the mountain of sand would cave in and suffocate his future.

I couldn't speak at first. I was subconsciously searching for an emotion reset button that would ground me, like a diagnostic scanner in my laptop, searching for threats to extinguish, so normal operations could resume.

After a few exchanges of how are yous, Brad began.

"You got a letter from an attorney, not Kurt Williams. It's from Minnesota. Explain to me what that's about."

"I'm limited to what I can say in here; everything's recorded, you know." Ryder spoke softly, leaning forward toward the glass.

"We're sick of the bullshit, Ryder. We can't even begin to sort through the lies. You've got to be straight with us if you expect us to bankroll your legal fees."

I swiped away tears.

"Yeah, I know, I know. I'm sorry. It's just that I don't want to make my situation worse." He looked over his shoulders in both directions.

We sat, silently waiting for an explanation.

Ryder continued, "Okay, okay, this is what's going on. I shouldn't be saying this over these phones, but a while back I was pulled over in Minnesota, and they found a needle. It was clean, but I still got charged. The lawyer is from a Minnesota law firm. Kurt knows about it."

There was no way of knowing how many more incriminating secrets Ryder had kept from us. All we knew for sure was that we didn't know the half of it.

Ryder's honesty about the needle ended up complicating his legal situation. We were careening without brakes or steering ability. It seemed every turn in this maze was a losing angle.

20

SPRING PATIENTLY WAITED BACKSTAGE FOR winter's unrelenting, laborious scene to end. Once winter made its exit, spring pounced on stage with a rapidly rising and powerful Red River demanding the spotlight. The early crest forecast projected our backyard would require a row of sandbags stacked two high. River Bend knew how to fight a flood from many years of harrowing experience. They'd began "Sandbag Central" at the Bison Stadium more than a month before the crest forecast, gathering volunteers to help fill and stockpile sandbags to be delivered to the front lines.

We were in our second home on the Red River. Our first River Bend home, on Elm Street, had been demolished as a result of the epic "five-hundred-year" flood of 1997. After that the flood plain, on which no one could build or live, was reestablished, and the city had forced us out using its right to eminent domain, which is why we moved a mile north into the Timber Crest neighborhood in 2007.

The boys were five years old during the 1997 flood, and they'd had plenty of questions about the river lapping up against the top of our three-foot sandbag dike. It was stacked along the back of our house and joined to our neighbors on both sides. If our dike failed, all of north River Bend would have flooded. The crest lingered and began to erode the sandbags. The city decided to put down an eight-foot earthen dike on Elm Street, in front of our homes. That ensured if our neighborhood took on water, our homes would be the only fatalities. We were literally between a rock and a hard place.

When I look back to that time, I can see it was a legitimate barometer of how Brad and I handled a threatening situation. We were both calm and assumed the best-case scenario would ensue. Our neighbor to the south had a walkout basement. They'd scrambled to construct a homemade contraption of scrap wood propped up with two by fours to support the seven-foot wall of leaning sandbags. It required 24/7 vigilance. If that blew out, our homes would have filled with river water in a matter of hours. Our neighborhood was at an eerie standstill as the National Guard patrolled atop the backyard dikes day and night. American Red Cross trucks had circulated the neighborhood to help the immense number of volunteers who'd built miles of sandbag dikes, one bag at a time.

The Red River flows north, and as it turned out, all the carnage in 1997 occurred two weeks later in Grand Forks, seventy miles upstream. River Bend was spared because unseasonably cold temperatures prevented widespread melting. When the river later crested in Grand Forks, the temperatures had risen to seasonal averages, in the fifties, and the river spilled over the dikes from the full-out thaw region-wide.

Like the slow-rising river that inched its way toward destruction, so too had been our sons' descent into the hell of addiction twelve years later. While Brad and I trusted our family would be spared, it quietly became life threatening one inch at a time.

Ninety percent of River Bend's population believed you'd have to be crazy to live on the Red River, certifiably nuts if you had one home demolished and made the choice to relocate on the river a second time. I guess we were nuts. Both Brad and I valued the view, serenity, and adventure with which those river lots graced the four of us. I'd had a balcony seat to behold the distinct change of seasons. I felt a primal connection to nature and the seasons that had me comprehend and internalize a truth I'd once heard that stated, "The only constant is change."

The Freeze had sent an e-mail to the billet families volunteering the team to come and throw sandbags if needed. As it turned out, two days before we were due for sandbag delivery, the crest forecast was reduced, and we were excused from the effort.

At long last, the day arrived when I drove to Detroit Lakes to meet Scott and interview for whatever this career opportunity might be. It had been over a month since I'd met Frank, and I had been thinking about Lakeland Marine every day since. Change was ahead; I could sense it, and I was on the edge of my seat excited to find out what it might look like. I hadn't talked to Brad about it much. He's not a fan of presumption, and has no interest in speculating outcomes without facts.

The route to Lakeland Marine began with a ten-minute drive through north River Bend, then along the edge of downtown, and across the First Avenue Bridge into Mayport. Highway 10 East opened up to sixty-five-mile-an-hour driving. This drive required only that I steer the car. The traffic was docile as the road unfolded, providing a panoramic view of Minnesota lake country. About every fifteen miles, the speed limit was reduced to pass through a rural town. Glyndon came first at twenty-five mph. It had one stop light and service stations on both sides of the road, a tattoo parlor that had once been a Mexican restaurant, the stucco walls, red-sided roof, and scalloped windows giving a hint of its past. Two blocks later, a dirt parking lot led to a family-owned market that featured seasonal produce from surrounding farmers. In May, they mostly stocked flowers to repot and arrange for decks and hanging pots.

In less than two minutes, I was through town and back up to sixty-five mph as the flat farmland transitioned into extensive moguls of freshly cultivated soil auguring the season of new beginnings. Grassy fields hosting grazing cows were peppered with cultivated hay bales—visual anchors placed much like yarn tie-downs in a homemade patchwork quilt. The scenery cycled between groves of trees, with occasional farmsteads still in view until the trees were fully bloomed in early June. Many of the farm families had built newer homes that were set apart from multiple outbuildings of various vintages. Steel-sided storage for tractors and combines overshadowed great-grandpa's leaning wood barn, its weathered red paint peeling beneath a mossy roof, crowned with a patina rooster weathervane. Rural mailboxes along the highway, like pushpins on a map, declared a family lived somewhere down the gravel country road. Railroad tracks came in and out of view. A generous horizon circulating fresh country air was the enduring backdrop.

Hawley came next and required a reduction to only fifty mph. Frontage roads that paralleled Highway Ten led to national franchises that hinted of a larger surrounding population. The Hawley Municipal Golf Course appeared after passing under some railroad tracks. Hawley was the first golf course I'd broken 100 on, when I was thirty-nine years old, just Brad and I. We'd stolen some rare quality time together. Once out of Hawley, the road rose at times, offering a view of treetops, with lush green valley below. Out of Hawley and into Becker County, lakes began to appear in the rotation of scenery.

Lake Park introduced turnoffs to the start of lake home country. A liquor store was the biggest building in sight, accommodating locals and the weekend lake goers on their way. Then, fifteen miles later, passing through Audubon meant Detroit Lakes was ten minutes ahead.

Escaping the mall for the day felt amazing. I'd traveled Highway 10 East hundreds of times in my life. It was the route our family took to Breezy Point to see my grandparents. Perhaps my stored memories had programmed my brain to release serotonin while traveling this childhood route. I recalled how my joyful dad sang his catalog of songs with improvised lyrics to celebrate his girls. We didn't have to ask or beg to stop at the Dairy Queen. "Ice cream is good for kids" was one of his favorite lines. His favorite DQ was the one in Staples, Minnesota, where they made their chocolate malts so thick it required a spoon, qualifying it as a meal so far as my dad was concerned.

As I got closer to Detroit Lakes, the Little River Band's song a "A Cool Change'" came on the radio. I hadn't heard it in years, and it was playing for me, I felt. I don't know if Mae sent it to me, or my parents, or the universe, but it provoked truth chills. I could feel starched hair follicles on my arms and scalp. The lyrics perfectly described how I felt and what this opportunity could offer me.

One of the basic truths about intuition is that "your body doesn't lie." I squeezed back tears as I listened to the song paraphrase my life in that moment. The emotional, involuntary reaction to a simple lyric was a sign to me that I was in alignment with a greater plan. I was so notably moved, in the presence of deep love, as though my mom or dad was rocking me as a child, shushing me that everything would be okay, singing these lyrics to me as a lullaby. I'd contained the extent of my emotions because I didn't want puffy eyes when I met Scott.

I turned left off of Highway 10, crossed over railroad tracks, and made the one-mile backtrack along a farmer's sloping cornfield to the Lakeland Marine property. This region of Minnesota landscape threw in lakes as randomly and frequently as stars populated a rural midnight sky. I turned into the parking lot and discovered the entire Lakeland property was spread alongside Loon Lake. I felt like crying with joy. I felt like I'd come home.

I entered the showroom, a large, white, steel-sided building. There was a lounge area with knotty pine walls, wicker furniture, built-in cabinets, and a countertop with a coffeemaker and various regional publications to take home. A plasma TV above had the Weather Channel on mute. There were two corner offices; one belonged to Scott, and the other to Troy Brennan, the business manager. Five more offices were set aside for the salesmen—and one for Shelia, the accountant who was known to all as the heart of the business. The showroom boasted a variety of new boats, including Southbay and Cypress Cay pontoons, Alumacraft fishing boats, and Larson sport boats. Plenty of sunlight was warming the showroom, and several of the offices had a view of Loon Lake. I'd arrived at the opposite pole of the isolated, windowless bed store in the mall.

Frank Peterson took notice I was on time and escorted me into Scott's office. At forty years old, Scott was a successful entrepreneur, and, in a matter of minutes, I sensed secure and familiar energy. He was warm and approachable, and I could tell early in our conversation that he was a man who didn't operate from ego. I would discover later that Scott was much like my father and my husband—grounded and intelligent without arrogance, kind and nonjudgmental, soft and strong. All three were attractive, athletic men, though not vain or flirtatious. They were loyal to the women they loved, and their driving motivation was to provide for their children in every way possible. They were all the type of men worthy of respect and trust.

Frank popped in and out of the interview, just as he had jumped around from bed to bed the day we'd met. Nothing here spoke of formality. I was completely relaxed as Scott and I became acquainted.

Ten minutes into the interview, Frank reappeared to ask me, "How are you at handling stress?"

He stood in the doorway of Scott's office as I answered without hesitation, alternating eye contact between them.

"If that's an important trait of the candidate for this position, then you've found your gal!" I beamed.

They both smiled, curious, I suspect. I didn't pause to formulate my answers. I had no strategy other than to be authentic and honest.

I continued, "I say that because for the past several years I've been living with ongoing stress due to my sons. To say they're having trouble finding their way would be putting it mildly. I'm accomplished at checking my troubles at the door. I appreciate work as a positive distraction."

I trusted that, between my body language and sincerity, I'd presented myself as confident and unassuming while describing myself as a proactive team player always seeking to be part of the solution.

We wrapped it up after an hour, and Scott assured me he'd be in touch with an idea of how I might fit into the business. He told me that if too much time passed to nudge him with an e-mail.

Later Brad and I sat down to discuss my interview. What if they make me an offer? I'd be giving up a solid sales opportunity with a benefit package only a major corporation could offer. I would have to make a 120-mile round trip daily commute, and gas wasn't cheap. Brad had a hard time believing they'd want a woman selling boats. Was it really going to be sales, or a desk job? I'd be starting from scratch again, a steep learning curve regarding boats in general, and their inventory. I'd never even driven a boat. My only pontoon experience was occasionally on my sister's over the thirty years they'd owned their summer home on Pelican Lake, thirty miles south of Lakeland.

I'd also had a conversation with the district manager of the mattress store the previous fall, when Brad and I had considered moving to Minneapolis. He had told me at the time that with a six-month notice, they'd place me in one of their Twin Cities locations. Brad definitely had concerns that if we moved to Minneapolis eventually, I wouldn't be able to generate enough income to make up for the cost of living increase. A transfer opportunity eased his concerns. A position at a marina in Detroit Lakes did not add up for him. On paper, the cons of accepting a position with Lakeland were many and obvious. I did my best to detach from the outcome, and Brad and I agreed to float the discussion until "if and when" an offer actually came in.

A week later, I got an e-mail from Scott.

"I apologize for being slow to respond back to you following the interview. Please do not take this as disinterest on my part. I am simply putting my ducks in a row so that I can put an offer in front of you that will be mutually beneficial. I will be in touch with you soon with my ideas."

Wow, what a teaser that was! Nine days later, the offer was in my e-mail inbox:

"First off, let me apologize for procrastinating on this for so long. What I am thinking is that I would like to offer you the following. You come on with us in the front desk position this spring helping us with customer service, data entry, website, etc. Gaining experience in our operation working toward working in sales heavier next year. Next year being January boat shows and following. I would be able to get you involved very lightly in direct customer sales from now until then. Most likely filling in for the other salesmen on the floor when they are tied up and letting them come in on the sale and help where needed. Upon assessment next fall, we would have you work the shows and being a backup to the sales staff. This would be an hourly position with some split sales commissions if the event arises. Please e-mail me or give me a call if you have any questions."

Brad and I discussed it over dinner. The reasons to accept, as I saw them: no more being isolated in a mall, and Lakeland offered a nonthreatening culture in the workplace. I could stay with my sister a couple nights a week on Pelican Lake and reduce my commute during the summer months she lived there. There was potential to earn commissions selling large-ticket items and time off from October through December. In years ahead, we could go south for those months. But more than anything, as far as I was concerned, I'd gotten too many signs from my intuition, though I didn't share that with Brad. He wasn't fascinated with my intuitive perspective and would never consider it to be a legitimate factor in the decision-making process. I blossomed in gray; he was rooted in black and white. The change would clearly be a risk. I knew it was my destiny, and risk didn't intimidate me.

The bottom line, Brad left the decision up to me, saying; "You're going to do what you want anyway." He still resented that I'd quit flying and lost an income and schedule he felt was optimum. Had I made the decision to appease Brad, I would have declined the offer. I replied to Scott's offer in an April 22 e-mail, the day after our twenty-second wedding anniversary.

"Good morning, Scott. I would like to thank you for all the time and effort you've put into creating this opportunity for me. I believe it to be a fair and reasonable offer that perfectly suits the future I'm pursuing. I'm confident I will exceed your expectations. With gratitude and excitement, I accept! I can begin Tuesday, May 7."

I wasn't the only one in the family with a newfound destination. Ryder's probation officer made arrangements for him to depart for Jamestown on May 7. The assignment would serve both as incarceration and rehabilitation. Ryder would be there for a minimum of one hundred days.

I was devastated and so afraid for him. We'd thought he'd been waiting for an open bed in a local rehab for a month's stay. The image of him living with criminals battling addiction seemed like a gross misfit from our subjective perspective. Brad and I were concerned that the more Ryder mixed with that crowd, the more he'd become one of them. We still believed in his goodness, in all his latent potential. Ryder was angry; he felt blindsided by the assignment. Those weeks in jail he'd had no idea Valley Rehab was on the radar.

We still didn't know if Jesse was leaving for the summer or forever. The thought of his complete departure weighed heavy; his presence in our lives held my heart together that entire winter. Of course I wanted the best for him, but I loved him and would feel a tremendous void if he was gone for good. Coupled with Ryder's situation, well, it was tough. My conflicting thoughts of dread clashed up against my excitement about Lakeland. The range of emotions that spun me daily made it difficult to stabilize as the days counted down. I continued to blame myself for Ryder's demise.

"I should have done something to save him; I'm his mother," echoed within me.

As it turned out, the night the Freeze had clinched the Western Division crown was their last victory of their awesome season. They lost two games in Dubuque, as well as game three in River Bend. Three and out. Brad had changed his flight schedule to attend that Clark Cup playoff game in River Bend and stayed up late to spend time with Jesse, as Jesse would be gone once Brad returned from his upcoming trip. For Brad, that meant four hours of sleep before twenty hours in transit and on duty, including the thirteen-hour flight to Japan. It was so like Brad to ignore his own comfort to make sacrifices for his boys.

The day before Jesse left for home, he sat down at the kitchen counter while I was making coffee.

"Good morning, Miss Dana," as he called me. "I was wondering if I could keep my suits in the bedroom closet until I come back in August."

"You're coming back to River Bend? For real?"

"Ah, yes, well my parents and I decided that was the best decision for me. It's good; I'm feeling good about it."

"Oh, Jesse, I'm so relieved. I didn't know how I was gonna be able to say good-bye!"

We hugged, and he went back upstairs to finish packing.

Thank you, Jesus; my heart couldn't handle saying good-bye to him and Ryder in the same week. Instead it was, "See you in a few months." It would be a short off-season, as it was already May, and he was scheduled to report back August 17.

The day before he left for Valley Rehab, Ryder was released from Cass County jail and came home to spend the night. He was humble, anxious about not knowing what to expect. After dark, I persuaded him to go for a walk with me. We walked by my folks' old home on Willow Road, the home I'd held my precious, fragile mom as God called her back.

Even though the walk to Willow Road was only four minutes, I rarely went by after we'd sold my parents' home. Why provoke sadness? There were so many happy memories that still lingered, but tempered by grief. That night it seemed like the right choice. As we passed by, Murphy tugged on the leash wanting to run up the sidewalk to see Muffin, my mom's Yorkie terrier, long gone.

"She wants to go play with Muffin," I said.

"You think she still remembers?"

"For sure; she had a lot of good times there with Muffin." I smiled

"Me too, Mom, I miss Gramzy and Papa every day." Ryder sighed.

"They're with you every day, Ryder, you and Avery. How else can you explain all that you've survived? All the risks you've taken because of drugs, it's a miracle you're not dead." I grabbed his hand to hold.

"I think so too. I pray to them. They hear me," Ryder whispered.

I could feel my throat swell.

"Keep praying, honey. Remember all those signs Papa gave us after he died?"

"Yeah, the high five, you mean?"

"Yes, I absolutely trust they're guiding and protecting us. If I wasn't so sure, I think I'd be a puddle of tears by now."

"For sure they are. I'm sorry, Mom; I'm sorry I've made it so hard on you and Dad. I love you." He squeezed my hand.

"Gramzy and Papa are getting tired, Ryder; you have to turn it around. It's up to you. Valley Rehab can be an opportunity to change, to start over. You're going to get out of it what you put into it."

"Okay, Mom, I know, I know. I don't want to talk about it anymore."

On May 7, 2013, I headed east to my first day of work for Lakeland Marine, and Ryder was transported west, handcuffed in a government van. Taking risks had been the mutual catalyst that launched us in opposite directions that day. The synchronicity of our departures was a positive omen, God's timing, I believed. The fruition of our journey was in the distance, far beyond even my assenting imagination.

21

I'M CERTAIN EVERY MOTHER IMAGINES the day she'll become an empty nester. I did. I'd wondered if ... my twins would attend the same university ... how far from home they'd move ... if perhaps one or maybe both would earn a tennis scholarship, ... or maybe if their leaving would be the first time in their lives that they lived apart from one another. With twins I'd always assumed my nest would empty overnight the autumn following their high school graduation. Instead, one was a dropout with a GED, working the night shift and slumming it in a house with a friend. The other was serving time in Valley Rehab, busted for possession of heroin.

No, I never imagined that scenario. Not even close.

My new adventure with Lakeland Marine could not have come at a better time. With a drastic change in routine, the emptiness in my home wasn't slapping me upside the head. It all happened inside of one week. Jesse was on his way home for the summer, Ryder was off to Jamestown, and I was beginning a lifestyle metamorphosis.

Ryder's van ride to Jamestown included a familiar passenger, his ex-girlfriend with the heroin in her purse the night of Ryder's arrest. She was still in love with Ryder, but he wasn't speaking to her. She too had been sentenced to drug court, then kicked out of Central Rehab for failing drug tests. Her family had cut her off long ago, tough love. They had refused to enable her. We had taken another path with him and showered him with coaching and codling and support in every way possible. Yet they were in the same van at the same time headed to the same facility and fate. Who's to say what is the best way to handle your kid on drugs?

Ryder was contained now that he was in Valley Rehab. Now he was the responsibility of the state of North Dakota. He'd get at least one hundred days of rehabilitation programming on the government's tab. This came as a financial relief for us because the bills had been piling up from treatment stays, attorney fees, medical expenses, and damage control to clean up his sordid path of destruction.

Ryder believed himself to be a victim, a mind-set he would have to change before he could begin healing. I'd spoken to him the first evening after he'd been admitted.

"I think about you constantly, honey, I hope you're okay."

"I'm not; this place sucks; I got screwed over. I don't know how I'm gonna make it through."

"It will be okay; you'll be okay."

I had no idea what to say to him. He wasn't going to hear anything positive from me, and I wasn't willing to foster his negative attitude.

"There's no way you're gonna understand, Mom; it's really bad. I have two cellmates; one is gay. I don't feel safe here. I gotta go."

He hung up.

I imagined Ryder sleeping near a cellmate who might attempt to rape him. Although rape had everything to do with violence and nothing to do with homosexuality, my fears ran wild as I felt helpless, unable to save Ryder from his consequences. I lay in bed that night trying desperately to spin my fears, failing to locate that trusting space in my bruised heart.

My first Sunday with an empty nest was Mother's Day. I felt like a failure; my only two children were on a fast track to wasted lives. It was my fifth Mother's Day since my mom had died, and I was lonely. I would have given anything to ride my bike to my parents' home and spend the day with her, doing nothing in particular, like we so often did. I probably would have given her a manicure and made a simple meal. My sisters Kelly and Ann would have driven to River Bend to hang out. I missed my parents terribly, the two people that treasured me most, witnesses to my entire life. Losing them in a matter of fourteen weeks left a wound that was slow to heal. Would my boys be on this same path if my parents were still alive? How could I have ever explained it to them?

I spent Mother's Day alone; Brad was flying. I received a text from Jesse, who was spending a week with his previous billet family in Nebraska.

They had grown very close the year and a half he'd lived with them. His dad would fly to Nebraska and help with the long drive home to North Carolina. Avery called too; he'd been up all night working, and I gave him an easy out from spending time with me.

I had a brief phone conversation with a bitter and angry Ryder, but, as usual, it was all about him. I reminded him that he had the choice to complain and be miserable or accept what the program had to offer him. Conversations with him felt like trying to untangle a heap of clothes hangers. The more aggressively you tried to break one free, the more tangled and resistant the heap became. Both ended in lingering agitation and frustration. His bitterness would be projected as sarcasm to the men in his group. It was a hurdle to his recovery that became steeper as the weeks progressed.

Twenty years earlier, I'd been in my last trimester of my only pregnancy. I'd been told early on, the day of the revealing ultrasound on March 4, 1992, that twins were a high-risk pregnancy. Brad drove us to the clinic in Edina, Minnesota, seven miles from our home near Lake Calhoun in south Minneapolis. Suspicious I was carrying twins because I'd popped out so far, we had joked, "Let's get a head count; take inventory." I'd asked the OB about it, and his reply was, "You're on the big end of normal, nothing to be concerned about." I'd wondered, at five feet four and 125 pounds' pre-pregnancy, why I'd be on the big end of normal?

I had a very strong sense that I was having a boy when I'd first learned I was pregnant. The ultrasound tech began by pointing out the head and spine. I asked, "Only one?"

When she said yes, I recall being relieved and disappointed in equal measures. Brad, destined to become a radiology tech seventeen years later, saw two heads. He stayed quiet, not wanting to be a buzz kill in case the head wasn't attached to anything, he claimed later.

The tech excused herself and returned with a more experienced coworker. She slid the wand across my slippery tummy and announced, "We've got double trouble!"

"Twins?" I asked.

"Yes! Would you like to know the sex?"

We'd agreed that absolutely we wanted to know. She stalled the wand higher up, then lower, and declared, "Boy, boy!"

I felt like I'd won a multimillion dollar lottery. Tears were flowing down my smiling cheeks.

Once out of the clinic, our first phone call was to my parents. They were overwhelmed with joy, and I wished I could have seen their faces.

My mom told me, "You're bringing those babies home." A prophetic statement indeed.

My dad said, "God blessed you double because you got a late start."

At thirty-four I was having my first babies, late by his measure. My mom had me, the fourth and youngest child, when she was thirty years old.

I had heard the words "high-risk pregnancy," but I didn't feel the threat. I'd assumed during the entire pregnancy that I would go full term and deliver two healthy babies. Healthy denial, it was my nature. The only complications were to my personal comfort, but I didn't require one day of doctor-ordered bed rest. By my sixth month, I'd looked like most women did full term with one baby. When the boys would shift positions, you could plainly see the outward indentation of a heel or elbow protruding from my tummy.

I'd gone full term, which for twins is considered thirty-eight weeks. I'd gained fifty-five pounds in all. The OB agreed to induce me to assure that Brad didn't miss the delivery because he had to travel. To induce labor, they broke Ryder's water because he was bigger than Avery, more able to endure the strain of delivery, they'd surmised. As labor progressed, Ryder was under stress, and it became critical that he be relieved of his trauma. Meanwhile, Avery floated in his sac. After twenty-two hours of labor, I was moved to the surgical ward, where a dozen medical professionals in gray blue gowns and masks were ready for a C-section, two newborns, and a postop mother.

We'd agreed on the names Ryder and Avery, but I left it to Brad to assign the names to each boy. They both were given my surname, Chase, as their middle name. I recalled the one feature I most wanted them to inherit was Brad's lips, their beautiful shape, full, and attractive. I could tell at first glance, when each baby was brought to me, on my side of the surgical curtain, that they both had their daddy's gorgeous mouth. Ryder weighed 7 pounds, 12.5 ounces; Avery 5 pounds, 6 ounces—a total of thirteen pounds of baby boys! At that time, the medical staff was unsure if they were identical or fraternal.

Ryder ended up in the neonatal ICU for five days. He'd suffered during delivery because I had spiked a fever and was slow to dilate. I asked the doctor if Ryder was going to be okay. He could tell me only that it was "too soon to tell." I was scared I might lose him and recall that even though I'd still have his twin brother, I couldn't face the pain of the loss. Ryder recovered quickly, and the OB told me he would be the one that may potentially give me trouble one day.

I didn't ask him to qualify his statement.

When the boys were ten days old, Ann and my dad drove to Minneapolis and packed the boys and me up and brought us back to River Bend, where we set up two nurseries in my parents' home. We planned to live there for two months, and leaned into the support of my extended family, most especially my parents. Brad flew to River Bend between his trips to see us. It became clear it was going to take a village, and by the time the boys were ten months old, we'd sold our Minneapolis home and moved to Elm Street, one mile from my folks.

Mother's Day weekend was also the annual fishing opener in Minnesota. Once the ice went off the lakes, it officially launched the season, which was why everyone in the region (except hockey and snowmobile enthusiasts) put up with the long, harsh winters. This was my first week at Lakeland, and it was the peak of the season at the dealership. Lakeland offered every service required by a boat owner, including annual and new dock and lift installation. Three hundred boats had to be moved from storage, cleaned and delivered. New boats had to be rigged and delivered, and plenty of sales traffic was still coming in.

The cold winter and spring of 2013 set a record for latest "ice out." Some lakes couldn't be fished for the opener. For Lakeland Marine, the long and stubborn winter set everything behind by more than a month, so the entire staff was hustling to please everyone, an impossible task. Memorial weekend was two weeks away, and lake home owners understandably wanted everything right now. Although this made for a very hectic, intense workplace, there was a mojo at Lakeland that made it all seem enjoyable, at least to those of us that weren't responsible for the deadlines.

Scott spent a couple of hours with me the first day touring the property and introducing me to everyone in what I quickly saw was a male-dominated business. Two buildings were separated by a sloped parking lot. The parts and service building included a retail area, service counter, and two large garage stalls where the marine techs handled the service, repairs, and rigging of new motors. Weather permitting, they worked outside as well. The surrounding property was full, including a number of shrink-wrapped new boats, used boats alongside a chain-link fence that paralleled the showroom, and four rows of parking for boats staged for service and customer pickup. All this adjacent to shoreline on Loon Lake, a small lake where the boats were test-driven.

The showroom was in a separate building, where I would be working, and was nearly double the size of the parts and service building. I met the three other salesmen. Derek was seven years older than me, native to the area, divorced with thirty years' experience in marine sales. He was a straight shooter with a playful delivery and knew just about everyone that walked through the door. After decades of heavy drinking, he was ten years sober and active in Alcoholics Anonymous.

Sam was soon to be forty, a happy family man proud of his beautiful wife and kids. He too was playful and took his job only as seriously as necessary and let the rest be a good time. Phillip, a few years younger than me, had a marine mechanic background and came into sales when back problems forced him out of physical labor. Troy Brennan, the business manager, had been working for Scott for sixteen years. He was Frank Peterson's son-in-law. Troy ran the business, and like Scott was approachable with no apparent ego.

They all would become like brothers to me, brothers I'd never had. Their love and kindness would bless me more times than I could imagine when I met them for the first time on May 7. I could hear Brad's voice, "Who's gonna buy a boat from a woman?" But I wouldn't be starting my career with Lakeland selling. I would be in a supporting role to start. Sales would come later.

My nicknames from the salesmen would evolve quickly, Frank called me "Mrs. C"; Sam, "Sunshine"; Phillip, "Darlin'" (though he respectfully called most every woman that); and Derek called me "Hot Stuff." But the comrade I would become closest to was Shelia—the accountant, the controller, the heart of the business. She was six years older than me, and we bonded quickly. One of my primary roles was to support her demanding position with data entry, and various mundane tasks to help her keep up during this crazy time of year. She treated me like a sister from day one. I quickly and happily learned that I had not just gained a new career, I had become the newest member of a fun-loving, hard-working, successful family.

Lakeland Marine in Detroit Lakes, Minnesota, felt like an anonymous escape to a jovial planet where I felt valued, protected, and isolated from the struggles in my life. Intuition had coaxed me into this blessing. It was a new beginning for which I was deeply grateful.

22

YEARS BEFORE, WHEN WE STILL lived in Minneapolis, I'd heard of a tragic story about a family. They had three children under seven years old. The oldest child was stricken with leukemia and the parents did all they could to save her life, spending every possible moment with her. The two smaller children, a boy and a girl, were taken care of by loving family members while their parents and sister were away for long hospital stays and lengthy trips to treatment. She recovered from cancer. Shortly after, her younger sister choked on a grape and died.

That story came to mind more than twenty years later. Intuition whispering? I wondered sometimes if we were overlooking Avery with the effort and attention we were pouring into Ryder's situation. Since moving out in December, Avery rarely came home and seemed to prefer his independence. I wished he was around more; I wanted to spend time with him, especially with Ryder and Jesse gone. I missed having a relationship with my sons. They'd been pushing away for so many years, keeping their distance physically and emotionally. It was hard for me to resign myself to their absence, and the disjointed way we felt as a family.

I asked Avery to help with Murphy when Brad was flying, and I was now gone for eleven hours on workdays. He loved Murphy and was happy to oblige. As it became hotter out, Avery also began to stay overnight because the air-conditioning at his rental didn't work that well. He had been living away from home long enough to have gained a better appreciation for the comforts of our home.

Occasionally we'd have a chance to talk, but he always seemed to be in a hurry to get going.

"Thanks for taking care of Murphy."

"Sure, Mom, anytime. I don't mind."

"Is everything going okay for you, honey?" He looked tired, and I could just tell he was feeling down.

"Yeah, I guess."

"Are you sure? It doesn't sound like it."

"No, I'm good. Kyle just owes me a bunch of money; he never has rent on time. I cover him so we don't get evicted. I'm just so sick of being broke all the time."

I refrained from commenting. He did not take advice well, especially about money.

"I know it's hard for you to have your brother gone. I'm sure you miss him, but this is a chance for him to get the help he needs. The path he's been on can only lead to one of three places—death, prison, or recovery. I hope you're learning from his mistakes."

"I am, Mom; I miss him even though he's a crab ass every time I call him."

"He's not happy. It's a big adjustment, but he'll come around. We just have to allow the process to help him. Are you still smoking pot?"

"No, Mom, I can't afford it, and I don't want to end up in all that trouble. It's just not worth it."

"I'm glad to hear it. I can't take both of you going down that path; I need you to stay clean."

"I will, Mom; don't worry."

Based on the abridged version of his life he shared with me, I chose to believe Avery was making good choices. It seemed he'd learned a lesson about drugs by watching his twin's downfall. Avery and I were both good at convincing me he was staying out of trouble.

We were scheduled to attend a family day at Valley Rehab the third week of June. For Ryder to return to our home once he was released, we were required to attend at least one of three scheduled family days that summer. We looked forward to seeing Ryder, and we were happy to make the trip.

We'd completed the necessary paperwork and mailed it to Bismarck, the state capital, to be processed for background checks. Avery didn't return his paperwork in time to receive clearance, so Brad and I made the trip without him. I was disappointed Avery wouldn't be coming along. It was sad to me that incarceration had been the reason they'd been separated for the first time for more than a few days. They were so close, best friends.

I'd read that it was healthy for twins to have their own identities, so we'd always intended to foster their independence. It's why we intentionally chose names that didn't rhyme. I didn't dress them alike or try to call attention to them for being twins. In kindergarten, we started them in separate classrooms, which they both ended up preferring. But the fact was, they had a relationship only twins can understand, and I was grateful for their bond, but I felt badly for these circumstances of their separation.

The day-trip west was a pleasant change of scenery and rare time alone with Brad. We had a coming and going lifestyle that didn't afford us much time together. We deserved better; we deserved to have life be more than just working and coping.

Ryder had been gone six weeks. His first week had been intimidating, but he'd become familiar with the routine and personalities as the weeks passed. The phone conversations so far had been brief and one-sided. He was still in full-blown victim mode. It was as though he wanted me to suffer, worry, to feel sorry for him. Ryder never felt like talking—he'd grow impatient if the conversation stalled, though he never asked me how I was or what I was up to.

I wondered if his demeanor in person would be less self-absorbed and glum. Traveling to visit my son in a division of the state penitentiary had me filled with a bundle of mixed of emotions. It was hard to witness his suffering, yet I was frustrated that he'd never listen to us and had put himself, and us, into this position. There were so many times we'd warned both boys where their choices were leading, and to now witness him in this hell—one from which we had tried to save him—was wrenching.

There was an unspoken, ominous, "I told you so" that gave us no satisfaction at all.

Inmates at Valley Rehab had the benefit of services and advice from licensed addiction counselors, social workers, and paraprofessionals, whose goals were helping inmates in overcoming addiction and personal problems and successfully working their way back to freedom—and staying clean and sober. Most inmates had come from the state penitentiary in Bismarck. Ryder, with his drug court sentence, was the exception. He was learning plenty about prison life and discovered that Valley Rehab was as high a level of incarceration as he cared to experience.

The final quarter mile leading to the Valley Rehab complex was winding uphill. The campus was comprised of a group of buildings that had been referred to as a mental hospital when I was growing up. As a young girl—when mental illness had a dark stigma attached to it— I'd heard stories of the "crazy people" locked up there. I'd pictured the complex as a foreboding institution—North Dakota's version of *One Flew Over The Cuckoo's Nest.*

The men's barracks where Ryder was staying was a two-story building with spiked razor-wire spiraling along the top of a ten-foot steel fence. A small yard adjacent to the housing included a sand volleyball court. Blocks away, his former girlfriend lived in the women's housing.

Inmates would earn privileges based on their participation and attitude as they advanced through various stages of treatment, which included frequent classes and therapy sessions designed to help them understand and address their addictions. Staff would grade them and promote them— perhaps—with reviews every three weeks.

At level one, an inmate was required to wear prison-issued clothing, a red polo and khaki trousers, and wasn't allowed access to the small weight room or volleyball court. Ryder made sure he passed through level one as quickly as possible and was soon lifting weights three days a week for forty minutes and playing volleyball as often as he could. He took advantage of every second out of barracks confinement that he could get.

On the day of our family visit, I had to leave my purse, cell phone, just about everything, in the car. As we approached the building, I was nervous; I wanted to find Ryder, pack him up, and take him home, all better. The weight of reality pressed hard against me. I felt powerless, and I guess I was.

We passed through a security checkpoint, signed in, showed our driver's licenses and paperwork, and were led to a classroom for orientation. When Ryder approached, the first thing we noticed was he'd put on weight, at least twenty pounds. He was getting muscular and looked so much healthier, thank God. His eyes were bright, and his skin was clear, with good color; his dark hair was short and tidy. His royal blue T-shirt matched his eyes. Ryder was so beautiful to me, every part of him—his oval face, almond-shaped eyes, perfect nose, and the handsome smile, like his dad. He lit up when he saw us; I opened my arms and held him close. After coffee together, we were separated for the rest of the morning.

The four-story building reminded me of my alma mater, St. Mary's High School in River Bend, which had been built in the 1940s. The room where we sat had cement block walls painted a soft shade that whispered lemon. Tiled linoleum floors were worn but waxed and clean. Old-style five-foot-high black chalkboards filled the wall space between the two doors in the front of the classroom. Narrow tables six feet long provided a place to sit and take notes. The morning program included such talks as "The Dynamics of Addiction," "Effects on Family," and "Communication Skills," and I found them enlightening and felt they did a great job making discussions relevant and beneficial. One of the presenters spoke of the importance of addicts attending Alcoholics Anonymous or Narcotics Anonymous meetings. I knew this was an opportunity to ask. I raised my hand.

"Are there circumstances when the meetings do more harm than good? What I mean is, can NA meetings act as a trigger for some addicts?" I was hesitant, not wanting to appear critical.

"I understand what you're asking. When you have a group of people talking about past usage, or current relapses, it can be a trigger for some," the speaker replied.

I nodded. He knew what I meant.

"My son has said it just makes him want to get high listening to everyone talk about it. And that's where he runs into fellow drug addicts; not all of them are feeling strong and committed, and they're looking for like-minded pals to take down with them," I explained.

"I won't lie; that's an element of the culture of meetings, or at least it can be, but not always. Two things: look for meetings where the group dynamic feels strong, feels right for you, him, and know that the addicts who have success staying clean are the ones attending meetings. Meeting makers make it, we always say."

This particular speaker had been an alcoholic for twenty years before turning his life around. He would know. He continued.

"It's not always a bad strategy to be reminded of the problems drugging caused you in the past. It's a reminder of why you want to stay clean and sober. That's how conversations at meetings can be beneficial; it's up to each individual's perception."

He smiled and thanked me for the question.

I had been sympathetic to Ryder's complaints about NA meetings. I believe that your thoughts and intentions—what you think and speak—create your reality. I've read that our brains cannot distinguish the difference between fact and fiction. So when you repeat, "My name is Dana, and I'm an addict," your brain then seeks opportunities to support your belief. It was a philosophical conflict with which I would continue to struggle. I knew very little about AA and NA meetings, and it was best I trust the system for Ryder's sake.

We had lunch with Ryder, which would be followed by an afternoon family group session. At lunch, I felt like I had my son back. Here was the Ryder I remembered before all the lies, avoidance, and the decay of his health and our relationship. We had a lighthearted conversation about normal stuff. I felt hopeful that he was on track to recovery, in the direction that would bring him back home to us ready to live a productive life.

The afternoon included all the guys in his group, about fifteen, ranging in age from eighteen to forty-something—all addicts, all convicted of some sort of crime. The circle included their counselor, Cameron, and one other mother, the only other parent attending this family session. I wished Brad, Ryder, and I could have met privately with Cameron, but it wasn't offered. This was the session Ryder was dreading, and the reason why, he'd confided to me, he didn't want us to attend.

Each inmate in the circle introduced himself and his addiction.

"I'm Ryder; I'm a heroin addict."

How does a parent absorb that? How can this moment be real? I knew why we were there, but seriously, how on God's green earth is this possible? I wanted to place an asterisk after his declaration and direct everyone to a footnote that read, "*though not a heroin addict in the true sense of the word—a temporary affliction that will pass completely and never return. Much like mononucleosis, it hangs around a long time dragging you down, but once it's gone you're over it completely … a complete mistake of a situation that will be cleaned up entirely … forever."

My denial was fighting for its life, like a fish being pushed around the desert in a stroller, I tried to protect it, but the blazing truth made it impossible to survive.

We'd been encouraged by a speaker in the morning session to be candid, authentic.

"Don't spare any truth about the suffering you've incurred at the expense of your loved one's choices," he had told us. That'd been the coaching recommendation for this session.

Neither Brad nor I were compelled to articulate the anguish and misery Ryder's addiction-fueled violations had pummeled our once blessed lives with. I'm not sure if it was because we felt sorry for him, or if we'd come in peace instead of anger, or if it was our nature to focus on the future. Perhaps it was because we had every angle of enabling unconsciously mastered. Instead we shared how much we loved him, believed in him, and how willing we were to support his recovery, and forgive.

During the earlier circle discussion, others had noted that Ryder had issues with his sarcasm and cutting others down. No doubt his badgered peers were seeking payback. I was concerned that our dialogue would become too emotional, and I wanted to protect Ryder. I didn't want him to come to tears, I know that's part of the reason he dreaded this day, this session. My maternal pattern was nearly impossible to break. I love him so deeply.

His counselor, Cameron, was young, early thirties I'd guess. She was upbeat, well-spoken, and engaging, and I admired her spirited energy and commitment. It had to be challenging to work with so much resistance. She asked Brad and me what our greatest fear was.

Brad spoke first. "That Ryder will be a victim of his addiction. That it will cost him his life, or the quality of his life. His potential is unlimited, but all that could disappear, forever. It would be a horrible waste; he's a good kid, a good man with a bright future."

I glanced at Ryder, several seats to my right in the circle. He was fighting his emotions that only a mother could perceive.

It was my turn. "My biggest fear is that someone else will pay a price because of his choices. If his addiction caused harm to someone or if his negligence cost someone their life, it would be harder for me to live with that, than losing him."

Grieving was one thing; I'd find a way to handle my own grief. What terrified me most was my kid being responsible for someone else's death, another family's grief. As his mother, I would feel responsible to some degree too. To be the cause of so much pain but powerless to influence healing, that helpless scenario petrified me.

God, spare us, please.

Ryder was honest too, "I'm not gonna lie, if I walked out of this room right now and someone handed me a loaded needle, I wouldn't turn it down."

I was astonished that he still felt that way. After the upbeat vibe during our lunch together and his improved health and appearance, I'd assumed he had more resolve than that. Obviously I had no legitimate perception of addiction, still. I thought our Ryder was back; I wanted it to be that simple. Clearly addiction was still his master. At least he was being honest, a positive step toward recovery and an indication of some growth.

Some of the guys in the group didn't say a word. One inmate was prone to rants to which his conclusions were completely unrelated to his opening statements; he seemed to like the sound of his voice. Many of them validated how fortunate Ryder was to have parents that still gave a damn, a family that loves him and stands by him after all the betrayal. The gay cellmate Ryder spoke of in our chilling conversation his first day was a Native American in his twenties. He was docile, the least threatening personality in the group. I found him to be endearing, sincere, and humble.

I also asked him out loud, "Ryder, if one of the guys in this group was released and able to come to our home, our family, and was given the opportunities and support you've had, what percent chance out of 100 would you give him to stay clean?"

He didn't think about it very long and replied, "Eighty percent."

"That's pretty good; you can do this; we'll help you," I said.

"Yes, those are good odds." He smiled and nodded

The next family day was scheduled on July 18, Ryder and Avery's twenty-first birthdays. I hoped by then he'd feel able to turn down a loaded needle.

On the way home, I felt heavy, drained. I turned and looked out the window at a line of dark clouds moving rapidly into the region. A torrential rainstorm was on the way to Valley Rehab that would cause minor flooding in some of the basements of buildings later that evening.

I was a native North Dakotan, yet I'd never seen much of the western part of the state, which boasted Medora, the vacation destination in the heart of Teddy Roosevelt country along the Missouri River, and farther west, near the Montana boarder, the Dickinson area was just beginning to steal international headlines for the oil boom. North Dakota had always been a proud state; now it was fast becoming rich and famous for helping America to become less reliant on foreign oil.

A mere eighty miles west of River Bend, bluffs and valleys took over from the flats around River Bend—something to do with the glaciers hundreds of years ago, I guess. North Dakota is a rich and varied state, and being from, and living in, North Dakota sometimes felt like coming from a family where everyone had big, unattractive noses. People would feel instant pity, as though that one feature defined you as unfortunate, at a disadvantage, a loser. Once aware, others would silently be thinking, Why put up with that if you don't have to? Any attempt to represent your choice to live in North Dakota seemed to come off as defensive. But Brad and I had made the decision to move them to my home state, believing they would have a greater chance of an innocent childhood, away from the big city and all those problems.

I said to Brad, "Overall a good day, but I can't get past the fact that he'd still use without hesitation. I'm glad he was honest, but he's been there six weeks; you'd think by now ..."

"That's why they keep them a minimum of one hundred days; it takes time. We have to look at the positives, and there were many," Brad offered.

"You're right; he looked so much healthier. You can tell he hasn't been smoking cigarettes either; his complexion was so clear."

Leave it me to notice he had a reduction of blackheads.

Cigarettes were prohibited at Valley Rehab. He was off everything; no wonder he'd gained so much weight. He needed every pound; he'd entered a skinny, grungy druggie. Was it possible he'd exit in sixty days healthy, recovered, and capable of living drug free? One thing I knew for sure was that so far, I had a terrible track record at predicting the future when it came to my sons.

23

O N THE WAY HOME FROM Valley Rehab, I dropped Brad off in Kellogg to resume his weekend on call. I returned home the evening of summer solstice. An empty house meant freedom to perform a feng shui blessing without interruption. There are any number of good times to perform a feng shui blessing, including at noon or midnight on a full moon, the winter and summer solstice, fall and spring equinox, or any time there's something magnificent occurring in the galaxy. Also, your birthday, anniversary, any day you consider lucky, or when you simply desire to influence positive change.

I'd become certified in feng shui in October 2008, two months after my dad passed away. I'd done some sort of a full moon blessing most months since. Because it represents the end of the lunar cycle, the full moon is considered auspicious. In feng shui, completion of anything is positive; it means all deeds are done, there is no more energy expenditure, and closure. Renewed energy is then freed up to invest in the manifestation of your next intention, your next desire, or the new season.

Summer solstice marks the beginning of summer. I considered most of my North Dakotan life that summer was the season of celebration. Though I was grateful for the warm weather, and for the opportunity to connect tactilely to nature and the relief summer gave to my spirit, I did not feel like celebrating. The summer of 2013 would open with a heavy, looming concern for my sons, especially Ryder. I was scared that he'd return home in a couple of months to the same addict lifestyle.

It had been a while since I'd had the house to myself. I would light all the candles I wanted, bang on my brass bell, and recite my prayers and intentions with no concerns of anyone walking in on me—definitely one of the advantages of an empty nest. The full moon ceremony I'd designed began with writing my intentions for each of the nine life areas represented in the Bagua, a life map of sorts: family, wealth, health, helpful people, children, knowledge, fame, career, and marriage. Next I went throughout the entire house ringing a bell to clear out all residual negative energy, effective because sound penetrates the space completely.

I understood feng shui to combine the power of intention and the law of attraction, even though I'd never read that specific claim. With my knowledge of feng shui, the décor I'd chosen was placed to enhance the manifestation of my intentions. My entire home subliminally represented my hopes and dreams. That awareness kept me in a continuous, albeit subconscious, state of attracting my desires.

Feng shui teaches that our homes have a pattern of energy flow. The living space is set to the Bagua, which divides the main floor, or a single room, into nine equal squares. On the main floor of my home, I had nine focal points, one in each area designated by the Bagua. For example, in our home in Timber Crest, the far left corner of the main floor was the wealth corner, where I placed a faceted crystal, a live healthy upward-reaching plant, and some décor pieces that collectively enhanced the corner. I chose items based on the color, shape, and substance of which each was made. Most importantly, the décor combination beautifully suited my tastes.

Step one in my feng shui blessing was to progress from one area of the Bagua to the next, lighting candles to illuminate the intention I'd written for the aspect of my life it represented. I'd placed at least one candle in each of the nine focal points on the main floor of our home. Next I would retrace my steps and pause to recite a prayer in each area. In the final step, I retraced my path and blew out each candle, releasing my intentions and prayers to the universe as I recited "this or something better now manifests, I am grateful." I'd move in a specific sequence from one Bagua focal point to the next until I'd performed the three-step blessing nine times—in an order considered auspicious according to feng shui.

Prayer and feng shui, I believe, each represent an approach of active surrender. They are action steps that release the outcome of a situation to God, to the universe, in hopes of positively impacting destiny. Surrender, after all, is a verb. Although prayer and feng shui might be judged as indirect efforts at best, I knew they were both ways of connecting to a higher power. I relied on both to live in alignment with my soul.

I continued to learn that letting go was the most powerful choice I could make. It was another paradox that I'd grown to trust. So much hadn't worked in our efforts to derail our sons' downfall into addiction. I believed that when nothing seemed to work, it was a sign to turn it over to God. Genuinely letting go is nearly impossible for most people; it requires tremendous trust. I'd discovered that when you try to control the outcome of a situation, you end up blocking the solution as well as the providence that's trying to come through.

Letting go of Ryder's situation was extremely difficult, and it felt counterintuitive on the surface, but I did my best to align with the deeper levels of wisdom. I had reached the point where it felt as though I was in a freefall that was best served by surrendering to the plummet—all the while keeping hope that we'd land safely at some point. Grabbing at branches on the way down, desperately attempting to sabotage the fall, it seemed, would only cause the descent to be more injury-prone.

In the previous six weeks, so much had changed about my routine, and my lifestyle. I was a fan of change. I felt it kept life interesting and gave me hope that the struggles we were having could change for the better. My sister Ann had arrived in Minnesota and would be living at her home on Pelican Lake for two months, while her husband commuted on weekends. I was excited about having her nearby.

Pelican Lake was a familiar paradise, and I arrived there after work on June 24, to spend the first night of many that summer. Ann was my big sis, and I wanted to relax and be distracted from my relentless orbiting heartache. With both of our parents gone, she was the next long-standing witness to my life. Eight years ahead of me, she'd always been there, looking out for me, caring about me. After squeals, hugs, and my tears, I set my overnight bag in a guest bedroom. We put on our walking shoes and set out to catch up in the scent of the evening breeze, a humid blend of lake, wildflowers, and mowed lawn.

"You look great, very fit; retirement suits you," I said.

"I feel good. Living in Colorado makes for an active lifestyle. The cold winter weather never lasts, and it seems to get back up into the fifties or warmer in a matter of days."

"I've got to lose some weight," I told her. "I'm turning into a tub of goo. I sit all day at my desk, and then all the hours commuting. There seems to be so little time to get much else done."

"You like it at Lakeland, though?"

"I love it. I'm so grateful to be out of the mall, away from River Bend. Nice people to work with—it's a very laid-back culture."

"I remember last summer; I think you only got to the lake a couple of times?"

"Not even. It was just that one afternoon with Avery and Brad. I'd vowed this summer would be different. Sure is ... who knew?"

I smiled, knowing I'd be staying with her several nights a week for the next two months.

I gave Ann an update on my boys, and then I purposely moved on to other topics. I didn't want to dwell on it; I needed distraction from it most of all. I still believed as a mother I could have, should have, done more, or done things differently. That was difficult to discuss. No one had answers for me, and opinions to the contrary didn't appease me. It left others feeling so helpless. I figured that the situation required that I deal with it, attend to it as I could, then otherwise keep it tucked away.

For over twenty-five years, even before I'd started dating Brad, Ann and I had walked this path on these blessed occasions together at Pelican Lake. Everything that mattered to us had been dispatched in our conversations over the years. There wasn't another place or circumstance that had me feel more grounded and peaceful than walking this familiar seasoned path with her. The trees canopied our route as we walked along, passing affluent lake homes. The layered shades of green sheltered us; trees, native foliage, meadows, and landscaped lawns eavesdropped and sent our secrets along in the breeze that floated over the lake, where our troubles slowly sank, dissolved, and were buried. I wished I could have drowned the curse of addiction and all the pain it bestowed—once and done, gone and away forever; like all the conversations from our past we couldn't possibly recall.

Inevitably our conversation always covered the topic of our weight and fitness. We'd always weighed within a few pounds of one another, and we considered 140 pounds to be the tipping point to get back on track with diet and exercise. I was now past that number and then some. As our walk wrapped up, our conversation came full circle.

"I wish I could play more tennis. It's just been once a week. Maybe I'll start packing my weights in the trunk and lift the nights I'm staying here."

Years ago, I'd participated in a training weekend to become a certified instructor to teach Group Power; a one-hour weightlifting class set to music. I'd learned the proper techniques to a full body weight-lifting workout, and I was able to do my own choreography. All I needed were my weighted bar components and my phone with iTunes.

"Maybe you'd inspire me. I want arms that look good in a tank top, even though I don't wear tank tops," Ann said with a smile.

"I think being flabby makes me feel weaker in every aspect of life. Probably sounds weird, but when I've been lifting weights consistently, and I can see the muscle tone, I feel more empowered," I said.

"Makes sense. At least it's one aspect of your life you can influence, when there is so much about Ryder and Avery that has you feeling powerless."

"All day at work they play a country music station. As you know, I've never been a fan ... *until now!*"

I stopped walking, put my hands on my hips, and gave her a feigned expression of astonishment.

"I swear to God, it's grown on me. I'm officially a country music fan," I confessed with a laugh.

Ann's lake place was only twelve miles from the entrance to WE Fest, an annual three-day mecca for country music fans. The first weekend of August, fans from all over the world arrive and take up hundreds of campsites next to the concert area. For three days, the biggest names in country music would perform from noon until after midnight, and I had never once considered going to WE Fest in the over twenty years it'd been held, practically in my sister's backyard.

It was ironic to me that country music was all about the South, yet it didn't get more rural, or more country, than the state of North Dakota and WE Fest in Becker County, Minnesota. That summer, I'd discovered a new genre of music in spite of my longstanding opinion that country music was for redneck hillbillies. Hearing "Pontoon" on the car radio back in March had been far more prophetic than I could have ever imagined. My favorites that summer would turn out to be Blake Shelton, Miranda Lambert, Eric Church and Dierks Bentley. Music that raised my spirits and lyrics that befriended my soul—another blessing I credited to the Lakeland Marine intervention.

We lounged in Lafuma recliners on the deck overlooking the lake with glasses of wine. Ann and her husband had been fans of the lunar cycle for many years, long before I was. They made plans monthly to watch the full moon rise. She had no interest in feng shui, but her home looked like it. It was always uncluttered, with the exception of vacations when her kids and grandchildren took over. And even then it was kept up to a standard far above average. A renovation in 2008 updated the original floor plan, and added on additional rooms. The result was an exquisite expansion with contemporary updates and design.

All three bedrooms were on the upper level. The master bedroom and the bedroom where I stayed had a view of the lake. The windows were intentionally free of blinds or curtains, with a clear and open view of the sights and sounds of the lake below. Waves washing ashore, loons calling, and moonlight filled our dreams. The bedroom walls and ceilings were blond knotty pine. Her wall décor was understated, definitely a "less is more" Zen vibe.

Their lake home was a proven sanctuary for me that summer. Four decks were at various locations around the house and yard. One, on the non-lake side, offered a view of the landscaped yard, featuring over twenty flower beds and a studio/garage outbuilding. This deck was great for days that the wind came out of the north, or if she wanted to keep an eye on the grandkids while they played soccer, croquet, or jumped on the neighbor's trampoline.

On our first night, we lounged on the lakeside deck that sat outside four sets of sliding-glass doors along the dining area, living room, and den. An elevated, panoramic view of the lake spread out below. A third deck offered a Jacuzzi and fire pit, partially secluded by trees, yet opened to a view of the water. The fourth deck was halfway down a slope and was terraced into the side of the hill, which was covered with yellow daylilies. Uneven, weathered, wooden steps led to the dock with a screen gazebo, Jet Ski, and pontoon boat.

The blessings of the day had indeed ushered in the season of celebration. We toasted: to sisters, to summer, and to the setting sun, leaving behind tiered ribbons of apricot light that the rising moon would soon climb.

24

WITH RYDER LOCKED AWAY AT Valley Rehab, I viewed the Fourth of July and celebrations of freedom and independence through an altered lens. Freedom was no longer an assumed aspect of life. I found it ironic that when I was surrounded by freedom, I never paid notice. Once it'd disappeared, it became front and center. I thought about all the parents that had sacrificed their soldier sons and daughters to maintain our freedom. How did I raise a self-absorbed son who cared only about serving his garish agenda? I couldn't separate myself from his choices completely; I felt partially responsible. Somehow, in some way, I wanted to right his wrongs, make it up to society.

July 4, 2013, Brad was flying. Avery was wherever he was, uninterested in joining my family at Pelican Lake. Fortunately for me, I had an extended family with which to blend. They understood my situation was difficult, and their unconditional love and support was a cushioned pillar I could lean into for comfort and support. I saw my nieces, nephews, and their families only about once a year. Any occasions that included a collection of my sisters and their families brought only the best of times.

Ann's three children, their spouses, and three grandsons filled the Pelican Lake home with joyful chaos. My nephew Eric, my sister Jackie's oldest son, and his family were visiting from Colorado and staying with the Thorson's, family friends who also lived on the lake. The entire family gathered at the Thorson's the afternoon of the Fourth.

Minnesota license plates boasted "The Land of 10,000 Lakes," and if you weren't at one of them on the Fourth, you were missing the good life. Boats, sun, sandbars, parties, skiing, swimming, fishing, and bonfires were full-on at nearly every lake property. The Thorsons had invited at least twelve families to a potluck at their newly renovated two-story log home, which sat level with the beach, making it easy for parents to keep an eye on wet kids digging in the sand, splashing, and swimming.

As much as I loved seeing my family, it was also difficult because it inevitably brought up the topic of my boys, and a simple "How are they doing?" had me strategizing a response. I'd tailor my answer, wanting earnestly not to bring others down with my struggles. That afternoon was the only day I saw Eric, his wife Beth, and their three young, beautiful blond, blue-eyed sons. Her grandparents, and then her parents, had owned the lake home next to Thorsons, where she'd spent summers growing up. It was a calm, sunny, eighty-degree July day as guests comfortably spread out throughout the yard and log home. I sat down at a picnic table across from Eric and Beth. Eric was the second of my parents' grandchildren, their first grandson, and I was seventeen when he was born. I watched him grow into the remarkable man he'd become. Beth was so sweet, as genuine and kind as any person you could ever meet. We hadn't seen one another in over two years, and they had no idea how bad it had become with Ryder and Avery.

"It's so good to see you. Is Brad coming; are the boys?" Beth asked brightly.

"No, just me."

"How are the boys doing? I know you had some struggles with them. Is it better now?" Eric asked.

"It's tough. I don't even know where to begin, and I don't want to ruin this awesome day."

My voice cracked.

"Oh, hon, what?" Beth put her fork down.

My eyes began to sting, and I felt the back of my throat swell.

"Ryder is in Jamestown at a treatment facility that's also incarceration."

I briefly explained Valley Rehab.

"Was he smoking pot?"

Both Eric and Beth forgot about eating.

"No, well, yes, that too, but he's actually in there for heroin possession, heroin addiction."

I felt like I'd just told them that someone had died. A part of me was dead, the part that believed my best efforts as a mom would be good enough. Beth's eyes instantly pooled with tears as she held eye contact with me, speechless.

"Oh, Dana, my God, I'm so sorry," Eric said softly, stunned.

I continued.

"I know it's horrific, surreal at times, to think that precious little boy became so lost. And we were right there when he went missing, right under our noses. I can't wrap my heart around it."

My eyes were spilling tears, but I did all I could not to actually break down and sob.

"Oh, Dana, oh my, I'm so sorry. I, we, had no idea." Beth spoke just above a whisper.

"I feel bad even telling you two. It's certainly not what you expect to hear when you ask someone how their kids are doing. I've just recently been able to say Ryder and heroin addict in the same sentence."

I twisted my napkin into the corner of my eyes to absorb my tears. I so didn't want to cry at this celebration. Fortunately, sunglasses were standard attire. I grabbed mine out of my purse and put them back on.

Their sons were nearby playing in the sand, tussling in a hammock. That was my life so many years ago, little boys, so innocent, just trying to keep up with them and all the fun they chased down.

"Your boys are so precious; it's great to see all of you. It's been too long."

It always tugged at my heart to watch little boys playing. I'd flash back to my own, and how perfect life had once been. I'd always assumed an idealistic life; never did I imagine I'd be pitied. It was a status that felt uncomfortable and didn't suit me. It was like wearing a wetsuit to a wedding reception; it felt unnerving and awkward on so many levels.

"I don't know what happened, how he got so off track. I needed to do something differently; I just don't know what."

"I hope you don't blame yourself, Dana. You're an awesome mother—you and Brad are wonderful parents," Eric said as Beth nodded in agreement.

"It's impossible not to take some responsibility. But honestly, I don't want to go on about it. It's so good to be with you guys; I wish it was more often."

I'd mastered the art of conversational shifts. If not, the topic could consume every conversation I had with others, and I didn't want it to be about our plight. I also realized that often, others wouldn't change the topic out of respect, allowing me all the space I needed to talk it out. There was a social etiquette I'd interpreted, telling me I could suck the life out of the room with my troubles, or graciously and efficiently steer the conversation into a new direction.

"Why don't you and Brad move out to Colorado and start over? Work for me, Dana; I'm desperate for an assistant. I honestly cannot keep up, and I don't want to work this much," Beth said.

Beth was a Realtor, and a magnet for success. Her honest, unpretentious, and professional demeanor drew clients to her. I would have loved to drop everything and say yes to her offer.

"Really? Wow, thanks for the offer, Beth. Honestly, I'd love to, but I don't think Brad would be on board for a longer commute. Otherwise I'd leave tomorrow. There's nothing left for us in River Bend."

As we continued talking, I felt my composure mellow, much like after the first two swallows of wine penetrate an empty stomach and loosen the knot of tension. I leaned into their compassion, and it rounded the edges of my despair. Eric's deep voice, his calm grounded energy, his paternal demeanor, gently resonated. It was as though he was a conduit for the essence of my dad's energy and love during that interlude. I'd imagined Eric to be much like my dad when he was forty—successful, devoted, respected, and raising a beautiful family of which he was proud. My parents' legacy of love was radiating; I felt it carry me.

Later that evening, back at Ann's home, we piled into their pontoon with sweatshirts and beach towels to protect us from mosquitoes. We returned to the Thorson log home at dusk, where we parked alongside their dock. In that area of Pelican Lake was Rolling Hills Resort, a family vacation destination that offered a step back in time to simpler days. Small log cabins filled the lake village, separated by paths to the clubhouse, tennis courts, and par-3 golf course. Every Friday night, a hootenanny was put on by staff for the guests. It was a quaint, nostalgic escape for families wanting to vacation in the slow lane.

We had an open view of the extravagant Rolling Hills fireworks display. Blocks away, a farmer's pasture was available for hundreds of spectators in lounge chairs or on the hoods of their parked cars to view the display above the treetops. A local radio station synchronized a freedom-themed playlist to broadcast in unison with the fireworks. Gratitude for generations of soldiers filled the thoughts of onlookers as the sky lit up with spectacular explosions of color. Springsteen's "Born in the USA" resounded from hundreds of boat speakers that floated in the bay.

Fireworks make magic seem real. How someone could pack a magnificent display of light and sound into a capsule that exploded on cue was a mystery that playfully beckoned me out of my paradigm of defeat. I was inspired by the sense that life is so much more than what I can see, understand, or explain. It stoked embers deep within me, the message that there was a purpose to my pain, our pain—a long-held whisper that someday I would write a book. I'd heard that message for over thirty years, but the notion to write a book had only simmered, and I'd never been compelled or disciplined enough to seriously attempt it. The truth, I intuited that night beneath the glow of stars and fireworks, was that Ryder, Avery, Brad, and I were currently living the story that was destined to be written.

I'd lived my entire adult life believing that "what you think about you bring about." In spite of my optimism and assumptions of only the best playing out in our lives, we were up to our necks in a situation I'd never even considered to be a possibility. Scenes of my children being addicts, incarcerated, had received zero playtime on the screen to which I projected our future. I had to wonder … if I wasn't thinking about it, how'd I bring it about?

The message my soul whispered, my intuition, was telling me that our experience would be a story that benefited others. These frightening chapters in our lives weren't due to any fault of character. Instead, our current, treacherous journey was God's will, and on a soul level Brad, Ryder, Avery, and I were willing to participate. That's the explanation I discerned, that explained how it was possible to have a life so contrary to what I'd envisioned.

My journey to become a life coach and feng shui practitioner had me well-read in the self-help and inspiration genres. Watching *Oprah*, I'd discovered many books and authors that had a profound effect on me. Gary Zukov's book *The Seat of the Soul* had influenced my perception of the meaning and purpose of life. I'd been striving to live in alignment with my soul's intentions and was discovering that it could be rugged terrain that required tremendous courage and conviction to endure. I was too far along the path now; to retreat or detour was not an option. I'd soon discover that Ryder wasn't the only addict in my family. How far would this story need to progress before I took action to manifest our souls' dharma?

Nearly an hour later, the fireworks display concluded. The cooling humid air blended with the scent of smoldering bonfires, as hundreds of boats progressed homeward. A slow-motion migration was illuminated by the collective docking lights from the eclectic fleet of boats. The unrehearsed parade floated along; it seemed no one was in a hurry for the evening to end.

In all, sixteen of my family members gathered that Fourth of July—sixteen exceptional people that I loved, laughing, sharing, and celebrating life at the peak of summer at our favorite place in the world, Pelican Lake, Minnesota. Regardless of what my future held, my family was there for me, always had been, and always would be.

25

'D TRADE MY LIFE'S EARNINGS to wake up to a typical life.

The boys' twenty-first birthday was approaching, two weeks to the day after the Fourth of July, and as it turned out, it was also a Family Day at Valley Rehab, and we planned a second trip. This time, Avery would be cleared to go with us. Their twenty-first birthday at Valley Rehab—certainly not the typical way to celebrate stepping over the threshold of manhood. Regardless, I looked forward to the four of us being together and my twin sons seeing one another for the first time in over two months, by far their longest separation.

I was spending the night at Ann's. I was tired and planned to lie in bed and fall asleep to the evening rhythms of nature closing out another day on the lake. I decided to call Ryder. The call rang to a central location, and Ryder was paged.

"How was your day?" I asked him.

"Okay, I guess. I learned how to set up a meth lab today."

He sounded smug.

Really? That's what he chose to tell me, with no regard for my feelings, what that would do to me? I was mortified, and so incredibly saddened by it. He was over halfway through his time in Valley Rehab, and this is what he has to say?

Moments of silence passed.

"Mom, are you there?"

"Yes, I am. I don't know how to respond to that. A meth lab, Ryder? What the hell?"

"Well, sorry, but one of the guys was just going on about it."

I took a deep breath and changed the subject.

"I'm hoping Avery will make it to Valley Rehab with us on the eighteenth."

"Ah … well … honestly, I'd rather you not come. It's just too hard seeing you guys, and I only needed that one family day to get released to live with you. So, just skip it, okay? … Is that okay?"

"If that's what you want."

"Hey, I can't really talk now; a bunch of guys are waiting for the phone. I hate talking when they're staring at me."

So, he now knew how to set up a meth lab. This had me understand the perspective I'd heard recently on an HBO episode of *Real Time with Bill Maher*. Actor Tim Robbins expressed the view that by locking away addicts, we're sending them to "crime camp" to mingle with the true criminals in society, and when they return to freedom, they can't get a decent job with a prison record. But they now have the new skills they acquired in prison. Would that be my son's fate?

I sobbed, overcome with anguish and fear. There was no end in sight. I feared it would be an endless cycle of drugs, consequences, treatments, legal entanglements, and attorneys until finally he'd end up locked away or dead. I let the despair I felt for his future, our future, grind away at my soul.

Why did this happen to us? I want what other people have, the normal concerns and victories. I don't want to be that family wrecked by drugs, dealing, addiction. I want my boys back. I want them in my life, caring about others, aspiring to fulfill their potential, discovering their gifts. I want to go back to the times when all they wanted was to snuggle alongside me as I read to them, their little fingers tangled in my hair, captivated with the Berenstain Bears and Clifford the Big Red Dog, familiar adventures, soothing them to sleep.

I cried it out until I had no more tears left. Once quiet, I could hear the call of a loon, a drawn-out plaintive beckoning, a yearning that was forlorn yet somehow comforting. It was a Tuesday night, and there weren't many boats passing in the stillness of midnight. The moon was two nights away from full, and it cast a drape of illumination across my sheets. But the light couldn't penetrate my soul. I lay there trying to contain my despair, but it was too much. It was impossible for me in that moment to believe that my son would ever heal, that he could evolve, that we would get out of this unscathed. I felt hopeless and afraid.

I sent a text to Brad: "If I met with a quick and painless death I would consider it a blessing." I meant it. I felt a jagged sense of relief that life was finite, knowing this suffering would end for me. I wanted to see my parents again. It was nearly five years since they'd passed away, and our son's demise had continually escalated ever since. I'd lived with varied degrees of grief, loss or despair every day for the last five years.

By day, I'd put on a happy face. No one would be able to guess the hell I was going through. I was accomplished at compartmentalizing. I was so incredibly grateful for the playful atmosphere at Lakeland, truly a godsend. The Fourth of July was the turning point of the season, a time when the staff could exhale. The push to handle the demands of seasonal activity would throttle back significantly. I went into one of the corner offices to do some filing. The sales manager, Troy, was a pleasure to work with, always sincere and delightful.

He asked me, "How's it all going for you, Dana? Are you liking it here?"

"I love it; I'm so grateful to be out of the mall. Everyone is so good to me. I've got to admit, though, I'm not sure I can see myself in sales," I confessed.

"Really, why is that?"

"I look at the four salesmen; they're outdoorsmen. They fish, hunt; they live in lake country, eat it, drink it, breathe it, dream it. Then there's me; I've never even driven a boat."

"Ahh, don't worry about that. Boats are easy to sell, not much to it really."

He smiled.

"You had a lot more to learn, with all the different beds you sold. And besides, sales are just about if people like you. You'll do just fine."

"Thanks, I appreciate the vote of confidence. Everything's been great, though; thanks for asking."

I sat on a bench in the shade under the front eaves of the showroom to eat lunch. A nest of barn swallows lived under the steel awning about seven feet from the showroom entrance. Frank had recently arrived early one morning with his shotgun and killed the parent birds. They'd been protecting the nest by swooping down on nearly everyone that approached the showroom. Not good, I realized, but I was still sad when I'd come to work, and the birds were eerily missing, while the orphaned babies remained in the nest.

I watched the baby birds chirping helplessly, hungry, with no parents to feed or protect them, yet they seemed to be surviving. I felt a knot in my stomach, and stopped eating. I lingered in the clear summer air, gazing at the farmer's corn field across the dirt road. "Knee high by the Fourth of July." It had been a good growing season. I went back into the showroom. The salesmen were sitting around watching the noon newscast. Nearly all the guys that worked at Lakeland were hunters. Killing birds because they were a nuisance was the law of the land.

"Those poor little birds are orphans now. Did you guys think of that before you murdered their parents?" I playfully scolded. We'd had an ongoing friendly battle over it.

They all liked to tease me, but I held my own. There was never a shortage of good-natured banter.

"Those babies are next," Derek said.

"Don't even think about it; those babies haven't done anything wrong. Leave 'em alone."

I said it lightly but meant it.

"I'm not so sure; next thing you know, they leave the nest, pick up where their folks left off, dive-bombing everyone, shitting all over the porch. Not good for business," Sam said as we all laughed.

Derek said, "Yup, better take care of business." He went outside.

I assumed he was going to trash the nest and do something with the babies. I knew he wouldn't shoot them with people around, but I was sure he'd find a way to get rid of them.

I felt my tummy knot up, tears swelling; I didn't want to cry at work. This was my escape, my distraction, but my emotions were stronger than my will. My eyes spilled tears, without crying; I had gotten good at that. I kept my head lowered, pretending I was looking for something in my purse, unable to stop the tears. But then the phone rang, and it was my job to answer it. I tried so hard to contain myself and speak normally. Finally, I managed a tortured response. "Lakeland Marine," was all I could mutter.

Derek had just come back inside when they all realized what was going on with me.

"Oh, hon, are you crying?" he said. "I'm sorry; hey, don't worry. I didn't kill them. Really, it's okay. I just kind of nudged them, and they all flew away. They're gone, flown off to find a new home."

He clearly felt bad seeing my struggle to hold it together. The other guys saw it too. They were sweet to me. "Free," a beautiful ballad by the Zac Brown Band, was playing in the showroom.

It was all a bit too much for me. And it was so not about the birds.

26

I T WAS TWENTY-ONE YEARS TO the day that I had checked into the hospital in Edina, Minnesota, at 8:00 a.m. to have my labor induced.

On July 17 that year, my obstetrician assured me, my twin sons would be born. It was my first pregnancy, and I'd hoped to endure labor without an epidural. The thought of that huge needle in my back made me wince. Do all first-time mothers begin labor with the thought of not taking pain meds? Why do we think that pain medication somehow diminishes the experience, that it is somehow less natural if the pain is removed or reduced?

By midafternoon, my best intentions vanished. I didn't care if they stuck that foot-long needle into my eyeball. Get that juice in me *now*! Once the drug took effect, the pain was greatly diminished, but there was a patch of my lower abdomen area that, for some reason, didn't numb. For the rest of the labor, there was an area the size of my palm, above my right hip, that felt the full-on labor pains. In all, it took twenty-two hours before my twins were delivered, C-section, the next day, July 18, at 6:25 and 6:26 a.m.

Now, twenty-one years later, the part of me that felt the full-on pain was higher up, in my chest—heartache.

Avery chose Denny's for his twenty-first birthday supper, so Brad and I met him there. Probably because of his nocturnal work schedule, Avery liked having breakfast for dinner. He'd been working the overnight front desk shift at a low-budget franchise hotel, following years of red-eye shifts at service stations. Being up all night and sleeping all day was a work schedule and lifestyle both boys maintained as soon as they were done with high school.

"Are you going out tonight?" I asked him, assuming he'd hit the bars on his twenty-first.

"Na, don't really feel like celebrating. I don't like the taste of beer or liquor either, or the buzz, for that matter."

"I wish your brother was here; I'm sure it's tough for you to be apart today."

"It sucks, but that's the way it is. I'm actually more upset about something else." He paused. "I got my hours cut yesterday."

"Why? What happened?" I asked. I could hear what Brad was thinking—another debacle to sort through.

"It's bullshit; the manager's kid needed a job, and he doesn't even want to work there. I've been the one training him. I had no idea he was going to be taking half my hours."

"Did you do something to give them a reason?" Brad asked. We could never trust that we were getting even half the story when he or Ryder told us something.

"No, that's what's so f'd about it. I work my ass off there, always show up on time, stay longer if they need me. Then some kid that's gonna quit after a couple paychecks screws me."

"Maybe you can go back to Holiday, they always need people. You left there on good terms," Brad offered.

"No, I'm getting my hours back. I'm applying other places too, though, to make up the difference until I do."

In spite of his frustration, he made an effort to relax and enjoy our meal together. We all felt the void of Ryder's absence but left it out of our conversation.

Life had become an exercise in numbing the pain by skimming across the top. Best not to plunge into the losses and disappointments because it was a bottomless dive, and the farther you got from the surface, the darker it became, and the less likely we could ascend to see the light of day.

Soon I'd look back to that dinner at Denny's as a benchmark. I'd recall that everything seemed fine at Avery's birthday dinner—well at least our family's version of fine, which included some nuance of disarray. Avery looked healthy, mostly pleasant. He even speculated he might try and take some classes in the fall. I would reflect, astonished that there was no indication tipping us off about how far gone his situation had become.

He seemed okay, other than his frustrations about work and missing his brother. He didn't look strung-out on drugs, unkempt. He wasn't acting slippery. He was just Avery, struggling, trying to live on his own. That's what I saw and felt. It seemed just another occasion, a vignette of our tainted normalcy. There was no intuition warning me, no barometric pressure shifting, no dark clouds building, or winds gathering velocity, or distant rumblings of thunder signaling that a disastrous storm was on the way.

I had Sundays and Mondays off. I was only able to play tennis once a week, on Mondays, at Island Park with my women's doubles group. I was gaining weight, being so sedentary during the workweek—eleven hours a day with the commute. Occasionally I'd play on a Sunday morning with Jack. Playing singles was far more physically demanding, a much better cardio workout because you hit the ball twice as much and covered much more court. Jack and I were fairly evenly matched, but Jack did not like losing to a woman, so we pushed ourselves, both eager to win.

One Sunday morning, after I hadn't seen Jack in months, we met at Elephant Park to play and chatted between sets. The conversation, of course, made it to my sons.

"How are the boys?"

"It's not good."

I recapped Ryder's status.

"Yeah, I wondered this winter when I saw him at the Freeze game; he looked awfully skinny."

Jack was truly concerned for me and my family. His three young adult children were thriving.

We were both soaking with sweat, sitting in a shaded corner of the court between sets, allowing our heart rates to slow a bit. He continued.

"It's just not fair. You and Brad are good parents. You didn't do anything different than any of us. I just don't get it," he said, shaking his head.

"I could lose my mind trying to make sense of it. I know I needed to get in their faces more; I was in denial that it would ever go this far, get this bad. I was naive, too trusting, for sure."

He tilted his head and leaned in toward me, like a big brother good-naturedly threatening to knock sense into me. He raised his voice.

"Well, I hope you're not blaming yourself?"

He paused and looked me straight in the eyes.

"You're not ... are you?"

"I'm taking some responsibility for it; God sakes, I'm their mother, how can I not?"

"It's not your fault, Dana, you have to know that." He was firm.

"Maybe I'll get to that belief someday, I'm not there yet."

"Well I hope you do. It's gotta be tough enough to get through, without shouldering blame for it too."

I toweled off my face and grabbed my racquet, ready to start the second set. I was craving the endorphins, the push, the distraction, the competition—*hitting something*! No matter how much I loathed my weight gain, I loved and appreciated my body on the tennis court. My recent weight lifting efforts were paying off. I was stronger. I was a coordinated, natural athlete, and that felt amazing. A lifetime of muscle memory playing tennis served me with the knowledge of what shot to take and the ability to make it. A tennis court was where I went to experience my best self. I'd won the first set 6-4.

"It's my serve," I said, then noticed I only had one ball in my pocket, and Jack had the other two. "*Gimme the ball* so I can finish kicking your ass."

The July full moon was on the twenty-first, my dad's birthday. Ann and I took our front row seats in the screen gazebo on their dock to watch it rise. Gazing into the fading light of the horizon, where the sky met the lake, only a sliver of distance shoreline divided the wash of blue, transforming delicately into gray. At night, in the gazebo, the absence of light dissolved the screen and created the illusion that you were floating in the lake. It was the middle of the week, not much boat traffic, so we settled into our quiet, private island, poised to soak in the benevolence of the full moon.

My dad's nickname had been Moon. Since his death, all four of us daughters felt a deeper connection to the moon. I felt like he was watching over me, us. He and my mom were helping to light our way, with their love and protection, in the dark hours of our struggle.

We gazed at the night sky in anticipation.

"How happy are we?" Ann asked playfully.

"For sure, it doesn't get better than this," I agreed.

She had a glass of wine, but I declined. I worked in the morning, and even one glass could cause puffy eyes in the morning.

"Too bad neither one of us can drive a boat. What a pair of helpless broads we are," I joked.

"You better get that figured out if you're gonna sell pontoons," Ann teased.

"Ya think?"

We laughed.

"I can't believe the Fourth has come and gone. Crazy, time, it just goes too fast in the summer."

Your boys are twenty-one now, how is it possible? How is Avery doing? Has he seen Ryder yet?"

"No, I don't know if he even wants to go to Valley Rehab. Ryder's been hard on him."

"How so?"

"Just so crabby. He also puts a lot of pressure on Avery to be clean, to be his sober buddy. Not that it's a bad idea, but it's not Avery's responsibility to make sure Ryder doesn't use."

"Well, at least Ryder has intentions to stay clean; that's an improvement."

"I'd like to get Avery into counseling. He won't talk about it much with me."

"Are you still opposed to counseling for yourself? I just think that could help you—that it's at least worth a try."

"I just don't feel compelled to search it out. It won't change anything. If it would fix the situation, I would. It's just one more thing to fit into my schedule, another insurance paper chase, and expense."

"But if it helped, it'd be worth it."

Ann was gentle. It was difficult for her to see me suffer and not be able to do anything to improve the situation.

"I really don't know what else I could be doing differently, or better. I take care of myself; I don't self-medicate with drugs or booze; I'm functioning and productive. And our marriage is solid. Sure I get down and sad about it, but who wouldn't? It's intense."

"Maybe a professional could help you with the intensity of it."

"It is what it is. I feel like before all this happened my life had a range of one to ten. One is the toughest times, and ten is the best of times. Now I feel like my range is one to five. Five is as high as life's gonna get."

Ann wanted to help me, but no one could, I believed. It was narrow-minded of me to not seek counseling, but it's how I felt at that time. Being here with her was the best therapy anyone could offer. The full moon didn't disappoint.

"I think the moon's almost up," I said, changing the subject.

"Happy birthday, Papa." Ann smiled.

I wouldn't be able to do a feng shui blessing in my home during that full moon. So instead, once I went to bed, I thought about my intentions and released them to the moon, now high in the midnight sky. That same moon was shining on my children. I believed that the source of all the blessings in our lives was also the source of our hardships. Like the moon, our lives had a rhythm and a cycle. All the suffering would be balanced out in time.

To everything ... there is a season ... a time to every purpose under heaven ...

I just had to continue trusting the divine plan and persevere until better days came around.

Little did I know the magnitude of the approaching storm. Better days were nowhere near the radar, and it would get way worse before it improved. It would in fact be several more years until I emerged from a cocoon of despair, that barely allowed me to breathe.

27

SHORTLY AFTER THE BOYS' TWENTY-FIRST birthday, Ryder earned a level three at Valley Rehab. This was a level, the institution deemed, that was an indication of his cooperation, attitude, and evolvement toward living on the outside, drug free. Our phone conversations were definitely becoming lighter, and Ryder was becoming more optimistic, finally shifting out of victim mode. I was relieved to hear he was evolving. His release date was projected for late August, and he had continued to take advantage of his weight room privileges. We actually had to send him larger T-shirts.

At Valley Rehab, next to the men's housing was a sand volleyball court. The women inmates would occasionally stroll past the court while the guys were playing. Not allowed to talk, this was as close as Ryder and his former girlfriend ever got to one another. Ryder's resentment toward her had gradually softened. In part because of the deprivation there, and the fact they were sharing newfound sobriety, both of them were gaining a commitment to changing their lives.

When the guys saw the women passing by, they whooped it up. The women played along too, so far as they were allowed to without breaking rules. Some of them would "accidently" drop something, then bend over to pick it up. That sent the catcalls to a fever pitch.

As difficult as it was to be locked up during the summer, it was less claustrophobic than a harsh winter would have been with little or no time outside. One day, Ryder was in a three on three volleyball match, with a group of guys hanging out watching them. When the women were spied a block away, the catcalls started, and some of the guys strut like peacocks. Their shirts came off, and they lined up against the fence. Ryder dropped to the sand, shirtless, and started doing pushups while his buddy counted loudly beginning at "100, 101." Blake Shelton's "Boys Round Here" played as the guys danced and grinded, much to the amusement of the women. They were belting out the lyrics, "Have ya ever got down with a redneck?" It was one of my favorite songs from my first summer as a new country music fan.

Brad and I were pleased to know that Ryder had taken up weight training. We'd tried in vain to get our boys interested in going to the gym over the years. One of the things I felt I had done right as a parent was to get them into tennis when they were young.

Avery is left-handed, and Ryder is right-handed—mirror twins, as it's called. Avery, however, made the choice to play tennis right-handed because he didn't want to be different from everyone else. As a result, he had an awesome two-handed backhand as it was led by his dominant arm.

The most successful men's doubles players in the world at that time were Mike and Bob Bryan, identical, mirror, twins, like Avery and Ryder. I'd had fantasies of my boys being doubles partners and going to the state tournament in high school.

One winter, when the boys were nine years old, we saw the Bryan brothers at a tournament in Phoenix. The boys and I had stumbled into them practicing on the tournament grounds. We watched them up close; only the chain-link fence around the court separated us. They were animated, gregarious, and totally aware of the set of twins watching them. After the match, they walked up and asked if we wanted autographs. I knew how special the occasion was, though my boys did not. We got autographed pictures and a memory I will always treasure.

We also watched James Blake practice. He was just coming back from an injury that could have ended his career, and his life. The Bryan brothers, James Blake and Andy Roddick, had won the Davis Cup in 2010, one of my biggest highs as a tennis fan. This was a generation of tennis athletes who were gracious and humble, including Roger Federer and Raphael Nadal, reigning champions. It was such an extreme departure from the egomaniacs headlining other major sports. They were tremendous role models, and it was another reason I'd wanted my sons to become interested in tennis.

In October 2004, I brought the boys to an exhibition match in Grand Forks North Dakota. They were eleven years old. Andy Roddick was playing Andre Agassi—are you kidding me? A dream come true for me. I remember I could see Andy waiting in the wings as the announcer hyped up the crowd building up to his introduction. It was like being at a rock concert waiting for the lead singer to appear. Again, I was way more into it than my kids, but I was trying to light their fire for the sport. If only our lives had continued to track with a shared passion for tennis. Would we have avoided this nightmare in our family?

The week following the July 21 full moon, my sisters and I reunited at Pelican Lake. It had been over a year since our sister's week in Kansas, and a rough year for me. Seeing my sisters would be medicinal—it always was.

While I was at work, Kelly arrived from Grand Forks, and Jackie from Kansas. When I turned the corner onto the deck, they were lined up reclining in lawn chairs talking, snacking, and gazing at the lake. We hugged one another, and I grabbed a chair, and we shifted to sit in a semicircle.

Jackie wasted no time. "How are you holding up?" She knew enough about my situation to know it was rugged.

"I'm doing okay, so grateful for Lakeland. My God, if I was in Dakota Mall this summer I'd lose my mind. I love the people, the culture, it's so laid-back."

"How about the boys?" Jackie asked.

"What can I say? It sucks. I'm in a constant state of despair, seeking out distractions."

I began to unravel. Here with my sisters I could lean in, and I allowed myself to do just that.

"I'm scared for Ryder to come home. If he relapses, he'll fail drug court, and be a felon for seven years. He has to stay clean, or all this will be for nothing. Then if he does make it, what happens when there's no accountability, no probation officer or drug testing? What keeps him clean then? There's so much at stake."

I was rambling, asking questions no one could answer.

"You and Brad are awesome parents; I hope you know that," Kelly said.

"I wish I knew what we should have done differently … I …"

Tears began to spill.

"Nothing," Jackie blurted before I had a chance to continue. "You two are wonderful, dedicated parents. I hope you know *it's not your fault.*"

"I'm aspiring to that. It's not something I can easily convince myself of though."

I wanted to believe it wasn't my fault, but that wasn't my truth. It was like getting a haircut that you hate while everyone tells you how cute it is. It doesn't matter what they say; you look in the mirror and see ugly.

"Dana, hear me; it's not your fault. God gives us children, but they're not ours; they have their own destiny; their souls have a journey that's God's plan," Jackie said.

I knew that was true. I'd felt it that night of the fireworks, that somehow this was meant to be our destiny. I could feel the depth of all my sisters' love. I was the kid sister, the wild one. They had watched out for me my entire life, caring about me, nurturing me.

"Sometimes I think that instead of trying to convince myself that it's not my fault, I should just accept some blame and work toward self-forgiveness instead."

This was the first time that notion had occurred to me, and it felt so right. The sentiment just spilled out of my heart, and the words formed as I spoke. I heard my truth as it leaked out of me uncensored. My sisters didn't respond. I could tell they were considering the idea but truly believed no fault should be assigned.

"One day at a time is how you get through it. Mom and Dad are watching over them, and you. They adored your boys," Kelly said.

I felt safe there. I could be who I needed to be. Here, in this circle of love, I allowed myself to dissolve, and to receive. How desperate I felt; how grateful I was for sisters, for unconditional love, to be witnessed.

In our three days together, we never left Ann's lake home. No shopping, no spa adventure. We didn't even go out to eat. We walked, talked, reminisced, drank a little, and laughed a lot. We soaked in the summer and the retreat atmosphere that the Pelican Lake home offered us; best of times, for sure. Mom and Dad were smiling down on us.

July was winding down. Late August would bring Ryder and Jesse back home. Ann would leave for the summer, back to Denver in a couple of weeks. Just when I was sinking into the rhythm of summer, the seasons would begin to shift.

In late July, there were two heroin deaths that startled me. One was Cory Monteith, from the hit television show *Glee*. The other was an acquaintance of my sons who overdosed in a bar restroom in River Bend. Both men had been clean for a while, and then took too big of a dose their first "high" back. By the grace of God, Ryder had been spared under the same circumstances seven months earlier. The waste and wretchedness of these lost young lives haunted me.

It was impossible to hear of those tragedies and not project it onto Ryder's situation. He was one slipup away from being an incarcerated felon once he returned home. Or worse.

... Whatever happens, I will find a way to handle it.

28

THE FIRST SIGN THAT AUTUMN was fast approaching was the scheduled billet meeting on July 31 for the parents hosting Freeze players. I hadn't been in touch with Jesse much since he left, but I knew he was working back home in North Carolina and excited to return to the ice. Brad was flying, so I attended the billet meeting alone. Because we had become a host family midseason last December, I never really got to know the other families.

I drove straight from work to the arena, excited to commit to the next season of hockey and have Jesse back. I could see what a blessing it would be to have him living with us when Ryder returned. He considered Jesse an important part of his plan for sobriety. He was the one peer Ryder knew he could hang out with and not be tempted to use. It felt as though my intuition to bring Jesse into our family had a purpose beyond the many that were already evident.

I recognized a few of the parents, but no one I felt I could pick up a conversation with, so I sat at a pub table by myself and listened to Terry welcome everyone and attend to the brief business. There were a couple of forms to fill out, including a waiver stating that neither parent is a felon. I took pause: What if Ryder had a relapse? That would change his status to a felon over the course of the season. I could feel the origins of a conflict begin to conspire within. Could we lose Jesse? I assigned my fears to my denial vault, that crowded, familiar storage compartment between my heart and solar plexus. I'd had enough heartache; there was no valid reason to foster potential dismay.

The next night Brad returned home from a six-day Asia trip. It had been a grueling summer for him. Between the reduced income with my new job and the cost of Ryder's situation, he had been flying more hours a month than ever trying to stay ahead of the expenses. By the time Brad would arrive home from Asia, he'd been up for nearly twenty-four hours. I never hit him up for conversation until he'd had a chance to sleep off some jetlag. The next morning, I shared my concerns with him.

"I went to the billet meeting a couple nights ago," I began.

"How was it?"

"Not much to it, really. I did wonder about something, though. I signed off that we're not felons. But the fact that Ryder could default to one left me uneasy."

Brad seemed unconcerned.

"That's something we can deal with if it were to happen. Chances are it won't."

"I wonder if we should present it to Jesse. I don't want him to feel stuck with us. Neither one of the boys were around much last season. This year will be different with Ryder home. I just wonder if we should give Jesse an out if he wants it. Better now than a few weeks or months into the season," I reasoned.

"Can't hurt. I'll text him."

Brad and Jesse had grown close in spite of the fact that Brad's schedule allowed him to see only three games all season. Their relationship was about mutual respect and appreciation, not about hockey.

Jesse's response was unwavering: "We're family, and family sticks together. I want to live with you guys. I love it there."

He looked forward to having Ryder around more. This first hurdle had been cleared.

Around this time, we scheduled a bathroom remodel for the boys that included a new shower, and new color palette to finally transition from the hot pink the previous owners had painted it. We'd never changed it, and the boys didn't seem to care. An improvement was overdue, and Jesse and Ryder's return was the best reason of all to make the upgrade.

I wanted positive and motivating decor on the walls. Ryder would be striving for sobriety, and Jesse was hoping to shine brightly enough to attract a full scholarship to a Division 1 hockey school. I ended up finding a wall stencil for the living room where the boys spent hours watching the plasma TV. It simply read: I CAN, I WILL, I BELIEVE. That seemed to be an affirmation that would serve all of us.

After Ryder told us not to travel to visit him, Brad and I were surprised when he invited us to come to Valley Rehab on August 4. With his release in sight, he wanted visitors. He was up for a level review, and once he reached level four, and had served one hundred days, he could leave within forty-eight hours.

This trip to Jamestown felt completely different from the one we'd made together in June. The once-hostile phone conversations had slowly become balanced, filled with optimism for a new beginning. The son who greeted us that day put my breath on hold. Standing before us was a beautiful young man in his prime. He stood taller, his chest and arms muscular. His eyes were clear, his smile pure, and his embrace strong and lingering. I held him tightly. "This is my Ryder; thank you, God."

The conversation reflected a new perspective, a commitment to live life with a sober compass, as though that would be a good thing, not something he'd been shamed into, or what was expected of him after all the havoc he'd brought to our family.

He held dear the comforts of home and family that he'd felt so far removed from, much farther than the one hundred miles that separated Jamestown from River Bend. Mostly, I think he realized he really had no excuse to be in this predicament. What, and who, was there to blame? The ignorance of reckless youth? The seduction of a chemical high? Grief? Self-absorption? Yes, all of that, but not the reasons of a broken home, living in a rough part of town, addiction in the family, or getting high to escape the horrors of abuse or neglect—all reasons he'd heard from fellow inmates. There was no reason to want to escape the beautiful life we had provided for him. He looked to his future intending to rediscover all the pleasures in his life before it had been reduced to the use and pursuit of drugs. This is what one hundred days at Valley Rehab had revealed to Ryder, and much more.

I was taken aback by my awareness of just how long it had been since I'd held hope for my son to return to us, healed, whole, the child we'd raised, a result of the foundation of love that every choice we'd made as parents was built upon.

Over the years, I had adopted a resigned acceptance of diminishing expectations. Ryder's mere survival would have been a sedate triumph. Hoping for the best had become a risky investment, with so much to lose. But some degree of hope had always dwelled within me, because it's how I'm wired, and he is my son. Hope was slippery; the amount of it I possessed was relative to the truth each day presented. Now there was legitimate evidence to believe that a threshold was near, one that offered us passage out of the unrelenting anguish that had prevailed every season for the past five years. Every storm runs out of rage.

The number of days left for lake lovers on their boats grew dreadfully finite. The challenge was to be fully present in the cherished moments of this final stretch of summer. The pace at the showroom had definitely mellowed, and it triggered justified confessions of burnout by the sales team. They'd been pushing hard since the boat show season had begun in the belly of winter, late January. Each of them took turns taking vacation days to spend escaping to a lake somewhere to fish, isolated from the rest of the world.

I had been a member of this family now for three months, though it felt comfortably like years. They appreciated my positive disposition, my aptitude for not taking anything personally, my approachability and sense of humor. They all took turns confessing their typical frustration with the other salesmen, knowing they could confidentially vent to me.

Politically correct was an overrated discipline none of us had much use for. It was a workplace where flip-flops, baseball caps, sexist jokes, and chewing tobacco were all acceptable. The culture at Lakeland Marine was like showing up for summer camp, one playfully productive day after another. We got the job done, but having a good time was the prevailing pulse. It turned out that 2013 had been the most successful year in the twenty years Lakeland had been in business. I felt privileged to be one of the players on this team.

What were the odds of this? I get a random customer who offers me this opportunity, a choice that blesses me with all this love, and joyful distraction. A job that I never in a million years would have sought. The decision to leave my sales job in Dakota Mall did not make sense on paper, yet I followed my gut and accepted the job. I flowed with the events that brought me to the decision to take a calculated risk and make the move.

Throughout my life, I had collected these types of experiences, each one building my confidence in my intuition to a point where I truly trusted it, relied on it. Benevolence from the universe is how I explained it to myself. Treat others right, and the world has a way of taking care of you. I prayed that same Higher Power would serve my sons too.

My last night with Ann on Pelican Lake had arrived. In all, she had been there eight weeks. In my purse calendar, I'd highlighted the dates I'd spent the night at Pelican Lake. I averaged three nights a week. Nearly all of those nights it was just the two of us, staying put, reclining on the deck staring at the lake flowing into dusk. It was cherished time for both of us.

On our final evening, we packed it in. We went for a walk, drank wine in the Jacuzzi, and toasted the moon from the gazebo.

"How happy are we?" Ann's favorite line always made me smile.

"How grateful am I? For you, for this summer, for everything it's served me with."

I could feel my throat constricting, the way it does when my eyes begin to tear up.

"Me too; it's been so special to have you here. This is my favorite place on earth. Over the years, with all the moves we've made, this home, this place, has never gone away. It feels more like home to me than any other address. It would have been kind of lonely if you weren't here this summer."

"Funny how that worked out, such an atypical summer with Craig working and away so much. Next summer will be so different. He'll be retired, and you'll have two new grandbabies."

The image made us both smile.

Ann's daughter-in-law, Sophie, was due in January, and her middle daughter, Hailey, was due in April; both would be their firstborn. They planned on long maternity leaves that included extended stays on Pelican the summer of 2014.

Ann's departure would mean I'd return to commuting back to River Bend daily. But the timing was right, as Jesse and Ryder would be home in a couple of weeks, and I'd need to be home every night anyway.

When I left in the morning, we were both on the verge of tears.

"We're not saying good-bye, 'cause I will see you soon enough," I said

"No good-byes. It was our special summer."

"I love you."

"Love you too." And off I drove along the winding mile, through the sloping farmer's fields, followed by a stretch of road canopied by the thick growth of sheltering trees, and to the stop sign where Westland Road meets County Highway 22. It marked another one of life's transitions; away from and moving toward a fresh assortment of blessings and challenges that was my life. It was a gorgeous summer morning, on the cool side for August—seventy-two degrees, low humidity, sunny. On the radio Kenny Chesney was singing the lyrics that always had me think of Ryder, *I see a kid coming in his own ... and a man learning to move on.*

By the grace of God, I prayed.

29

SATURDAY, AUGUST 17, WAS THE last night of my empty nest for quite some time. Jesse was in Minneapolis on the last leg of his long drive out from North Carolina and staying overnight with friends before the final 250 miles west to River Bend. He'd arrive Sunday. Ryder was scheduled to get out of Jamestown on Monday, and would drive home with Avery, who was set to pick him up early that morning. Jesse and Avery were key players in Ryder's sobriety plan. He knew the company he kept could make all the difference. Jesse was perfect for the role, and Avery certainly knew how much was at stake for his twin. I was so excited to see all three of them. It felt like everything was falling into place. I was imagining a great season of hockey, Ryder beside me, both of us cheering on Jesse.

I was frustrated with Avery, though. All summer we had played the "please text me when you feed the dog" game. I'd last seen him a week before at the house.

"When you don't text me, I have to wonder and worry all day at work if Murphy's okay. One simple text, and you make my day. Is it too much to ask, honey?"

"No, Mom, I will. I'm sorry, but I wouldn't forget; she's my sugar bear," he'd said with a warm smile.

I was grateful that with Jesse and Ryder back in the picture, I wouldn't have to rely on Avery anymore.

On the drive home from work at five that Saturday, there was still no text from Avery. I wondered if I'd find a starving canine that was forced to do her business on the carpet. As I entered Mayport, I considered stopping by Avery's house to check on him, but decided against it in case Murphy was desperate. I didn't want to delay another thirty minutes. Once home,

I could tell by Murphy's demeanor that she was on schedule, that Avery had taken care of her. He wouldn't forget his sugar bear. I tried to get in touch with him all evening to talk about his upcoming road trip to Valley Rehab, but no response.

Ryder called me at nine thirty that night; he was excited that he'd be home in less than forty-eight hours.

"Mama, how are you?"

"Good, except I haven't heard from Avery all day. He was supposed to feed Murphy and text me. I've been trying to get a hold of him since noon."

"I think you should go over there and check on him."

Ryder sounded very concerned.

"Really? Ugh, I really don't want to; I'm all ready for bed."

"Mom, you have to, or I'm gonna sit here and worry, wondering what's going on."

Welcome to my world, I thought. I got dressed and headed over. I'd only been by Avery's place twice since he'd moved out the previous December, but I'd never gone inside. He lived in a rundown, ramshackle neighborhood even though it was just a couple of blocks from the Mayport police station.

On my way there, I was stopped at a red light near a trailer court. I was startled when a little boy, younger than eight, I was guessing, crossed the intersection on a scooter. Dressed in dark clothing, he was difficult to see. My God, where are this child's parents? Where is he going alone in the dark? I wasn't sure if I should call 911 or try to catch up with him to see if he was okay.

I drove on to Avery's neighborhood. The view across the street from his rented house was of vacant lots where there once were homes that backed up to the Red River. The 1997 flood had led to blocks of demolition. With few homes to supply porch lights and TV rays streaming through the windows, the street he lived on was darker than most. I didn't want to be there, especially at night.

I parked in front of his house and turned off the ignition and headlights. It was a hot, still, muggy summer night, and I could hear the chorus of riverbank creatures, crickets, frogs, and who knows what else. A distant train whistle blew; the heavy, humid air held the warning. I paused to observe for a minute to be sure I was safe to approach the house. One of the window shades was open, and a light in the bedroom was on. I got out of the car and could see someone frantically pacing back and forth; I couldn't tell if it was Kyle or Avery. A neighbor's fat Chihuahua bounced by and barked at me, and if not for the barking, I would have thought it was a rat.

I knocked on the front door; no answer. I could see it was Kyle pacing in the bedroom, with what looked to be a phone in hand. I kept knocking and looking over both shoulders to make sure no one was coming up behind me.

"Kyle, it's Dana. Answer the door."

More knocking.

Now I could see he had a drill in his hand. What the hell is going on? What am I doing here? Where is Avery? I went back to the car as Ryder called again.

"Oh my God, Ryder, I don't know what's going on." I explained the scene.

"Mom, Mom, go knock some more. Kyle will answer the door; you have to see if Avery's okay!" he pleaded.

"I'm scared, Ryder; this is a shitty neighborhood. Damn, all he had to do is send a simple text."

"It's okay, Mom; you'll be okay."

"Ryder, this is how I've lived these past years, scared as hell that something bad was about to happen. It's horrible; you two have got to get your shit in a pile—I can't keep living like this."

I was glad he had a play by play, an insight to what I'd been going through.

I continued.

"Are you sure you want Avery to bring you home from Valley Rehab? He can't be relied on."

"Mom, just go and knock some more. You've got to check on him."

Kyle finally answered and let me in. Avery was lying on the sofa in the living room, sleepy, sweaty, alive. "Yeah, hey, I'm sorry, Mom; I fell asleep; all good." He was extremely groggy. "Been working so many overnights, I'm beat," he mumbled.

I drove home, heart pounding; I was frustrated and relieved. It didn't occur to me that he might be high, or that Ryder had reason to believe he may be in trouble. I was so used to their lives being upside down. So used to trying not to feed my fears—denial. If I had tuned in, I would have perceived the rumble of squall, the front moving in.

I drove past baseball fields where they used to play little league. They loved baseball, playing it and watching it. I used to drop them off at the Redhawks' games. They'd chase around shagging foul balls that left the stadium. They'd be so excited when I picked them up, hot, sweaty, all smiles, carrying baseballs wherever they could fit them. I could never have imagined how fragile their innocence was back then, how tenderly I'd needed to guard it, to guide it.

It was too late now.

30

JESSE ARRIVED IN RIVER BEND on Sunday. It meant so much to me that he wanted to be in our home, with our family. That afternoon he reported to a mandatory team meeting. Nothing was assured for the players; half of those who reported to the Freeze that day would not be signed for the final roster. In his last year of eligibility for the USHL, Jesse had finished the 2013 season strong and was considered to be one of the leaders returning to the lineup. In his first week back, he had already attracted a number of media interviews. He was a magnet for attention—approachable, good-humored, handsome and always humble. I had no doubt when he left our home at the end of the season in the spring of 2014 that he'd have his pick of great offers from universities.

The next morning Avery left River Bend at six to bring his brother home. It had been 105 days since they'd seen one another. I wondered if he'd been up all night, if he was safe to drive, if his car was running well, the tires fine—I worried about everything that occasion. My entire world was in that red 1999 Mitsubishi headed back east to River Bend—and home.

Ryder was required to report to his probation officer as soon as he got to River Bend. By one that afternoon he was home—my beautiful, healthy son, beaming with freedom and possibility.

Our eyes met, and his smile reminded me of a ten-year-old I once knew, who had just hit a home run.

"Hi, Mama, I'm home!"

I was instantly in tears. He held me and swayed back and forth holding me tight. A moment too rare in our lives, a moment of hope, gratitude, and deep love mutually felt and expressed.

Ryder spent the next week getting his schedule together, and he had a lot on his plate already. He was required to meet with his probation officer, attend Narcotics Anonymous meetings, find a sponsor, and be ready for random drug testing. We weren't concerned with him getting a job until he'd established a recovery routine.

It looked promising that he'd be able to join the dock-and-lift crew at Lakeland Marine in early September. It would be about eight weeks of work hauling docks and lifts out of the lakes for homeowners. It was hard physical labor, in wet suits, chest deep in lake water. The weather would gradually get colder, making work conditions more uncomfortable as the season progressed. There was a part of me that didn't want Ryder to work for Lakeland in case he turned into a whiner, and hated it. But he was excited for the opportunity, and grateful to get any work. Scott had no problem giving him a chance. Over the years, Lakeland had hired a number of men from various work-release programs, and I knew some of the guys on the dock-and-lift crew had done their share of hard living. If Lakeland would hire Ryder, it was yet another blessing from the Lakeland Marine intuition intervention.

That first week back, Ryder went over to Avery's house one evening, and while Avery was sleeping, Ryder decided to dig around a bit to be sure Avery didn't have any drugs or paraphernalia, as he'd promised. His commitment to sobriety was intense, and he wanted to be sure he could trust Avery to be on his recovery team.

It didn't take long to find a pipe with a thick residue coating the bowl. He darted up the stairs to the attic bedroom.

"Avery, get up—dude, wake up, now!" Ryder's voice was abrupt and angry as he paced.

"What the fuck, dude, I'm asleep bro, chill." Avery was groggy and disoriented.

"Is this your pipe dude? What the fuck, just being around this shit gets me revoked!"

He held the pipe up, and then threw it next to Avery on the bed. The sheets were barely hanging on the mattress, yellow sweat stains, in desperate need of washing. There was no bed frame, just a box spring and mattress on the mangy carpet. The room reeked of stale cigarette smoke. There was no clear space to step without walking on dirty clothes. A window air conditioner was noisy and barely functioned; the air was stale and clammy.

"Fuck, Ryder, don't be throwing shit at me." He slowly sat up. "That's Kyle's pipe."

"Don't fuckin' lie to me bro. No more lying!"

"Jesus, Ryder, I just woke up; you come in yellin' and throwin' shit. What the fuck? Why do ya gotta be all wakin' me n shit?"

Ryder grabbed Avery by his T-shirt with both hands and shook him.

"You weren't even sleeping, you're probably so baked you passed out, you fuck!"

Ryder slapped Avery across the face. "Dude you promised drugs wouldn't jeopardize us hanging out. I need you Avery."

Ryder was between rage and tears; his body was shaking; he leaned against the wall and sunk to the floor.

"Wow, Ryder, seriously, don't be coming in here fuckin' with me. I just woke up, and you're in my face smackin' me and being all sober; move around dude."

They gradually calmed down, went outside to smoke cigarettes, and continued talking. Avery admitted he was using, and he wanted help. He was an addict, he told his brother—to an extent we would learn about soon. Avery had been afraid to tell Brad and me because of all we'd been through with Ryder. He didn't want to pile it on, taking our devastation to a new low. Avery didn't want to be the one to tell us, but he was desperate to come clean. After clearing the air with each other, Ryder and Avery hatched a plan. As soon as Brad was home from Asia, Ryder would come and talk to us about his concerns and suggest we do an intervention. They trusted we'd do anything we could to help.

Two nights later, Avery was carjacked, an incident that found itself all over the local news.

The August 28, 2013, *River Bend Forum* ran this story:

> RIVER BEND—A Mayport man told River Bend police Sunday night that he was assaulted and robbed after being pulled from his car.
>
> The incident reportedly happened about 10 p.m. in the 400 block of 21st Street South.

Police Lt. Sam Holmes said officers encountered the victim at a service station in River Bend and asked him about what appeared to be an injury to his head.

The man told the officers he was driving his vehicle when a man with a pistol walked into the path of his vehicle, forcing him to stop.

He said another man pulled him from his vehicle and struck him in the head with an object.

The victim said he was robbed of a small amount of cash and that he saw a total of three men running away.

Holmes said the assailants were described as black males and two of them were wearing dark-colored hoodies. The victim told police the third man wore his hair in dreadlocks.

The story featured a quarter-page photo of Avery holding a bag of ice to the back of his head, blood running down his neck. He was talking to a police officer.

Avery called to tell me. He said after it happened, he drove to a nearby convenience store for help because he'd seen a cop there as he'd driven by minutes before he was attacked.

I wondered if the thugs thought he was Ryder, still dealing and carrying drugs or money on him. The two of them switched cars occasionally.

I watched several newscasts, and found the entire situation surreal. What was this really about? On the 6:00 p.m. television news, the announcer made a comment that put me on edge. "Police report that there is usually more to an incident of this nature than what is evident immediately. They're continuing to investigate many angles of the crime. The public shouldn't be concerned that this sort of incident will reoccur. Stay tuned."

Even though I felt like pieces of the story were missing, I was offended that my son was being treated with suspicion when he was the victim of a crime. It was disturbing to wonder how much worse it could have been, and what provoked the assailants to attack Avery. It wasn't sitting well with me. I didn't tell anyone about it, even though everyone was finding out. Because I'd kept my surname, I had a bit of anonymity with Avery and Ryder. I was a Chase, and they were Madsen's. It was a connection many people who knew me would not have made automatically after hearing just a quick sound bite from a newscast.

Avery had accepted an invitation for an interview with a local radio station, after which the interviewer told him, "You seem like a nice young man." There was also lots of action on Facebook, and I told Avery to stop going public with it. Stay quiet and lay low, I advised him.

Brad returned home from Asia the next day, and I told him right away, offering him no time to recover from jetlag. I expressed my apprehension about it, aside from my obvious concern for Avery's safety.

Avery came over that evening before he went to work. He gave Brad his rendition of the incident. It had occurred near Avery's first rental home in River Bend, where he had been living the year before. It wasn't a safe neighborhood, which made us frustrated that Avery still hung out in that part of town. Avery justified being there by saying he liked the slushy drink served by the service station where he once worked. Really?

This was the night before Ryder was going to have the conversation with us about staging an intervention. Avery knew he was one night away from going into treatment, assuming everything went according to plan. He had a lot of mixed feelings about what'd happened with the carjacking and what was soon to happen. After they'd talked through the carjacking incident, Avery lingered.

"Are you okay, Avery? Seems like something else is bothering you." Brad asked.

Avery was on the living room couch, leaning over, elbows on his knees, looking down at the carpet, gently rocking himself, twirling some hair in his fingers.

"No, Dad, I'm good; it's cool. Thanks, I gotta go to work, though."

"Okay, take it easy. We're here—anything you need, let me know. Glad you're okay; love you."

Hours later, his fate took a horrible turn. The *River Bend Forum* headline said it all:

Major River Bend Heroin Seizure Leads to Arrest of Alleged Carjacking Victim

RIVER BEND—A man who reported being carjacked by three people last week in south River Bend was arrested Tuesday night in connection with what River Bend police are describing as the city's largest heroin seizure in recent memory.

The seizure of 12 grams of white powdered heroin came about as a result of the carjacking investigation and a joint narcotics investigation with the Mayport Police Department, River Bend Police Lt. Sam Holmes said.

"We haven't seen anything close to this in the last decade as far as this large of a seizure," he said.

Through their investigation, police gathered information that led them to identify a vehicle believed to be involved in illegal drug distribution, Holmes said.

The vehicle, a 1999 Mitsubishi Eclipse that Holmes said is registered to the alleged carjacking victim, Avery Chase Madsen, was located Tuesday night at Madsen's workplace in the 3500 block of Interstate Boulevard.

A police dog sniffed the car and alerted to the presence of drugs, which led to a warranted search that yielded heroin, the prescription drug hydromorphone, a digital scale and $1,300 cash, Holmes said.

Madsen, 21, who has River Bend and Mayport addresses, was arrested at about 10:30 p.m. on suspicion of heroin possession with intent to distribute and possession of a Schedule II narcotic, both felonies, as well as misdemeanor possession of drug paraphernalia, Holmes said. Madsen did not have a prescription for the hydromorphone, he said.

Holmes said investigators continue to look into Madsen's claim that he was assaulted by three men after being forced from his car on the night of Aug. 18 in the 400 block of 21st Street South.

Holmes has previously said officers encountered Madsen at a service station in River Bend and asked him about what appeared to be an injury to his head. Madsen reportedly told the officers he was driving his vehicle when a man with a pistol walked into the path of his vehicle, forcing him to stop.

Madsen said another man pulled him from his vehicle and struck him in the head with an object. He said he was robbed of his cash and that he saw three men running away.

Holmes said he couldn't comment on whether the carjacking incident may have been drug-related.

"What we can state is we've had some concerns about what exactly happened there," he said.

The heroin bust is significant, he said, because police have intelligence that heroin distribution is on the rise in the metro area, he said.

"Certainly this does show we're doing everything we can to prevent heroin from getting a foothold here in the city of River Bend," he said.

We learned later that Avery had planned to unload the heroin he had left the night he'd spoken to us. Once and for all, over and done with and ready to get clean and enter treatment, and start a new drug-free life.

He'd been that close—so tantalizingly, frustratingly close—to avoiding this disastrous turn of fate. Was it horrible luck, karma for his sins, or our souls' collective destinies influencing the delicate order of the details of our story?

Wednesday I was at work in Detroit Lakes, a world away from River Bend, it seemed, until my cell phone rang. Avery broke the news to me in a phone call from Cass County jail. The connection was poor. I had to go outdoors to improve the quality of the reception. A beautiful summer day was about to go black.

"Mom, Mom, please help me; I'm the same as Ryder. I'm addicted to heroin. I need help; I want help; I don't want to be an addict." His voice was weak; I had to keep asking him to talk louder to understand what was going on, where he was, and what had happened.

"I got picked up last night; the cops found drugs in my car. I'm in a lot of trouble, Mom. I need a lawyer. It's bad."

I promised him everything that we could do would be done. I called Brad's cell and left a message to call me. He was on the golf course. I called Kurt Williams, the attorney we'd hired for Ryder, and left a message.

Identical twins; maybe I should have seen it coming. But how could any mother see this coming?

I didn't have the full extent of the situation until I went back into work and read the article online. Oh my God, how can this be possible? How could he, after all he witnessed Ryder go through … all that we'd been through? I should have been paying more attention. I was their mother. There must have been something I could have done to prevent this from happening. Ryder had only been home from Valley Rehab ten days. We made it ten days without a kid in jail. Why is this happening to us? Why our family? I was growing numb from the outside in.

My shock and grief quickly turned into horror as my next thought materialized. Avery knew the boy who had died of a heroin overdose in July. His family lived in Avery's old neighborhood, where the carjacking occurred. Did Avery sell him the fatal heroin dose? Oh my God in heaven, please don't let this be true; this cannot be true. My worst fear was dangling, like a machete, suspended by a thread above my throat. I was imploding with terror.

31

I GAVE SHELIA AND SCOTT a brief version of our crisis. They understood and assured me it was no problem for me to take as much time away as I needed. Brad called, and we spoke briefly before I got behind the wheel.

On the drive home, I didn't turn on the radio or listen to iTunes. Music would have been a joyful distraction, but it would have felt inappropriate, like playing an Irish jig at a funeral. My physical body and my cognizance teamed to quiet my emotions and transport the human being through the required motions. I processed only the necessary fragments of reality: turn left here, slow to twenty-five mph, check the rearview mirror, and resume cruise control. It seemed as if the car remained stationary as the road and countryside slid past. I guess that's what being in shock feels like. You separate into the physical, emotional, and mental aspects of yourself, and functioning goes on autopilot. Once you're somewhere that it's safe to collapse, then all aspects of one's self become integrated again.

The only influence I allowed was the quiet stillness of my moving car. I focused on my breath, which seemed to be the only thing I had control of. I inhaled "be still" and exhaled "God's grace." *Be still, God's grace. Be still, God's grace* is the mantra that carried me home. I kept a rosary in my car, and I held it and rubbed the light-blue glass beads between my thumb and index finger. *Be still, God's grace.* I entered a meditative state. Becoming hysterical wasn't pragmatic; I didn't cry on the way home. Rather I maintained a stoic trance. Every frightening thought that entered my mind I released and returned to ... *Be still, God's grace.*

I'd been a flight attendant for twenty-three years. Each year the FAA required us to attend recurrent training, going through emergency drills in mock airplanes. I remember thinking all those years, if I was ever in an aviation accident, I wouldn't be the one that got hysterical and panicked. The mistake that I imagined I was at risk of making was that I'd underestimate the severity of the situation and fail to act with appropriate haste and concern.

When I was on that fated DC-9 in 2005 and an emergency evacuation was required, I'd handled it just how I'd imagined. The entire time I was assessing the situation and moving forward to evacuate the passengers. I'd been completely calm, no different than how I felt grocery shopping, simply moving forward making the required decisions. I never stalled because of fear, never felt panic. I was oblivious to the fact that there was every reason for a deadly and imminent explosion. I didn't smell fuel in spite of the fact that six hundred gallons of fuel had spilled onto the scene. My presumption that everything would be fine served the situation well. I was able to lead every single passenger to safety.

My nature was, and is, to assume the best possible outcome, always. It seemed that inclination was a double-edged sword. That tendency is also what had me falsely assume none of this hell would burn down my family. "It could never happen to us" was a lie that I'd bet our lives on. That's what I had to forgive myself for. I had blindly trusted the notion that just doing our best was good enough. That somehow being good people, happily married, committed and caring parents, would be enough to live a blessed life, to keep our sons off drugs and free from pain.

It was my fault for not watching out for the demons and taking them seriously when they came calling to claim my sons. Now I knew what I needed to forgive myself for, but I also knew that no one could ever hold themselves responsible for the tragic circumstances we were facing. The moment I knew what to forgive myself for was the moment I realized it wasn't my fault. No loving parent could shoulder responsibility for what was happening to us; it was way, way, too far gone.

To everyone else, it was just another hot August afternoon. The heat and humidity were too intense to enjoy being outdoors unless you were on a moving boat or in the water. It was one of the rare days in North Dakota and Minnesota where the term heat index is mentioned in the forecast. The conditions were a perfect boost for the crops, a final push toward ripening before harvest. Roadside farmers' markets were stocked with homegrown tomatoes, peppers, potatoes, and watermelons. Lawns were still fully exposed, lush green carpets yet to be covered with autumn's cascading colors. It appeared to me that all of nature was cast in a wheat-colored haze—the farmers' fields, the lakes, waves and beaches, even the clouds. My world was melting, dissolving; the only buffer I perceived was a timid, thin glaze of August, quickly running out of time.

As I got closer to River Bend, I felt the intensity building. I would soon be crossing the border into North Dakota, where my son was rapidly becoming notorious. I would choose to not read another word online, in a newspaper, or watch a newscast. I didn't want to know what was being broadcast about my son. It was already far too real to me than I could stomach.

There were times in my life that I had loved River Bend, and times that I couldn't wait to leave it far behind, but I'd never felt ashamed to be there because of who I was. If I could have, I would have turned the car around and headed east until I arrived at Breezy Point, 1962. Then I could perch on my grandmother's lap in the kitchen and watch for hummingbirds seeking the feeder filled with her homemade sweet red nectar. We'd wait patiently hoping for the flurry of tiny wings and a toothpick beak to feast on the juice. That's how joy seemed—a swift eruption of brief pleasure proceeded by hours, days, years of waiting in hope for joy to return.

I felt humiliation and revulsion for what Avery had done. I felt grief and despair for what he was going through. I was petrified for the future we had to face.

Once I got home, I went upstairs to our bedroom, where Brad and Ryder were discussing the situation. Jesse was at practice. As I ascended the staircase, I felt the tremble of collapse spreading throughout my body. Brad stood as I entered. I slid my arms around his waist, buried my face into his chest and his strength, sobbing.

32

TRYING TO PROCESS THE REALITY of our situation was like trying to consume a heaving plate of food in two swallows. Most importantly for Avery, we retained Ryder's attorney, Kurt Williams, considered one of the best defense attorneys in the state. He was intensely busy, though, so we'd learned to wait to hear from him about developing information.

Our most concerning detail was whether Avery had sold the heroin to the young River Bend man who had overdosed and died, which not surprisingly was also what state prosecutors wanted to know. The first thing police did once they confiscated Avery's stash was take it to the lab in River Bend and test it to see if it matched the heroin that killed the young man. They would have a huge victory on their hands if they'd arrested the villain who had supplied the fatal dose. And if it was true, what we had on our hands was the worst possible situation. Avery would be going away for a very long time. The emotional prison would be even worse, and I would be in that cell with him.

Bail was set at $50,000. Our first major decision was whether to bail him out. We could come up with the money, but it would take several days. Ryder had been through the legal system enough that he served as our interpreter, explaining what was occurring in Avery's world as a newly arrested inmate—and a detoxing heroin addict. Ryder was fluent in the language of arrest, incarceration, and addiction. Ryder was also aware of the ramifications regarding felony charges and state versus federal processing. We sorted through the first round that afternoon gathered in our master bedroom.

"You've gotta bail him out. He's gonna rot in there. He's dope sick right now; it's horrible."

Ryder felt only compassion for his brother.

"We have to see what Kurt says; there's always more to it than what we know," Brad said. "Even if we did, it's going to take several days to come up with the cash."

"You could get a bondsman to put up the cash; they just take a cut. You could have him out by tomorrow."

Brad was firm.

"We're paying an attorney to help us make the right decisions, and until I hear from him, I'm not going to make a move."

"Avery's in the classification section of jail. He's on lockdown for over twenty hours a day, stuck in a tiny cell. Until they classify him as a nonviolent, non-sex offender he'll be stuck in there. Detoxing is like the worst flu ever, puking, and your body feels like you got hit by a truck."

The rest of the day was a flurry of decisions and information piling up. Federal marshals had arrested him, but the State of North Dakota wanted him too. The state would seek to use Avery as an example of what happens to felons who bring heroin into North Dakota communities; the punishment would be severe. If he became a federal prisoner, we assumed all the time he spent in county jail wouldn't count as time served once he was sentenced. We had no idea how long he'd be sitting in Cass County Jail. He was sick and needed help. It was all speculation and confusing for Brad and me.

That was why we'd hired Kurt Williams.

In Avery's brief calls home, he pleaded for us to bail him out. We didn't promise him anything until we knew more. Ryder witnessed the helpless anguish Brad and I suffered through. He realized for the first time what he'd forced us through the past several years.

"I will never put you through anything like this again. I can see what it's doing to you guys."

That meant something.

I went to bed that first night of Avery's arrest in a level of despair that was charred blackness; nothing good in my life mattered to me. I didn't try to search the horizon for a bright spot projected somewhere in the future, to leak some solace into my heart. Denial had abandoned me to face reality. A primal instinct within me knew I had to allow the totality of our circumstances to hit me square in the face, penetrate every cell.

181

Being in union with despair was the only way to transcend it. I wept until I dropped off into sleep.

The next morning, Kurt called to tell us the batch of heroin in Avery's possession did not match the dose that killed anyone. Oh my God in heaven, thank you. He discouraged us from posting bail. His strategy was to get in contact with local treatment facilities and get him moved into treatment as soon as possible. Avery needed and desired professional care. The time spent in a treatment facility would also be considered an extension of incarceration.

That day the *River Bend Forum* had another article (I was told) about Avery's arrest. Next to it was an interview with the River Bend family whose son overdosed in July. Ryder had spoken to the family, and they knew it wasn't Avery who sold the fated supply. They were not pleased that the articles were run next to each other, and I was grateful for their grace and God's. Even though we didn't know what the ramifications were of the heroin Avery had sold, and it made me nauseous to think of what those might be, I had some peace that he was not responsible for that young man's death.

Once we'd dealt with all we could, I lay in bed and watched the US Open tennis tournament, the tonic I needed to distract and soothe me. I wanted to lose myself in a full day and evening lineup of early round matches. I was limp from all the crying. I recalled that a year ago it was Andy Roddick's retirement that triggered my tears during this grand slam tournament. Things had certainly changed.

The 2013 US Open in Flushing Meadows, New York, was celebrating tennis great Arthur Ashe's accomplished life. It was the fiftieth anniversary of the March on Washington and the forty-fifth anniversary of Arthur Ashe winning his first US Open as an American amateur and a US Army lieutenant.

During a rain delay, they played recorded footage about Arthur Ashe, his tennis career and his life. One quote resonated; I believe it was a quote from his wife or brother: "In times of blessing and in times of challenge, he found a way to help others with what life presented him."

I heard again that quiet voice within telling me that what we were going through as a family was bigger than the heartbreak, the humiliation, the loss and suffering. How else could I explain this horror playing out?

All that we were and had been as parents, the little boys they once were, the unconditional love, opportunities and support we'd offered them every step they took. This nightmare we were living made no sense, unless it was destined to serve a higher good.

I recalled a book I'd read years ago by Martha Beck, a life coach. She explained a paradigm in life she referred to as Square One, as in back to square one. It explained that we arrive back in Square One in three possible ways: great opportunity, shock, or through a voluntary spiritual awakening. I was back in Square One due to devastating shock. Her advice for navigating square one was to live one moment at a time, rely more than ever on intuition, and keep telling yourself, "I don't know what I'm doing, and that's okay." By gently proceeding forward and following your intuition, you will find your way, quite possibly, to the greatest blessings of your life.

What I believed to be true about intuition is that it's the voice of my soul. My intuition was telling me that when a situation makes no sense in the human realm, when there is no earthly explanation for it, then it has God's fingerprints all over it. I trusted my intuition, and I trusted God, and in that moment it gave me the strength I needed to survive until the next moment. Maybe our trials will serve someone in some way in the future. Who knew?

I'd only spoken with my sister Ann and Erin, my best friend, about Avery's arrest. Ann would keep the rest of my concerned family informed. I didn't contact friends or family, but of course everyone who loved me was reaching out with calls, texts, and e-mails. It's my nature to isolate and deal with my struggles by letting in as few people as possible. It took too much precious energy to discuss and update the situation with anyone other than the professionals we needed to help us. Four days after Avery's arrest, on the last day of August, I sent out an e-mail to all my friends and family. I was grateful for the outpouring of love and support.

Dear loved ones,

I cannot adequately express my gratitude for your love, prayers, and support. I know you all understand that I'm the type of person that grieves in private. It's all so raw right now that I cannot talk about it without extreme emotion, so I'd rather not talk to anyone about it beyond Brad & Ryder.

For years now I have been managing despair. Because I've prepared myself for the worst with Ryder, when the worst now shows up, only it's Avery, I've not been completely blindsided. Yet it is shocking nonetheless as I've had many conversations with Avery that led me to believe he was headed in a very different direction.

Ryder is doing really well, amazing really how far he's come. Brad is a rock, and taking everything with complete bravery, no anger, no blaming.

I called God this morning and asked "Seriously, WTF?" This is what he told me:

"This ongoing hardship with your children comes from the same source as all the blessings you've had over the years. It's all from me. You've known and believed that trust is 100% or 0%. You cannot kind of trust someone or something. Your trust is 100% and that is what you need to lean into. Trust that all of this is part of a bigger plan I have for your family. That trust will be blind, but my vision will eventually be clear to you. Until then lean into all that you know about coping and despair management. Lean into your circle of loved ones and hang on. Your parents are here and they have been devoted not only to protecting your children, put holding you and Brad as well.

"It's not your fault. I know you believe that now, as far gone as everything has become. No human, no parent can take responsibility for this much demise. Ryder & Avery have very strong souls, with a destiny that is not to be denied. I brought them through you and Brad because

I knew you would handle it, and allow it, meaning that you would cooperate with my will even though it makes no sense. Everything I've had planned has taken place. It is, and will continue to be in my hands. All you can do is follow what your feelings guide you to, and continue to release it to me.

"I know you're willing and committed to finding a way to serve others through this journey. That is another reason why it's happening to your family. You will come to understand how that will become a reality in time.

"Be brave, seek joy, manage your despair and recognize your blessings."

Please keep praying for us,

Love,
—Dana

The next loss I forecasted was Jesse. How on earth would his mother allow him to live with us given Avery's situation? The assumption that he would be placed in another home sent me to one of the darkest moments of this entire chapter of events. Jesse was a sober brother for Ryder; he was our son in so many ways, and now I would have to give him up. I sobbed as deeply as I ever had; I'd lost too much in too short a time.

Jesse was gone most of the time with tryouts, practices, meetings, and preseason games. The Freeze still had cuts to make, but he was a returning star who had helped take them to the Clark Cup finals. Surely he was safe from the chopping block.

"We have to let Jesse's parents know what's going on," I said to Brad, crying. "They'll probably pull him from our home."

Brad didn't want to lose Jesse either.

"It's not like Avery's coming home; we know we're not going to bail him out now," Brad said.

"Not telling them is shady. When I completely reverse the situation—let's say our son was living with a family in North Carolina, and their son was just arrested for dealing heroin, wouldn't you appreciate a call from the parents?" I explained.

"Yes, of course, you're right."

I was hoping he would volunteer to call them, but I knew it would be up to me. I needed a few days to get my nerve up, to process the projected loss, to prepare my heart as best I could.

Our first visit to Avery in jail came three days after his arrest. We entered the assigned area and took our seats next to the phones in front of the glass. Avery appeared and sat down. I began to cry and did not stop until we left fifteen minutes later. His orange sweatshirt was dirty around the cuffs and frayed. Dark circles recessed his eyes, and his complexion was broken out with raw, bloodied blemishes. His hair was slick, in clumps. He was treading murky water in an infested swamp. He twirled a piece of his hair to soothe himself.

There was very little to say. We'd learned the hard way with Ryder that you don't speak about your legal situation over the tapped phone lines. The conversation was a collage of general sentiments.

"I love you. I'm sorry. We're here. Hang in there."

I remember the first letter Avery sent us from jail, desperately pleading with us to bail him out. "Please help me out of here, and I will do whatever it takes to make things right. I will be so grateful ... I hope you will always love me; I will always love you and be your little boy ... please bail me out mom and dad ..." He included a drawing of four stick people and a dog.

It devastated me. I recalled, when they were out of early elementary grades, and thinking to myself, which stickman drawing will be their last?

How do you know when it's the last time they see the world through the innocence of little boy eyes?

33

A COUPLE OF DAYS LATER, I finally found the courage to e-mail Jesse's mom, Tamera, and attached a letter. I didn't want to put her on the spot with an unexpected phone call with jarring news that required an immediate response. I was honest about Avery's charges, and our plan to get him into treatment as soon as possible.

I was astonished by her response. In part it read, "You're family to us, and when you hurt, we hurt. No need to stress out about it with us, nor do you need to ever speak about it with us. It's hard enough without reliving it. I'm always here if you need to talk, It's *not* an issue for us, so please take that worry off your plate."

I've never been so touched by such remarkable compassion. Her only request was to let her know if having Jesse in our home was causing too much strain with everything else going on. She and Jesse's father would understand, she wrote. I cried with relief and gratitude. Losing Jesse as part of our family, and with that all the joy I anticipated with his upcoming hockey season, would have been like blowing out the only candle left burning in the cave. I will never forget her empathy as long as I live. I felt witnessed as a mother by someone I respected so dearly. More than ever, I looked forward to her next visit to River Bend for the season opener just a few weeks away.

Labor Day weekend we were expected to join Brad's family at a small annual reunion at Sandy Shores Resort on Little Detroit Lake. With everyone, it would only be twelve of us. Avery clearly would not be attending, and Brad hadn't told his family about the arrest. We had no idea if they knew somehow. The story of his arrest had made it as far as the *San Francisco Chronicle.* Like my side of the family, Brad's too was filled with successful, accomplished adults. His father and brother were engineers, his sister was an attorney, and his mother was a retired art teacher.

We dreaded this year's reunion for obvious reasons but still felt obligated to attend. Brad's dad reserved the time-share condo every year and was traveling from Phoenix while everyone else was heading over from Minneapolis. Because of work, I made it only to the Saturday afternoon and evening gathering. Brad's younger sister, Megan, whom I treasured, let Brad know that she and her husband were aware of it but had not shared it with anyone else. His brother had a thirteen-year-old son and sixteen-year-old daughter, and none of them had any idea of the chaos. We told them Avery had worked all night and didn't feel good—or something like that.

The sky and forecast threatened rain. We were surrounded by ominous clouds in every direction, but on Detroit Lake there was an opening in the sky that strangely remained all afternoon and evening. The intense two-week heat wave was beginning to taper. It was a perfect day: no wind, the air and water were gentle and warm.

Brad rented Jet Skis from Lakeland Marine, and by the time I arrived Saturday afternoon, everyone was content to take a break, so Brad and I went out alone. I sat behind him and leaned into him, embracing all that he meant to me. My handsome, sturdy husband was my strength, my partner. Our love, the bond we shared, held me up in the darkest hours we'd just survived. Our marriage was blessed with trust and respect. His commitment to me and the boys was immeasurable and pure. We lived a mostly independent, low-maintenance life with a lot of time apart. But that didn't divide us. Instead it made us appreciate one another and the little time we had together, especially moments like this. We belonged to one another, soul mates; I believed we would survive all of this, together.

It was the type of scene you fantasize about in the frigid shadows of winter—disappearing into a summer afternoon on a Jet Ski, blending with water surrounded by the majesty of lake country on a hot summer afternoon. The speed of the Jet Ski stripped away the aura of anguish in which I'd been swaddled. Warm water splashed, drenched, and cleansed. My tears of the past week were replenished. I was transcended. Being on water has a way of meeting many needs, filling the emptiness, buoyancy gently rocks a silent lullaby; the water's an accomplice for escape; it's warmth and mystery is seductive.

For that tranquil ride, I left the hell we'd been going through, and connected to the pulse within me promising that better days lay ahead, and that our luck would change. It had to; I believed it had to.

Ryder and I also went out on the Jet Ski together. The healthier and more fit and muscular he became, the more he resembled his dad. I couldn't even recall the last time I'd had fun with him.

"I hope you like being in the lake," I told him. "You'll be spending a lot of time in them this fall."

"I love it, Mom. I'm gonna like working for Lakeland."

"It's hard work, but you'll be surrounded by nature. It will be good for your soul."

"I'm just happy to have a job, and be out of River Bend. Thanks for hooking me up."

We ventured far enough away that we could no longer see the dock. My child could never know how deeply I loved him. I would do anything to save him from himself.

"There's something about water," I purred as we were heading back.

"For sure," he nodded as water from his hair dripped down my cheek. The tender blending of mother and son, a moment, an emotion, I'll hold in my heart forever.

We later played ping pong in the rec center of the resort. All trash talk and banter, we had a blast, both playing to win. I beat him two out of three. *Gimme the ball!*

Their two teenage cousins were different from our boys in every way imaginable. They loved to be the center of attention. Both were talented, intelligent students, and, God bless them, they were at gawky teenage stages, all hyper and socially clumsy. My sons at that age had been unassuming and mellow. The cousins' zeal perpetuated that sense of awkwardness that arises when someone tells a lame joke that falls flat, followed by unnerving moments everyone feels compelled to smooth over or tolerate silently. My lingering expression of obligatory feigned amusement was required to mask the actuality that I found them to be entirely draining.

On the drive home, we recalled bumbling snippets of the gawkiness of the afternoon that showcased the vast differences between those two and Ryder and Avery. Brad joked, "I'll take my two heroin addicts any day over that!" The three of us busted out laughing.

I gazed out the windshield, beholding a spectacular sunset. The setting sun traced an orange neon outline of the cloud it hid behind and sent boldly streaked angelic rays to the earth below. A day that I'd dreaded turned out to be breathtaking. Life can be that way sometimes. Providence can sneak up on you, like a hummingbird. That sinking sun took an exhausted, played-out summer by the hand and put her to slumber. Tomorrow's sunrise would commence autumn 2013—a new month, the next season of our journey.

34

O N SEPTEMBER 4, BRAD'S FIFTY-THIRD birthday, we learned that Kurt Williams could no longer represent Avery because of a conflict of interest. It seemed that another attorney from the Woodland Law Firm was representing someone connected to Avery's case. We didn't get any other details. It felt like a big setback, and we were devastated. Kurt recommended a local attorney, Tom Anderson, and we got in touch with him immediately.

We met Tom and two associate attorneys at Anderson Law Firm, a two-story, renovated 1930s home near Island Park, in an older River Bend neighborhood that was a blend of residential homes and businesses. Inside were beautiful dark hardwood floors that creaked with history, built-in bookcases, old-fashioned register heaters under the windows, and a brick fireplace. The renovation was impeccable, uncluttered and traditional. The former upstairs bedrooms were now offices for the attorneys and support staff.

Meeting Tom and briefing his team on our situation for the first time felt surreal. They knew nothing about our family story: Identical twins, heroin addicts, drug charges, unrelated legal cases. I did not know where to even begin explaining our entangled saga. Here we were, an intelligent, attractive, articulate couple, and our story was so pathetic, so contrary to appearances. Summarizing it to someone who knew nothing about our family felt absurd, as if we were making it up. It couldn't possibly be true. It sounded like a contrived pulp fiction plot written by an aspiring novelist. In response, Tom was both thoughtful and confident, in a most assuring manner.

When he later met with Avery in jail, he looked him in the eye and said, "You are and will continue to be my priority until we get the best possible outcome for you."

191

Tom immediately went into action and got things moving for Avery, including the furlough order that would move him into a treatment facility the next week. Tom Anderson turned out to be a stroke of luck; his expertise and commitment to Avery was inspiring.

Avery had been detoxing in a jail cell large enough only for a toilet and the gym mat he slept on. He was allowed outside of the cell only four hours a day. The little bit of tortured sleep he was able to get was on a one-inch-thick mat that afforded little comfort atop the concrete floor with no pillow. He was anxious to get into treatment not only because he'd get out of Cass County Jail, but because he truly wanted to overcome his addiction.

News of Avery's bust was still buzzing in River Bend, and I was grateful I didn't work in town. I did my grocery shopping in Detroit Lakes. The only time I went out in public in River Bend was to walk the dog or to play tennis. If I had been working at the mall while all this played out, I would have been a terrible mess, worried who'd turn the corner into the store and bring up the topic.

The immensity of the situation felt similar to a death in the family. Most conversations I had included an extended condolence from whomever I was speaking with. I genuinely appreciated the concern and love, but I really hated to be the person others felt sorry for. I'd always been one to make others laugh. Over the years, I'd had more than one friend tell me I was the funniest person they knew. The best facets of my personality were mostly dormant and had been for years. I missed the person I once was, and the lifestyle that'd inspired my lighthearted sense of humor.

I wanted our family and friends to continue to hold us in their prayers and thoughts, but didn't want to be surrounded by an energetic circle of worry and fear. A week after I'd sent my first group letter, I sent a second to update everyone.

Initiation to Shift

Thank you for all your prayers and concern, for holding our family in your thoughts. And for allowing me space to process this in my way. I don't like to talk about it with everyone that loves us because it seems to keep the intensity alive, and it drains my energy to replay it. Brad

& I are dealing with each nuance as it unfolds, and we're looking to the future and better days.

There is a term in weight lifting called "the new normal"; that's when you increase the amount of weight you put on the bar, increase the amount of weight you bear. It serves to make you stronger. It takes you to a higher level of fitness and health. It brings visible, tangible results.

Our family situation has forced me into a new normal. There has been a weight increase on my shoulders, my heart. Initially the extra weight is difficult, you dig deep and push through it … Gradually the physical & emotional adjustments are made and greater strength is gained, and it all feels mostly manageable, a new normal.

My new normal is not to interpret this situation as a hardship only. Although it felt like a version of death when it began to unfold, it is not loss of life. The death I see now is what I hope is the death of this chapter of addiction in our family. The bottom, the darkest, anticipating the severest of consequences is where we have been dwelling this past week. God willing it won't become darker.

Please shift with me out of the human place of judging all of this as horrific, painful, devastating, and exclusively negative. On the earthy plane that is how all of this appears.

Instead shift out of your human perspective into your soul's perspective; shift away from judgment and into curiosity …

What if this is all playing out in perfect accordance with God's plan?

What if this is part of a plan that ultimately leads to serving others … a plan that has no other route to be fulfilled other than this succession of catastrophic events?

What will be the blessings that unfold because of this?

What am I going to learn about love, family, life, and the depth of character of my family and the loved ones that support us?

I wonder how all this will come together to serve a greater good?

Meanwhile imagine Avery's in boot camp for life lessons. Pray for his evolution, health, and recovery.

I appreciate you more than I can say.

Love, Dana

The Freeze had its first preseason game on September 6, and Ryder and I went. With the temperatures in the eighties outside, it was fun to show up to a hockey game in T-shirts and shorts; Ryder was excited to attend as many games as possible. He felt he missed out the season before and regretted it. He and Jesse were becoming very close, which made my heart sing. There were hardly any fans there, to be expected, as it was a balmy September evening. Though the season opener was only two weeks away, the Freeze still had cuts to make. I actually looked forward to winter knowing we'd be cheering Jesse on in his final USHL season.

The Saturday before Avery was transported to River City Recovery treatment facility, I traveled to Mentor, Minnesota, to teach a feng shui class, something I would have canceled had I not committed to it so long before. I would have preferred to isolate on a day off. Before I left town, I stopped at the library to get a book on tape for a change of pace. I picked out a novel, and the book *Heaven Is Real*, which caught my eye for some reason. It's the true story of the four-year-old son of a small-town Nebraska pastor who during emergency surgery slips from consciousness and enters heaven. He survives and begins talking about being able to look down and see the doctor operating and his dad praying in the waiting room. The family didn't know what to believe, but soon the evidence was clear.

I decided to listen to that first. As it began to play, a car pulled in front of me, the license plate said COLLEENS. Colleen was my mom's name. It was September 14, what would have been my parents' sixty-fifth wedding anniversary. It had been five years since they'd died. My mom was letting me know: Colleen's heaven is real. She and my dad were with me, protecting, guiding me and my family. Her presence and the message were as real to me as if she'd whispered in my ear.

That Monday, Brad, Jesse, Ryder, and I went golfing at El Zagal, a par three, nine-hole course across the street from where our old house had once stood on Elm Street. It was the course where Avery and Ryder learned to play. It was the course my dad played after he'd retired his River Bend Country Club membership because he no longer had the stamina to play eighteen holes. The last time I played golf with my dad was his eightieth birthday, Ann, dad, and me. The summer before he died, 2007, he'd go to El Zagal and hobble through seven holes and have to call it quits. He was determined to hang on to the small grasps of pleasure left to him. I learned perseverance from my dad. He never gave up on anything.

The third hole had an elevated green. Avery had scored a hole in one on that hole when he was ten years old. He kept the trophy on his dresser; it was there in his bedroom, waiting for him to come home.

I recalled a Hopi prayer: "Do not stand by my grave and weep; I am not there; I do not sleep." I felt my parents' essence when I was on a golf course, or passing their home on Willow Road. I didn't go to their graves much; it's not the place that I felt connected to them.

That September day the course was mostly deserted except for Jesse, Brad, Ryder and me. Along with my golf bag, I carried memories from this neighborhood golf course across from the house that our little boys lived their Tom Sawyer, Huckleberry Finn years, all innocence and adventure.

We'd talked for months that we'd all play together some day, and we did it. The nine holes we played would become an endearing memory of our time with Jesse, not because it was remarkable, but because it was one less regret for which I would have to find room.

35

AVERY WAS MOVED TO RIVER City Recovery on Monday the sixteenth of September 2013. Once he was processed and settled in, we would be able to go visit him in a day or two. I couldn't imagine what he'd been going through. I knew only that he was in pain in every way that was humanly possible. My love for him was far stronger than my disappointment.

I was running errands that afternoon, on my way to the mall. On a stretch of Nineteenth Avenue North, past the airport where the speed limit is briefly fifty mph, a car cut sharply in front of me. I laid on my horn, which happens maybe once a year—traffic in River Bend does not often spark road rage. Then I noticed the license plate WRITE. The universe had curious ways of getting my attention.

On the way home from the mall, my cell phone rang. Tamera was calling. I had been thinking about calling her, since she was flying in for the Freeze season opener that coming weekend.

"Hello, there! Been thinking about you; so excited for this weekend!" I said.

"Yes, well, unfortunately, I have some bad news."

I could hear it in her voice, and I felt my stomach shrivel. I held my breath.

She continued, "Jesse was cut today, the final player."

I was speechless, stunned.

Tamera continued, "I know, hon, it's awful. Why did they lead him on this long? It's just awful."

"Oh my God, Tamera, I can't believe it. I can hardly speak."

"Are you home? Can you be home soon? I don't want Jesse to be alone."

"Yes, of course; I will be there in ten minutes. How is he?"

"Shocked. They didn't let on in the least. It makes no sense how they treat these boys."

When I pulled into the driveway, Jesse was sitting on the front steps; he was in a somber daze, so unlike him. I walked up and hugged him, and I started to cry.

Jesse had not seen it coming. When he first arrived, the coaches had cut some of the older guys in their last year of eligibility, like Jesse. After he survived that, he felt he was safe. He thought if he would get cut, it would have been then.

All the grief I'd felt, believing I was going to lose him—I guess—had prepared me for this in a strange way. It was devastating, for sure, but the blow wasn't straight on like it would have been had my heart not already visited this possibility. Fate, intuition, has a way of bringing me along in my life.

Ryder and I had started our new journeys on the same day, on May 7. Ryder and Jesse had returned to River Bend within twenty-four hours of one another on August 19. Now Jesse and Avery were beginning a new direction as well, both on September 16. Synchronicity, I believed, was an intuitive indication that it was God's timing.

Word spread fast, and within an hour Jesse was picked up by the New Jersey Hitmen, and in forty-eight hours he would be packed and driving to the East Coast. Brad was on an Asia trip and never got to say good-bye in person.

The morning Jesse was departing; I was in the kitchen getting ready to leave for work. I didn't want to wake Jesse, and I didn't want to say good-bye at all because I knew I'd get emotional. So I simply left him a note: "I hate good-byes. I'm sure you do too. I will send you an e-mail later. Drive safe, have fun, be great! We love you. We thank you. Our family will always be here for you. Love, Dana."

Just like that, this beautiful young man we loved, who had lifted our spirits with the pursuit of his dream, was gone. All the excitement and anticipation for the upcoming season was extinguished in the time it takes to blow out a candle flame. I had to trust it; that was all I knew to do.

Avery requested that Ryder, Brad, and I go to my parents' graves at the cemetery that night at seven and pray for him. He knew at that time he would be alone, and he'd be praying too, all of us connected in prayer. He also wanted me to ask my sisters and his cousins to join in prayer wherever they were at seven. My sister Ann sent me a beautiful prayer she wrote, and that's what I read. I was relieved to know he was willing to pray. I believed both Ryder and Avery would need to find God to have a chance of surviving and overcoming their addiction.

It felt as if my heart was in a three-way tug of war. I was forced to let go of Jesse, drop the rope, and watch him leave. The dark pit of loss I'd felt weeks ago, believing he would be placed with a new family, had somehow prepared me. If not for that, I would have been completely blindsided emotionally by his abrupt departure from our lives, even though that's part of what we signed up for when becoming a billet family. I'd never imagined it would happen to Jesse a second time, especially the way he'd contributed to the team during the playoffs at the end of the previous season.

I recalled one of the things Terry had told us about Jesse's previous billet family in Nebraska. For more than ten years, they'd hosted players—one would leave, another would arrive to take his place. Jesse's billet mom could not move on with a new player when Jesse was traded to the Freeze midseason; the loss was too devastating. He'd lived with them for eighteen months. I now knew exactly how she'd felt. One day it was sunny and seventy-five, the next day below zero at midnight.

Then there was the emotional tugging with my own boys. I recall reading in a self-help book suggesting that to qualify if a situation was worthy of worry, you needed to ask yourself: "Will this matter in an hour? ... tomorrow? ... next month or next year?"

If the answer is no, then let it go, the book advised. We had to face the truth that Avery would be a felon for his entire life. Ryder was one relapse away from being kicked out of drug court and being slapped with a seven-year felony charge. And they were both battling heroin addiction.

Avery was in treatment, out of jail, remorseful, seeking to be healed. His sentencing lay ahead, and we could expect him to serve from two to five years. Ryder was free, with the temptations and the challenges of living sober while most everyone he knew was in party mode. They both were walking a shaky line between addiction and recovery. One doomed step and our family could once again be swept away in a reckless current with grave consequences. They were twenty-one years old; yes, all of this will matter, next month, next year, and for the rest of our lives. It was worthy of worry indeed.

Brad and I had so many dreams that dissolved into despair and disappointment. Now we simply hoped for their survival and recovery, their freedom, to stay alive, that would be enough. We'd forgotten what it felt like to truly hold the best and highest aspirations for our children. The money we'd been saving for college since they were babies was now being spent on treatment, attorneys, emergency room bills, skyrocketing car insurance, bail, and damage control.

It had been a gloomy, wet fall; the river was rising. One afternoon, after several warm, dry days, I took Murphy to Trefoil Park, where we used to bicycle from our old home on Elm Street. I'd bike, and she'd run alongside me on the leash. The park was along the Red River, and there was a dam where people fished. There was a blacktop hobby landing strip for remote control airplanes. Mostly there were trees, a walking path, and open space for Murphy to run. The two of us came here often over the years, in every season.

It wasn't uncommon on weekdays to be the only ones there. On that gorgeous autumn day, no one else was around, and I let Murphy run off the leash. She'd matured and would mind me when I'd call her back from chasing a squirrel. She was tired after half an hour, so she and I lay in the leaves, under a tree, and we rested. It was calm, sunny, sixty-eight degrees, peaceful. Autumn leaves, the color of golden coins, with brown and red in the mix, floated down in slow motion. Squirrels gathered acorns preparing for the winter ahead as they scampered over crunching fallen leaves. The smell of a wood-burning stove blended with the tranquil, warm air. The grass was now dormant, no longer in need of mowing. Mother Nature was offering me her wisdom—autumn, the season of surrender.

So much of the solace I sought could be found by simply observing nature, by slowing down and tuning in. That's what I was doing, grounding myself. I lay on my back in contact with the slope of the ground beneath me from head to toe. I imagined all my worries, my anguish, my losses, to be leaving my body. I surrendered it all to Mother Earth, knowing she could handle it. My connection with nature was profound, and it was healing. Tears slid out of the corners of my eyes. The enormity of all that had happened in the past seven weeks, the trauma and losses on so many levels, were moving through me, out and into the earth.

I knew the only way to navigate emotionally was by allowing my hopes to be greater than my fears. It was essential that I view my circumstances from the perspective of my soul, instead of my human perspective. The human perspective was laden with fear, it was attached to outcomes, it judged circumstances as good or bad. My soul whispered that this was merely a human experience, it would pass, life was more than what I could perceive and all the pain would serve me and make sense at some point. I needed to transcend the heartache the best I could one moment at a time, and trust the higher plan. Replace judgement with curiosity, allow God's will to flow through me, and believe that I would survive.

The previous month felt like hitting ice on the highway at sixty-five mph—don't panic, don't hit the brakes or accelerate, or turn the steering wheel, hold steady, allow the car to slow down, and steer your way through it one foot at a time. Pray for a dry, stable patch of road to regain control. By the grace of God, you'll return home safely.

The remainder of October drifted by. Avery was passing several drug tests a week—if he didn't, he would be sent back to jail. He was so grateful to be out of county jail, and mostly through all the physical withdrawals from heroin. He was surrounded and supported by professionals teaching him about living sober. Most weekends and some evenings, he was awarded passes to come home.

Ryder loved his new job at Lakeland. It took him a couple of weeks to get acquainted with the crew; several of the near dozen men had been working together for many seasons, installing and removing docks. By three weeks into it, Ryder was one of the pack, and found the two guys he rode with, Roger and Nick, to be an amusing comedy team. Roger was older, animated, and unpretentious. Nick was a few years older than my sons. He was the reserved, cool straight man. He'd play a distinguishing, providential role in my life years later.

Their work days included drives in and around beautiful Minnesota lake country from one picturesque lake property to the next. Once at the site, they'd climb into the lake in wetsuits, shouldering the dock as a team. Ryder's forearms were black and blue for weeks, until his upper body, already muscular from lifting weights at Valley Rehab, gained the additional required strength. He never complained once to me about the physical demands and the increasingly chilly conditions. Shelia had told me that over the years they'd had plenty of guys that had quit after one day of dock removal.

One day, Ryder and I had commuted together; I came to pick him up at the Lakeland Marina on Detroit Lake. When summer was in full swing, the marina was in the thick of the action, next to the Detroit Lakes Pavilion. While I was waiting for him to change out of his wetsuit, his foreman came up to my car to chat.

"I just wanted you to know Ryder is doing a great job for us. He's a good fit, and a hard worker."

Matt stood, a big, broad-shouldered man, at six feet five. His lineage was Hawaiian descent, and he was deeply tanned from a full season of outdoor work next to the water. Everybody working at Lakeland knew who I was and that Ryder was my son, and that our lives weren't perfect. I truly appreciated Matt letting me know. I felt proud of Ryder, a feeling I hadn't experienced in far too long. The blessings of Lakeland Marine continued.

Ryder was still riding the wisdom and fortitude he'd gained from Valley Rehab, and keeping up with all the legal requirements of his drug court sentence, which included weekly NA meetings, meeting with his probation officer, wearing a patch that was tested for drug use weekly, and taking random drug tests.

His relationship with his former girlfriend was on again, and she was released from Valley Rehab in mid-October. They now had a shared commitment to sobriety, and they became inseparable when he wasn't at work. It concerned me. In my perfect world, they'd both move on and find new friends with no connection or history with drugs or addiction. I wanted him to start over with a fresh demographic of women to date. I knew I had no influence over him in matters of love, or anything else, it seemed, so it was a battle I declined to enter. It was possible that she might be good for him, depending on her commitment to sobriety, but it was simply one more thing for me to turn over to trust.

On October 18, Avery's bail was reduced from $50,000 to $2,500 at a bond reduction hearing. On October 22, he completed treatment. I was not able to attend his completion ceremony, but Brad was there. Now the decision to post his bail was easy. We paid the bail, and he came home. We now had both boys back home, where they belonged, where they'd have the best chance to change their lives for the better. Avery's court date had not been determined yet.

Ryder had seen enough of the boating industry and the culture of Lakeland to decide to enroll at Minnesota State in Detroit Lakes in the marine tech program once he completed drug court. That meant his first semester would be in the fall of 2014. We planned to attend an open house at the Minnesota State campus after work on October 29. This was the same school Brad had gained his radiology technician degree from in 2009, while still flying full time. He graduated with a 4.0 and received the Edward Mallinckrodt Award of Excellence, in recognition of outstanding performance.

Ryder was feeling anxious about touring the school and tried to talk me out of going. I wouldn't let him out of it, and we arrived and parked on campus. He didn't engage with anyone we passed by in the halls, though they were all very friendly and welcoming. We dropped off some of Brad's old textbooks to donate to the rad tech department. As we passed the rad tech classrooms, Ryder stopped me. There was a five-foot silk screen banner that featured a near life-sized photo of Brad operating radiology equipment. Ryder took a picture on his phone and sent it to Brad with the message, "The students here are really old." That seemed to lighten him up a bit.

We made it to the marine tech classroom, and I recognized the department head, as I'd met him a few weeks prior when he'd stopped into Lakeland Marine. Ryder relaxed and could see it was a hands-on learning environment, one that didn't intimidate him.

His future was starting to take a new shape, straighter lines with a lighter shade of possibility filling in the middle.

36

LATE OCTOBER, RIVER BEND WAS one gusty day away from becoming barren. Trees were stripped down, creating piles of autumn leaves that briefly insulated neighborhoods until they were raked, hauled, mulched, gone. The stark topography lay harshly exposed in wait for winter's assault to begin. November felt like a home that'd been stripped in the final days of moving, when all that's left are stacks of boxes, bare walls, exposed wiring, and a dark glare reflecting off naked windows. Winter was encroaching, the season of isolation, and November days were filled with resignation, melancholy, and a steady transition into seclusion: darker, colder, shorter days.

Ryder was laid off from Lakeland for the season. He and Avery both needed jobs, but the search was limited when you're a pending felon.

Avery stayed out of public as much as possible. He attended outpatient programming at Prairieview two nights a week. He also went to NA meetings and spent a lot of time with his sponsor. Ryder was usually with his girlfriend. The boys slowly began to sink back into that "up all night, sleep all day" lifestyle, though they were at home most of the time. We'd given them an 11:00 p.m. curfew. I was bothered that they'd park on sofas watching TV shows that depicted crime, life incarcerated, and drug cartel-themed crap. That made me nuts; for hours that garbage would download into their brains. They were getting lazier; their bedrooms and cars were trashed. Old patterns were surfacing; it was concerning.

On the first Saturday of November, I returned home from work and took a long nap. Because of that, I ended up staying up much later than usual. At 1:00 a.m., Ryder started screaming for me. He and his girlfriend were in the basement, and I was in my second-story bedroom. I thought he was just being demanding.

"*Mom, Mom*, where are you? Come here. Where are you? Help me, please!"

"Jesus, Ryder, I'm coming. What the hell?" It was a pet peeve of mine when they attempted to have a loud conversation with me from a different room.

"Oh my God, Mom, she fell, hit her head; she's not breathing; God, Mom, please help." Ryder was frantic, and sober, it seemed.

I felt no panic whatsoever. I never assumed the worst, still, after all the shit storms my sons had initiated. When I got downstairs, she was flat on her back unconscious. I knew CPR, and rescue breathing, from my years as a flight attendant.

I listened for breath, and there was none. I told Ryder to call 911. I gently tilted her head back and her chin up and began rescue breathing. Ryder remained frantic but gave the operator all the information required to dispatch an EMT team to our home.

Then he ranted. "We were watching TV … she got up to stretch … I heard her hit the floor … didn't see her fall. Mom, please help her, I don't want her to die; I love her, Mom; I can't lose her."

He was pacing, breaking down.

She was not responding to rescue breathing; her eyes were transfixed, then a shallow breath, then nothing. I began chest compressions. Ryder continued to pace, scared she was dying. I remained calm. The compressions began to work. She made a feeble attempt to push me away, still incoherent; she was simply responding to the discomfort, but responding nonetheless. I told Ryder to open the garage door so the EMTs could enter easily. The entire time I remained oddly unconcerned that her life was at stake. I wasn't suspicious that the situation was drug related, even though I had every reason to expect foul play based on their history.

She began breathing on her own but was disorientated when the EMT team took over. I briefed them on what I knew and what I'd done, and Ryder filled in details. She was able to speak and told them she hadn't taken any illegal drugs, that she was a recovering heroin addict, been clean six months.

"Congratulations," one of them said.

An hour later, they left; she was fine. I went to bed, grateful no drugs were involved. I said so to Ryder. He thanked me.

Sunday I'd committed to painting a room for a dear friend of mine, Christeen. She was a healer, a tender, petite, fairy of a person. Erin and I gave her a feng shui consultation as a birthday present. She wanted help with her extra bedroom, where she did various types of energy work with clients. Christeen was an addiction counselor, psychiatric nurse, and tai chi instructor, with gifts far beyond her remarkable credentials. She wished to create a room that would inspire and support her desire to write a book.

I'd already done the consultation, which included a recommendation to change the color of paint on the walls. I spent most of Sunday painting the room as part of her birthday gift. I'd known, believed, that the best way to get what you want in life is to help someone get what they want. The notion that I was supposed to write a book persisted. Intuitively I had a feeling that my gesture had more to do with my book than Christeen's. That evening, I thought about what my book might be like. I felt intimidated, doubtful that I could ever write well enough to be published. I also felt it was quite enough just to be living the story; I couldn't expect myself to write it too.

The idea of writing a screenplay occurred to me later that evening. Maybe that would be easier, less eloquence required. If I was going to get published, it couldn't be amateur, so maybe a screenplay would require less talent. That was my erroneous assumption at the time.

The next morning, I went to the dentist. Love going to the dentist, and love getting my teeth cleaned.

"What do you have planned for today?" the hygienist asked me.

"I'm going to reprimand my sons; they're lazy, don't help me with the housekeeping, and I'm sick of it."

Posttreatment, Avery had now been home for a few weeks, and Ryder for over two months. They'd tried unsuccessfully to find jobs. It seemed the initial motivation to embrace sober living was waning. As the weeks progressed, daylight was shrinking, and the mood in our home became dimmer. Reality was setting in for both of them, and they had too much time on their hands. When I returned home, we had the talk. They needed to get steady jobs. Ryder couldn't sit around until spring when he'd be back on with Lakeland. Girls had been sleeping over behind my back when Brad was flying. Avery was lazy, and Ryder was breaking our rules, just like old times.

"I want you guys to start reading, get something positive and life affirming into your brains. All that crime TV you watch has got to stop. What you put into your mind is what turns up in your life. You've got to make some changes if you are going to remain sober."

They didn't respond, just looked down, displaying shame like puppies that got caught raiding the garbage.

"When you sneak girls over to spend the night when Brad's gone, it makes it look like I can't hold down the fort. I'm not keeping secrets from him."

"Okay, okay, Mom, I won't do it anymore," Ryder said curtly.

I showed them a list of all that we've provided for them, and then I made a list of what we asked of them. It was overtly lopsided.

"We don't ask for much, and you've got all day to get it done." I took a breath, trying to remain calm. "Remember the last time Brad and I took vacation?"

They both looked bewildered, trying to recall.

"You were three years old. We didn't want to leave you behind, and we don't dare leave you now. We've sacrificed above and beyond; the least you can do is keep your rooms clean, quit trashing the house, and respect our rules."

I was irate.

On that November 6th it was the first birthday I'd worked in my entire life. I could have taken the day off, but Lakeland Marine was one of my favorite places to be, so why not spend my birthday with people that cared about me, a place that made me so very happy? Scott bought pizza for everyone still on staff during the off-season.

The next day, Ryder and I exchanged texts.

"I'm getting kicked out of drug court for when I relapsed they're taking me to jail right after court at 5"

"what??? call me"

"can't I'm in court I'll call u asap"

"I didn't know u relapsed What did u use?"

"it's been two weeks I told u about it"

"no u didn't tell me"

"will call u if I can after drug court if I can't I'll call u from jail but I'm gonna see a judge tomo and bond out so I can come home for another month or so"

"How can you bond out? There's only $50 in ur checking account"

"I've got $900 in my room"

"where"

"never mind Avery has it"

"WTF don't lie to me"

"ok it's in my room I'll call u when I can can't talk anymore getting handcuffed"

Is this what my life was going to be like, forever bracing for the next catastrophe? Scrambling to respond to their crises, watching them diminish their opportunities in life by making one corrupt decision after another? Do we need to throw them out and let them drown in their mistakes? I cannot continue living this cycle, wondering how far, how bad, how deep they're going to get buried. What mother could?

The relapse was two weeks ago? Then it wasn't the Saturday night I did CPR? Or was it? Did he have the time mixed up? I was confused, and destroyed. He'd been one relapse away from being kicked out of drug court and going back to Cass County Jail to serve out his deferred sentence. Ryder would now carry a felony for seven years, and end up incarcerated for up to six more months.

He was in jail for two days. I didn't schedule a visit or deposit money into his phone account. The boys knew if they ended up back in jail, they weren't getting bailed out by us. Yet no matter how many boundaries we set, it was impossible for me to stop loving them, stop caring about them, to let go and allow them to plummet. Is that what it would take?

I searched Ryder's room and found the clues that confirmed usage: Q-tips (to stop the vein from bleeding), a rubber band (to get the vein to pop), thumbprint-sized baggies (for doses of heroin). I sat on his bed for a moment feeling hollowed out by resentment, betrayal, loss. The void inside of me began to numb. Is there a chance in hell for a happy ending to all of this?

Avery was upset about his brother's relapse. Ryder had traded a food coupon for phone minutes and called Avery from jail. I asked Avery what he'd said.

"He doesn't want me to stress out over it, doesn't want me to use because I'm upset," Avery said softly.

That was so unlike Ryder, to think of someone other than himself.

The next morning, Sunday, at 9:00 a.m., Ryder walked into my bedroom. They released him; the charges didn't stick; that was a choice his probation officer could make. A second chance, thank God; I was so happy to see him, so relieved.

"Looks like I caught a break, Mom. My PO must have changed his mind. The guards came to my cell and said I could go home. We'll know for sure Tuesday when I meet with him."

Tuesday came, and his luck vanished. The guards had made a mistake. Ryder would have to "give himself up," bail himself out, and then await a court sentencing date. He'd be going back into jail; it was just a question of when and for how long.

The next day, he and Avery spent the entire day applying for jobs. At 10:00 p.m., they called me from a public phone. They were in the mall parking lot, twelve miles from home. They were out of gas, phones were dead, and it was freezing outside. I stopped at a gas station, filled the portable gas tank, and drove to the parking lot where they were stranded. God help me, will they ever figure it out?

The next morning, it was time for another talk.

I began.

"I'll always regret I didn't do more to influence you two in high school when all this shit started. In these months we have, while you're still living here, I want us to talk about life, teach you what I know about intuition. I want us to read my book about intuition together and talk about it."

They agreed, so I got out my copy and began to read. As I spoke, they could barely keep their heads upright; their eyes were floating, heads bobbing, incapable of holding eye contact with me, delirious actually. They looked like stoned bobble headed figurines WTF?

"Are you two high right now? Are you?" I was trying so hard not to lose my temper.

No, Mom, no; it's just that, well, we're tired," Avery said.

"Yeah, Mom, just keep reading," Ryder said, yawning.

I started to feel like they were a lost cause. It they weren't high, then what was going on? I grew increasingly upset.

"Chins up please; eyes up here, please." It was absurd; I felt like it was story time for sleepy toddlers.

They couldn't manage it. I left the room crying and went to my bedroom. They followed me up the stairs, apologizing.

"We're sorry, Mom; give us another chance. We love you, Mom, please."

It meant a lot to me that they pursued. I wasn't trying to be dramatic, I was hurting, frustrated. I knew they loved me, though. We agreed to try again another day.

The next Saturday, I got home from work at 4:00 p.m. Avery was disturbingly despondent. He sat on a loveseat near the TV and kept nodding off. I told him to go to bed. It was like he didn't hear me, kept nodding off but wouldn't lie down to sleep. Was this what addicts did, the "nodding" I'd heard of when they're riding a heroin high?

I went over to the couch, put my arms around him, held him, and told him I loved him. He didn't seem to know I was there, didn't seem to hear me.

I was numbing into a statue, rigid from the lack of connection to anything or any thought that could soften the brutal reality that my sons were heroin addicts, and there was nothing I could do to save them. I would live out my days and years going through the motions of a vacant life, darker, colder, frozen.

How do you live as though your children don't exist? How do you exist if your children don't live?

37

WHAT IF THIS IS ALL playing out in perfect accordance with God's plan?

What if this is part of a plan that ultimately leads to serving others ... a plan that has no other route to be fulfilled other than this bundle of events? What if our souls collectively agreed to come into this lifetime together to live this story?

Those were questions I'd proposed in my letter inviting my loved ones to shift in September, shortly after Avery's arrest. Two months after I had written that, I wondered if the purpose of our struggle was to somehow offer our story to help others, and until I did, the problems would continue. Reverse karma? Maybe if I began to write the screenplay, committed to it, only then our family would begin to heal. It's possible that was the higher truth of our circumstances. I didn't tell Brad about the idea; I knew he'd consider it an overthought long-shot notion on my part.

On November 23, I posted my screenplay idea on a website where hundreds of freelance writers could view it, and those interested could pitch me a proposal. When I advertised the job, I had listed it as a screenplay, which is what I had in mind. The first e-mail I got was from Mac, a writer and editor who suggested that perhaps a book would be a better first course, and then a screenplay could emerge later. That felt true, I knew he was right. We agreed to speak the next day, on November 24, my mom's birth date. When I woke up that morning, I told myself if I saw deer out back during our phone conversation that I'd hire him without sorting through the dozens of responses filling my inbox. I hadn't seen deer since the previous spring. Thirteen deer came in and out of view in the hour we spoke.

In our initial collaborations, it became clear that it was my book to write. Even though the first few pages Mac sent me were written well, it wasn't me; it wasn't my voice. My intuition was so clear and compelling that I was the only one that could write our story, and that I was capable. The enormity of that challenge was eclipsed by the trust and resolve I felt to do whatever it was going to take to save my sons.

So Mac agreed to act as proofreader and clean up grammar, sentence structure, and logistic details of that nature. The content, the words, the story, the voice, the style would all come from my heart, my head, my pen. I would come into an experience of writing that was extremely challenging, but at times it felt ethereal as though I was a conduit for pages already penned from heaven.

The night before Thanksgiving, a temp service called the boys and offered them a day's work bagging birdseed. It was the first day of work for Avery since he'd left treatment. There'd been nothing but closed doors for young able-bodied men with pending felony charges. I was grateful they had a day's work, even though it meant Brad and I would be alone for the holiday.

Until my parents passed away in 2008, Thanksgiving had always brought together twenty or more extended family members. There were often more, depending on in-law obligations. The kitchen would be full with me and my sisters preparing the feast, laughing, joking.

That year there was no need to dig out the extra dishes and silverware. There would not be a family celebration. I cooked only because I knew Brad appreciated a traditional turkey meal, and the many days of leftovers. Once the turkey was in the oven, I made the green bean casserole and sweet potatoes and put them in the refrigerator to heat up when the turkey was done. Next I followed an inclination to search the boys' bedrooms.

I found a syringe under Avery's mattress. Beneath Ryder's mattress were two needles, a small box with a scale in it, and inside his retainer case he'd hidden thumbprint size baggies. I sat on Ryder's bed feeling stony, remote. Was this some kind of a cosmic joke? Or curse? Who spends Thanksgiving like this? How dark was my world going to get? I felt a detached resignation—that there was nothing more I could do. *This is who my children are*, I thought. Each new crisis with them had left me increasingly battered and fatigued. My strength and conviction to keep trying was dissipating. If they were going down, I wasn't going with them, I resolved. Under the glass top on Ryder's nightstand he'd kept the program from my dad's funeral. On the cover was a photo of my dad smiling, taken just a couple of years before he passed away.

I gazed at his photo and whispered, "Protect them, Papa; help them find their way."

I'm the mom who couldn't let my babies cry. If it meant getting out of bed for the fifth time in the night, I did. "Let 'em cry it out" never worked for me. My maternal instinct was to protect my children no matter the foe—to save them from danger and continually believe in their goodness. How do you save them from addiction? If Brad had been treating me the way the boys were, I would have divorced him long ago.

I had to quiet my maternal instinct and listen to logic. As a mother and a woman who relied on intuition, a logical approach was like writing left-handed, or driving on the left side of the road; it was messy, awkward, and required concentration and discipline. It meant tough love. I had to realize that by allowing, helping, protecting, I was actually making it worse. I was beginning to understand that I was part of the problem. I had to let them "cry it out."

Brad and I had tread the periphery of enabling for a long time. The cusp where parental instinct ended and enabling began had seemed negotiable and fluid. But now I understood we were past the line. Our approach was no longer working, probably hadn't been for too long. Unconditional love and support, thousands of dollars for attorneys, treatment, drug debt, cleaning up their mistakes, had done all it could. It was time to get out of destiny's path. By doing everything we could to help them, we'd become part of the problem.

I didn't love them any less. If letting go meant losing them, I'd have to find a way to accept the loss. I so believed in an afterlife, that it's a good place, that if that's where they end up, it's not a bad thing. They will be with my parents, and eventually so will I. It had come to that. It was like trying to get comfortable in a bed of broken glass.

Brad and I settled into the living room overlooking the river. The only evidence that this was a holiday was the smell of turkey wafting through the house. That was the single common thread to Thanksgivings past.

"I went through the boys' room, just had a hunch." I showed him what I'd found.

"What the fuck? Is this shit ever gonna stop?" Brad spoke softly, shaking his head.

"We can't save them. I want to salvage what's good in my life. We've got to let go, let them fall. I'll hope and pray for the best, love them as much as always, but I've got to walk away from it," I said without tears.

"The problem is where are they gonna land?" Brad replied. "They've got to break the cycle. I'm not even angry anymore; I feel sorry for them."

"I feel like we're becoming part of the problem. If we don't make a strong statement now, they'll think once they're out again they can come home and do whatever they want," I said.

Brad had come into a tender resignation.

"School has always been tough for them; they're scared of all the limits that are set on them now. I'd rather have them in this cycle than dead," he said.

"We need to call their probation officers, tell them what we've found, and then take their lead. They need to go to jail or a halfway house until their sentencing. Being at home running all over us isn't serving anyone, and I'm sick of it," I said.

"I think we should let their attorneys know, and let them decide who finds out and what should happen next," Brad said.

"You're right."

I moved to the kitchen table to gaze out the window. I put on my headset, played iTunes, and began peeling potatoes. Just a dusting of white was on the lawns, not enough snow to cover the brush and trees. The Red River was beginning to freeze. The banks were solid ice, but the center was flowing as the sun shone down on the current and burst into thousands of bright, dancing facets of light. I too had frozen up around the perimeter, thicker skin. It wasn't apathy; it was a new angle of trust.

We'd done all we could do for Ryder and Avery. By letting go, I believed I was making space for miracles, for destiny; this would be a threshold for a higher purpose. I needed to embrace whatever was possible in my life, even if it didn't include my boys. I knew that letting go, allowing them due consequence, was the key to a different future for all of us. Maybe not the future I'd hoped for all of their lives, but one with possibilities I was just beginning to imagine.

After dinner, I hatched a plan to confront them.

"Why don't we split them up when they get home? That way we can get the story straight from each of them and see what adds up."

Brad agreed.

When they arrived around 8:00 p.m., I had Avery come up to our bedroom and left Brad and Ryder in the living room.

"Tell me what's going on with your drugging, and don't lie, please."

"Okay, Mom, I'm not gonna lie." He looked me in the eyes. "I did relapse," Avery confessed.

"What happened? It had to have been that Saturday when I came home and you were so out of it. Ryder finally yelled at you to go to bed."

"Yeah, that was part of it."

"Tell me about it. Did you get drugs from Ryder?"

"No, Mom, I just ran into a guy I know at Holiday getting gas. He owed me money, and he gave it to me instead of cash. I was having a weak day. I'd found some triggers when I was going through stuff you guys moved back from my house while I was in jail."

"Tell me what you used. Was it in the house?"

"No, I was in the car, in the driveway. I crushed it up and injected it, a painkiller. It was stupid, fucked up. I'm really sorry I did it; I regret it. It doesn't make me want to keep using, Mom; I don't want to go back to being an addict."

"We're going to let your attorney know. If you need to go to jail or a halfway house, so be it. Apparently living here isn't part of the solution."

"He already knows, Mom. I told him and my counselor. You and Dad are the only ones I didn't tell. I didn't want to let you down. And I won't let you down again; I won't, Mom."

"What did they say?"

"That it was a relapse, and that we just have to get back on track and push ahead. Figure out what I need to do so it doesn't happen again. I'm meeting with my counselor Monday. I didn't lie about it to any of them; I'm not doing that anymore."

"Who's Abby?"

"She works for the Feds; like a probation officer, kinda. She wants to come and meet you and Dad, and see where we live."

"That would be great, but it has to be Tuesday or Wednesday next week, before I leave for Denver."

"Okay, I'll tell her. And, Mom, for sure the best thing you can do for Ryder is to get out of River Bend. Me too, but I'm probably going to be in prison longer than him. Just try and get out of here as soon as you can. For both of us."

By then Brad was done with Ryder. He too was forthcoming.

"I'm not going to live my life as a drug addict. I know you don't believe me, and I know I have a lot to prove, but you'll see; I'm gonna beat it. I'll let my choices do all the talking. That's why I'm wearing the patch, I want you guys to know I'm not using."

I thought about what everyone else I knew was doing on Thanksgiving—family, laughter, sharing the day, relaxing, catching up. Not us. When would it be normal again? Ever?

Brad and I regrouped and agreed that given the little time each of them had before sentencing, we'd allow them to stay home. If not, we knew they'd end up couch surfing at user friends' homes. Avery's hearing was late January, and Ryder's was the week after. The important thing is they were honest to their attorneys. At that point, I did believe they both wanted the life we'd set them up for, but wanting and committing were two different things, especially with addiction in the mix.

When I went to bed that Thanksgiving night, I felt different. I saw the boys in a way that had me trust that they had a chance, trust that they wanted a different life for themselves. Mostly I trusted myself to be able to let them go and leave it to God. It was time for me, for Brad and me, to have a life outside of the dark tunnel of addiction in which we'd been held captive for years. I was thankful for the clarity and peace.

The following Monday, I went to play tennis as usual. The night before, Avery told me he wanted to move far away once he'd served his time, to Florida maybe. I made the quick assumption that he wanted to move there because it would be easy to get drugs. Instead of clarifying, I jumped to a fear-based assumption and let it take me over. Letting go was clearly going to be a process, not a once and done.

While on the tennis court I focused, continually blocking out my concern about Avery and bringing my attention back to the point, the ball. Thank God for this sport.

During a lengthy rally, I saw a rolling ball from the court beside us headed toward my partner's feet just as our opponents were setting up for a decisive point-winning slam. I called "ball," ending the rally, which was my right to do when I have a legitimate distraction.

"Come on, that was a put-away shot," one of our opponents snidely remarked.

That, I thought, was a seriously bitchy thing to say, and I was furious and offended. Do not accuse me of calling "ball" just to save a point. I don't play that way, never have. If she only knew the emotional battle I waged every day. Tennis was my haven, and she ruined it for me that day.

"I have the right to call a ball in the court when I see it. Take the point if you want it," I said curtly and turned my back, returning to the baseline.

I was too close to the edge. The only other words I had were to my partner to vent. I left immediately after the match. Once I brushed the snow off my car and got inside, I burst into tears. Thanksgiving, Avery moving to Florida, the f'd up life I was living trying to be brave when everything I had tried for my whole life, my children, was the worst possible mess. Two boys, both addicts, felons, awaiting sentencing. How's this going to end?

It all came out. I cried all the way home, then headed straight to the couch, and cried some more. I was sobbing as hard as I ever had.

"God, please help me," I asked between sobs.

I settled down a bit when my sister Ann called, a call I'd been expecting so we could plan my arrival to Colorado.

She could tell right away that I was upset.

"What's wrong? You don't sound good."

"I'm okay, but sometimes it all gets to me. I just needed a good cry."

"I want to help; I worry about you. We've got to get something figured out for you."

"Some things can't be fixed. All I can do is get through this as best I can. I'm doing that one day at a time. This just happens to be a rough one. I'll be okay."

"You're right. Can't wait to see you."

Later that day I finally asked Avery why he wanted to move to Florida.

"Is it because you can get hooked up with drugs?"

"No, Mom, of course not. I said Florida because it's far away. Could be Texas, Arizona, just far away. I'm not that person, Mom. You'll see, I'm not going to be an addict."

"Okay, glad to hear it, honey. I love you."

"Love you too, Mom."

On Tuesday, Brad was home, so we went to our favorite Indian restaurant for lunch.

"We really have to start making a plan to get out of River Bend. The boys have told me more than once that living here makes it so much harder," I said.

"I was thinking about it on this last trip. Remember my buddy John; he had that lake place on Big Pine near Perham?"

"Yep, I remember."

"John never goes to his lake place anymore. Maybe we could rent from him. He might have it for sale, though. I could find out."

"Yes, for sure, get ahold of him. That would be awesome. What's his place like?"

"Very nice, gorgeous view, right on the lake, great kitchen; He loves to cook. I'll check with Murray; he rented it last summer."

Two days later, I left for Colorado and basked in relief to simply get away. I needed a vacation to escape my life, and I hadn't since our sisters' week in June 2012.

It was five days of shopping, working out, sleeping in, and being a sister instead of a mother. We went to Ann's daughter's home one evening, and the three of us chatted.

"What do you do to take care of yourself? Do you have a good therapist?" Paige asked.

"Tennis is the best medicine. I'm back to playing twice a week. I don't see a therapist."

"Therapy might be helpful. You have to do something for yourself."

"I know that sounds like a reasonable choice. But here's the deal. I'm finding my way. If seeing someone would change my life, I would do it. It comes down to managing my despair, and I'm doing that, in my own way, pretty well most days, considering …"

Ann nodded. "Yes, you're amazing."

I continued.

"Honestly, I'll tell you when you need to start worrying about me … when my marriage is crumbling, when I have no interest in tennis, or work … when I've lost touch with my intuition … when I've let myself go."

Paige just smiled. She could see I was handling it, and pretty well, in fact.

Brad spoke to John. His home on Big Pine Lake was available for us to rent. The boys weren't the only ones who wanted to move away from River Bend. Every time I left the house, I hoped I didn't run into anyone I knew.

What do you say to the mother that's living my life?

………….."Hey Dana how was your Thanksgiving?"

38

I CONSIDERED NORTH DAKOTA WINTERS TO be a three-act play. Act one, "The Holidays," spread from Thanksgiving through Christmas. In this stretch of winter, there were plenty of distractions from the climate bearing down as most people prepared for the holidays and the accelerated social calendar. Once the holidays passed, the second Act opened, "The Tundra," which stretched until the end of February. Eight weeks of frozen tundra, with no expectations of relief—though an occasional jump to twenty or thirty degrees could feel like spring break. In this stretch, all you could do was suck it up and take the beating. March began Act three, "The Teaser." Winter could continue, or it could spike into the sixties for a few days; there was no telling from one year to the next.

December 2013 was colder than average, with daytime temperatures rarely rising above fifteen degrees, and it was frequently below zero at night. Winter solstice was December 21, the longest night, which made it auspicious for feng shui. It represented the rebirth of the sun, and the light beginning to increase each day as the earth's path moves closer to the sun. In the fading gray of late afternoon, Erin and I returned to Trefoil Park by the dam on the Red River. She'd been struggling for a reasons of her own. Over the years, we'd done all kinds of blessings in this park, in every season.

We met on Elm Street near the park entrance. It was closed for the winter, so a gate blocked cars from driving in, but the city still plowed the walking path. We were both bundled up for the brisk winter day in boots, gloves, scarves, hats, and layers of clothing beneath long wool coats. With multiple layers of insulation, our voices were the only clue to our identities, though we'd be the only ones venturing in the park that day. Since ideas of that nature occurred quite easily to me, Erin often left it to me to come up with details of the blessing we'd perform.

I thought a walking blessing would be best, to keep us moving through the cold air. I brought a yellow candle protected in its glass container, keeping the fragile flame shielded from the wind. Side by side we followed the half-mile path through the snow. I began the blessing by expressing my hopes and intentions for family. Then I passed the candle to Erin, and she did the same. Wealth was the next intention, and we progressed one by one through the rest of the Bagua: health, helpful people, children, knowledge, fame, career, and marriage. Our phrasing resembled a spontaneous, unfiltered prayer. We took turns holding the candle as we spoke, allowing one another to expel every thought and wish. We concluded each intention reciting, "This or something better now manifests, I am grateful."

When we finished, we blew out the candle, our breaths visible as vapor in the damp winter air. Our noses were red from the cold, and our gloved hands were stiff, but we'd conquered the elements. I felt a sense of completion, a victory of sorts by communing with nature despite winter's oppression. Our lives weren't easy, but we kept trying, kept believing that a power greater than ourselves would lead us where we were supposed to go, and sustain us through our struggles. Better days lay ahead, we'd hoped.

Winter solstice marked the darkest day of the year, the least amount of daylight. That's how 2013 had felt, my darkest year, and I hoped it would forever maintain that distinction.

Winter is much like the color white. Technically, white isn't a color. Rather it is the lack of pigment. Winter in North Dakota is best described by what's lacking. You cannot walk onto the deck of your house in the early morning and hear the songbirds trying to outmuscle one another with the pitch and draw of their magnificent notes. Rabbits, squirrels, and deer appear only briefly in search of nourishment. Neighborhood dogs aren't outside long enough to bother barking, and there are no passersby to alarm them. Children's laughter carried in the breeze and the buzz of lawn mowers and sprinklers are all mute. The fragrances, colors, and visual depth that grass, shrubs, trees, flowers, and gardens grace our senses with all vanish. The landscape is stark, one-dimensional, barren.

The pleasure of being outdoors is replaced with an active and unrelenting assault on your personal comfort and an ongoing battle to seek warmth. Winter is the season of deprivation, seclusion, and hibernation. The pace of life lurches, and home becomes a sacred shelter to recoil and nest. The winter months are an invitation to retreat, recharge, and pull back from social engagements. Everyone accepts the excuse, "It's just too damn cold to go out tonight."

Winter is a dictator forcing its agenda on everyone regardless of status. It's the season that taught me that you can't always have life on your terms. Every day you wake to stingy daylight, discouraging weather forecasts, and the surrender of warm weather conveniences and pleasures. For months it seems there's no end in sight, forcing the resignation to endure it and mark one more day off the frigid calendar. Winter was the season that mirrored how I'd been living for years.

Being cold is a low-level pain. It's an irritant though, not a crippling one. At times, in North Dakota, the emotional ache of deprivation and the long winters elicit a sense that you're merely surviving, not necessarily living life to its fullest.

Winter has its ways of strengthening character.

When you're forced to reconcile to the harsh conditions of winter, you learn to hold on, to remain steadfast. "This too shall pass" is the mantra that becomes internal to your emotional fortitude. North Dakota winters taught me as a young girl resilience, patience, and perseverance. I learned how to drive on ice, to operate a snow blower, and to always leave home prepared. I was forced to be brave driving alone in the terror of a whiteout with no idea where the road was, driving an inch at a time relying on luck and timing to arrive home safely.

The wisdom I intuited from a lifetime of North Dakota winters prepared me, made me tough enough to survive the heartbreak and devastation that had become a part of every season that my sons were lost. Innately I understood, no matter how dark, cold, and desolate life became, that it wouldn't last; spring would eventually arrive. The cycle of seasons remains, always and forever.

As a commuter to Detroit Lakes, I'd become a daily spectator of the changing seasons, driving two hours round-trip, mostly through rural countryside. My interaction with nature in winter was primarily visual; I could only view it through a window. The disconnection was much like visits to my son in jail. Through glass I could see orange clothing, dark circles of tortured sleep, pale skin from lack of sunlight, and the slouched demeanor that confinement bred. But I was separated by the walls and window. I couldn't touch him, feel his warmth, and embrace his broken spirit in hopes of absorbing some of his grief and blending it with my own. That's what winter mostly was, a yearning, an awareness of what was missing, a long-distance separation, where the distance wasn't miles; it was the passage of time.

Christmas was white in River Bend that year, but there was less snow than usual—just a little over a foot. The four of us traveled to Minneapolis to spend a mellow holiday with Brad's family. I hadn't bought any gifts, so on the way, we stopped in Albertville, Minnesota, at a massive outlet shopping mall and let the boys pick out their gifts from us. We didn't talk about the boys' legal situation with Brad's family. We ignored the events of the past year and pretended it was just another Christmas, to come together and then move on.

On December 30, we met with Avery and his counselor from Prairieview. I was grateful for the opportunity. The family session was scheduled to conclude his outpatient treatment. He'd been attending twice a week since his release from inpatient treatment in October. Ryder couldn't be there, though I don't recall why.

Gwen met my eyes. "How did you feel last summer when Avery was arrested?"

"I was already in hell; I didn't know it had a basement," I said quietly.

Gwen nodded.

"Everyone tells me it's not my fault," I continued. "But I'd be lying if I said there was nothing I could have done differently, or, well, better, I guess."

"What do you believe your role was?" Gwen asked.

"There were different choices I could have made. I may have tried to maintain harmony to a fault. I needed to be less concerned about my children liking me, and stand up stronger as a parent."

"But do you realize that Avery made those choices, and that he's the one responsible for his actions, not you?"

"Yes, but if my kid had graduated cum laude from Notre Dame I sure as hell would have taken some of the credit, so why wouldn't I take some of the responsibility for this?" It was a candid question that I didn't expect anyone to answer.

"So how is taking responsibility serving you?" Gwen asked.

I got the feeling she'd heard it all many times before.

"Trying to convince myself it's not my fault has never felt true. What's felt more authentic is to accept that I missed some opportunities; I allowed my optimism and denial to detach me from reality."

I looked over to Brad and Avery, and took a deep breath.

"So I've tried instead to forgive myself. And I have forgiven myself. So it's serving me by becoming self-aware, and to learn from my mistakes."

Avery was the most emotional when he spoke of his sponsor and all the guidance, advice, and support he'd provided.

"What do you love most about Avery?" Gwen asked me.

"Everything," I said instantly. I turned and smiled at Avery with tears in my eyes, and added, "But what I love most is his sense of humor."

When he was asked to express to each of us what he loved best, he put us together and said how much he appreciated having parents who are united, who love one another, who are together. Indeed, we were all blessed in that regard.

Later, at home, I asked Avery what he would have said if he'd answered that question just about me. He said what he loved most about me was my unconditional love, never deserting him, never giving up on him becoming a better person.

A horrible year was coming to a close, and the tundra stage of winter 2014 was beginning. Although we'd lived in a constant state of uncertainty, we did know that in 2014 both of our sons would be state and federal prisoners. All we could do was wait for their court dates to arrive, and the details of their sentencing, their fate, would be filled in. Our best guess was that Ryder would serve two months, and Avery two to five years. I did feel a sliver of tainted relief knowing that for a period of time they'd both be the government's responsibility, sober, and I would have an interlude from unrelenting consequences. Peace had a high ransom.

Perhaps the most lucid testament to how intense 2013 had been could be found in the contact list of my cell phone. The phone numbers I'd acquired included: a psychiatrist (to prescribe Suboxone for Ryder); Lost and Found ministry (though I never did call them); office and cell phone numbers for two attorneys; one state and one federal probation officer; two numbers for Cass County Jail; three numbers for Central Rehab, two for Prairieview, three numbers for Valley Rehab—one for his counselor and two others for phone lines to try to call Ryder's floor to get him paged to the phone; two sponsors for Avery; Securist, an inmate phone card purchasing service; and one contact listed as Bail, though I have no idea who would answer if I called that one. And, not in my list of contacts but dialed, 911.

Seriously, who is the mother living that life? I wasn't even sure if I knew.

39

As January 2014 rolled in, Brad and I debated whether to sign a six-month lease for the lake home in Perham, thirty miles east of Detroit Lakes on Big Pine Lake. The primary consideration was getting Ryder out of the gates with a strong start. Once he was done serving his time, he would be completely free, with no probation or drug testing, which was a bit daunting, a high-wire act without a net. In the spring he'd be working at Lakeland Marine in Detroit Lakes. In early January, Ryder, Brad, and I made a trip to Perham to see the lake home. Winter seemed even more desolate out in the seclusion of Minnesota lake country. Some of the homes were year-round residences, but mostly it was seasonal properties that were locked up for at least six months of the year.

We trudged through the snow with Kate, the next-door neighbor who kept watch on the place for John. The property was a year-round home, insulated and with a good furnace, not a drafty cabin full of cobwebs. Lakeside, the house was all windows with a second-story view of the lake. I imagined relaxing in the summer sun on the second-story deck overlooking the lake, sitting level with the tree branches full of leaves and birds: the purr of trolling boats, the singular trickle of a fish jumping in still water, the humid air filled with the scent of bonfires from a nearby campsite, the lonely call of a midnight loon—lake recollections that seemed a lifetime away. It would be the perfect escape. Brad didn't want to keep John waiting too long for an answer to his generous offer.

"It's bigger than I thought, and I won't have to bring one kitchen item from home. I love the bay window and the view," I said.

"Yeah, it's pretty stark out here now, but summer, with all the trees filled in, it's beautiful." Brad had stayed there several times with a group of guys on golf weekends.

"I love it," I said. "But seriously, don't rent it for me. Even with his reasonable price it's still a lot of money for us. I don't mind the commute to River Bend. If we do this, it's for Ryder."

I left the final decision up to Brad. I'd learned over the years that when it came to decisions that involved a lot of money or lifestyle change, the less emotionally invested I was the better. I'd made a point not to try to talk Brad into or out of anything. I offered my opinion but left it at that. Taking that angle, I never had to shoulder the responsibility of persuading Brad into a choice that turned out poorly. The truth was we shared core values and usually agreed on big decisions even though he processed primarily from logic and me from intuition.

I also believed as good or as bad as an assumed outcome appeared, there was always more story than I could ever project. I'd learned that the downside of most decisions was usually obvious, but the blessings were a mystery revealed later, once the leap of faith had been made. Destiny always sprinkled in details of providence when you're willing to take risks.

I felt the only justification to rent the home would be to get Ryder out of River Bend and away from negative influences. Otherwise we didn't need to spend the money. Sure, it would save me an hour commuting each day, but money saved on gas didn't rationalize the added expense and responsibility.

Two days later, Brad signed a six-month lease that would begin on April 15. As it turned out this peaceful lake home, with the treetop view of the lake, would be where the most of the pages of my book would be written.

In mid-January, Brad began a six-week medical leave, and with him at home around the clock, we maintained order with the boys, who were working several nights a week at a birdseed plant. Otherwise they spent time with their sponsors and went to NA meetings. Mostly they were home evenings passing time watching TV. I was free to work boat shows out of town without worrying about the situation at home. It was a rare sense of freedom that I hadn't known since I'd quit flying in 2007. Back then, when it was my turn to leave on a trip, Brad was home holding down the fort.

I wondered if things would have turned out differently if Brad had been the full-time local parent instead of me. The boys had taken advantage of me, the softer parent, and the solo parent much of the time.

Avery's court date, which had been scheduled for late January, was pushed out another six weeks at the request of his attorney, who thought it would help Avery's case. Ryder's girlfriend was transported to the women's prison in New England, a small town in Hettinger County, in western North Dakota, at the end of January. She would serve her remaining time there until early July.

For Ryder's sentencing on February 4, we dressed as if we were going to a funeral. The boys wore nearly the same size as Brad, so his wardrobe supplied all three of them with pleated trousers, collared shirts, and neckties. The county courthouse was an older four-story brick building that took up an entire city block near downtown. It was four blocks away from Anderson Law Firm, six blocks away from Island Park and Prairieview, and one mile east was Woodland Law Firm. Geographically, our situation was uncomplicated.

Ryder left to meet his attorney at his office. Avery and Tessa, a friend, rode with Brad and me. We arrived at the courthouse before Ryder and Kurt. After passing through the metal detectors, I found the property tax office on the first floor and paid our taxes for the year, mixing the mundane with the intense. Brad seemed edgy, so I said as little as possible. Avery was a full size smaller than the shirt and pants he had on. He'd worn athletic shoes with a grandiose red and white checker shoelace pattern. He was so endearing to me.

We all assumed Ryder would get six to eight weeks in Cass County Jail, and then be free just in time to resume working with the installation crew at Lakeland Marine following the ice-out in early May. Then off to live in Perham. At least the end of the legal web for one of our sons was in sight. Or so it seemed.

Kurt Williams seemed to always have a somber demeanor about him. That wasn't a bad thing, certainly an attribute you want in your attorney. But on February 4, he'd seemed especially intense, nervous actually, and so was Ryder.

Four more of the boys' peers joined us outside of the courtroom. Months later, we'd find out one of them had been used by the police as an informant against Ryder, though that day he acted like a supportive friend. Kurt and Ryder left to take their places in the courtroom, and the rest of us filed into the wood pews to quietly observe.

The judge read aloud my letter requesting that Ryder serve time in River Bend so we could continue to visit him and remain an influence. He read another from Cameron, his counselor from Valley Rehab, asking for leniency. Next the judge read the list of violations Ryder had incurred while in drug court. Brad and I were astonished. Although the legal jargon was difficult to interpret at times, we both understood that Ryder had not been forthcoming about the number of times he had violated probation: flunked drug tests, missed appointments with his probation officer, traffic tickets—the list went on. We were devastated. It was an assault of betrayal taking my insides by the fistful and squeezing hard.

It quickly became clear that there was strong opposition to the time frame Kurt Williams was seeking. Ryder's probation officer did not believe six weeks would be enough time to set him straight, and he told the judge and the courtroom audience that Ryder wasn't ready to become unaccountable in six weeks. He told the judge that over the years a number of his probationers had come back and thanked him for the additional time they'd spent incarcerated at his request. It's what helped them turn their lives around, he said, and was what Ryder needed. The Probation Officer had a profound influence on the judge. I kept my palms up, resting on my lap, open to receive the entire hearing. I'm not sure what I was hoping to receive, whatever was best for Ryder, I guess.

The judge sentenced Ryder to a year and one day, less the time he'd served at Valley Rehab—seven months in Cass County Jail. One word echoed within me: trust. I kept repeating it silently as I absorbed the judge's decision. It seemed there was no chance Ryder would return to Lakeland in the summer. The lease Brad signed for the house was all for naught; Ryder wouldn't be free until late August. When Ryder realized what was coming down, panic set in. I watched him speak frantically to Kurt but couldn't hear what he was saying. Kurt looked down, his head alternating nods between yes and no gestures.

It was too late for a different outcome. The judge dismissed court, and Ryder was taken into custody and off to seven months in jail.

Brad was very tense the rest of the day, furious about Ryder's continued deception. I stayed away from him, and he went to our bedroom with a six-pack of Leinenkugel and chew.

Later that evening, we got a call from Ryder.

"You guys have to get me out of here and into treatment. Call Kurt and have him get me into Central Rehab. I got screwed by that judge. I can't spend seven months here. I need help; I need treatment, not jail," he demanded.

He did not ask. There was no "please," no "thank you." Just an abrasive demand that we do what he was saying.

Avery had reminded us that the first week in custody Ryder would be locked down for twenty hours a day until they classified him as a nonviolent, non-sex-offender, at which time he'd be moved to G-Main and have more time outside of his cell. Ryder knew what he was in for and wanted out.

I didn't promise Ryder anything. Brad and I agreed we weren't going to give in. We had told him and Avery at Thanksgiving that we wouldn't be spending any more money on attorneys once they were sentenced. It would be up to them to get it right from that point forward. Brad was angry and frustrated and didn't plan on visiting Ryder until tempers settled.

A couple of nights later, I attended a sixtieth birthday party for one of my tennis buddies. It was all women tennis players. No one knew what was going on with my children. I tried to just enjoy the occasion for the positive distraction it offered me. I stayed only long enough to kill time until I had my first chance to visit Ryder at the appointed time.

I felt defeated driving back to that jail, and sad that Ryder would be there until the end of summer, seven months away. I found my way through to the colored tiles, and the door that matched the badge I'd been given. I sat down and waited for Ryder to appear. He entered and sat across from me and picked up the phone receiver. He looked impatient and didn't bother saying hello.

"Well, are you guys gonna help me out, get me into Central Rehab?"

He spoke to me like I was the enemy.

"No, Ryder, we're not; we're out of money. We told you that you'd have to make better choices," I said softly.

"I have been making better choices; I got screwed!" With that, he stood up shoved his chair back against the wall and flipped me the bird and walked out.

I was stunned. Our visit was over in less than thirty seconds. When I went back down to hand in the badge in exchange for my driver's license, the woman asked, "Are you leaving already?" I held back tears and nodded yes.

I returned to my car and felt myself crumbling. Neither of my sons had ever treated me with hostility. Tough love was unfamiliar to all of us. As I drove away, I called Brad and told him what happened.

"That's why I didn't want to go see him yet. He's pissed off, acting like an asshole. Don't take it personal. He needs time to settle his ass down. He'll come around; just take it easy."

I drove home with the radio silent attempting to contain my emotions. When I passed Elephant Park, my eyes pooled with tears, blurring the streetlight rays to appear eight feet tall. Once in the house, Brad hugged me; I wept until I was exhausted, and crawled into bed.

Ryder called to apologize at ten thirty, but I was asleep. Brad texted me so I'd see the message when I got up in the morning. It meant a lot that Ryder came around that quickly.

Avoidance was a dance we'd mastered to sidestep confrontation physically and verbally. I was accomplished at glazing over the clues and hoping for different facts to come into focus. It was like approaching roadkill; I'd see the heap on the shoulder of the highway. I knew it'd be grisly, so as I drew closer to the carnage I'd focus ahead and allow my eyes to blur slightly until I passed the casualty. That way I never knew for sure what it had been, impossible to calculate the loss if it'd been someone's pet. I didn't want enough details to make a connection.

Tough love felt counterintuitive; I didn't know how to trust it. We knew we had to do something differently because the open heart and purse approach wasn't working. If we didn't hold our ground, they'd never believe us when we told them we'd had enough. The truth was that "more than enough" was a destination we'd passed years ago.

Weeks later, Ryder told me that he'd had a vivid dream his first night back in jail. My parents appeared to him and told him, "We love you and always will; we've been protecting you and Avery, but we're getting tired. You need to find God, Ryder; it's time for you and your brother to turn to God."

40

I N MID-FEBRUARY, I EXPERIENCED WHAT I would characterize as possibly the worst seventy-two hours I'd had as a parent—a mix of extreme anxiety for Avery's health, immense frustration at how as a suspected addict he was perceived by the world in general, and how fragile my emotions had become. The events of the past year had abraded my protective armor down to the thinnest of layers.

Shortly before those three days in hell, we learned that his sentencing would not occur at his next court appearance on April 15 but at a later hearing. We'd assumed that, like Ryder, Avery would go to his hearing on the fifteenth, be sentenced, and be led away to prison from the courthouse.

Instead that meant he'd be at home until late May at least. With Ryder in jail until late August and Avery home until late May, it appeared that it had been a mistake to rent the home on Big Pine Lake for the summer. Brad wouldn't consider asking John to get out of the lease. He felt an obligation to be true to his word and commitment.

All of this—the jail terms, the hearings, the schedule changes—was wearing, certainly, but I also realized that it could be years until my twin sons would see one another without the separation of glass. I couldn't imagine how difficult that was for them; they had struggles only a twin could understand.

Then, very unexpectedly, there was a glimmer of hope during this bleak time, an opportunity to look to the future.

Two weeks after Ryder returned to jail, Avery got an e-mail from Cahill Hedland Production Company, which was casting young adults from all fifty states in a reality/stylist show. The team would travel to the contestant's hometown for the filming. The show's producers felt that by doing style makeovers on the various chosen candidates, these young adults would gain a new self-respect and thus be more inclined to turn their lives around. I loved the idea of it, but how on earth did they find Avery?

We sat on his bed, read the e-mail, and then did some research. We learned they were heavy hitters in the production industry, and it looked to be totally legitimate. "Wow, Avery, it looks to be legit. That's so weird. I wonder how they found you?" I was sitting next to him as he scrolled through the website on his laptop.

"Yeah, for real; I must of shown up when they did a Google search for 'fucked up kids in North Dakota.'" We laughed. I could hear the gurgle of lungs damaged from cigarette and pot smoke.

"Something like that, sure, because it's a makeover program to help the contestants get a fresh start. You'd be awesome on that show, Avery, with your sense of humor."

I nudged him with my shoulder.

"Honestly, Mom, I don't care to be in the spotlight, at all. But maybe somebody we meet can help you get your book published. I'll do it if it helps you."

I had recently finished the first draft.

"Who knows? Let's answer the questions, and see what happens. You can always say no if they offer it to you."

I felt intuitively that we were beginning to attract a higher frequency of events, people, and opportunities. Even if this particular offer didn't materialize, it was still a sign to me that better days lay ahead. The conversation that evening became more meaningful in hindsight. It was upbeat, and hopeful, and I felt so connected to Avery. The problem began the next morning, a Sunday. Avery woke up with a slightly swollen bottom lip. He was icing it to bring down the swelling and soothe the mild burning sensation. I wondered if it was a spider bite, or some kind of allergic reaction. Whatever it was it wasn't bad enough to keep him from going out to apply for a job in south River Bend that afternoon.

When he got out of the car to walk the short distance into the store, his lip began to expand so rapidly that he had trouble breathing, which frightened him enough that he called 911 for an ambulance even though the ER was only five blocks away.

The doctors who treated him offered no diagnosis, just two medications, Benadryl and a prescription for a steroid. He called home around eight to tell me he'd be home after he picked up the medicine.

Watching TV with him later, I saw his lip was getting worse, and he turned to me and asked, "Where's Ryder?"

"Honey, he's in jail; you know."

"Oh, yeah, yeah, I forgot," he said, shaking his head as if to say, "Of course, how stupid of me."

Several moments later: "Where's Ryder?"

"Avery, are you feeling okay? You know Ryder's in jail."

"Oh, yeah, yeah; that's dumb, I know."

Then again, "Where's Ryder?"

Something was very wrong.

Then he also began obsessively picking at his ever-expanding lip as his entire appearance seemed to deteriorate in front of me. His behavior became odder and darker.

Brad had been working on a car in the garage, and at around ten I went out to tell him, "Avery's kind of loony; he keeps asking about Ryder, and his lip is getting worse. It's strange, like his personality is altered in a dark way. It's not right."

"Get the info out about the meds he's taking and read what it says about side effects." He was leaning over with his head down staring at the engine of the car.

"Okay, but then I'm going to bed. Are you gonna be up for a while? I think one of us should be watching him."

"Yeah, I'll stay up with him for a while."

The side effects included hallucinating, paranoia, and agitation. When I got back into the living room, the situation was getting worse. He was also becoming paranoid. He jerked abruptly, startled, and threw his empty bottle of soda at the person he "saw" approaching him.

"Avery, what are you doing?" I was getting scared.

"Mom! Didn't you see that? That dude was coming at me!"

He'd lost touch with reality, and he looked freakish with his lower lip by then grotesquely swollen.

At midnight, Brad took Avery back to the ER, and I went to bed.

At four, Brad came and woke me up.

"I can't stay awake anymore. Avery's been up all night, still hallucinating and hyper. You need to take over."

"What'd they say at the ER?"

"Quit taking the meds; the combination sent him into orbit, I guess. They suspect he's allergic to Benadryl and added that to his records just to make sure it doesn't happen again."

"That's it? No diagnosis? What about his lip? We still need to get that figured out."

"Yeah, well, I'm beat. Let's hope it starts improving."

With that, Brad went to bed.

I was dumbfounded that the hospital would release Avery without diagnosing and treating the lip. We weren't any closer to a solution than when Avery had called 911. It was gut-wrenching to look at him; I was sick to my stomach, and Avery was a mere shell of himself.

As the sun rose, Avery became less frantic as the medications wore off, though he was still obsessed with picking at the chapped skin on his lip. He finally fell asleep for a couple of hours, but his lip was as bad as ever, red lesions and ballooning when he woke. At eleven, I brought him to Heartland walk-in clinic. While his behavior was more rational, he was so embarrassed by his appearance that he pulled the hood of his sweatshirt over his face to hide his lip. I quickly explained our situation and the lack of response at the hospital to the reception nurse, who asked Avery for his ID. When he stepped up to give her his driver's license, she saw his face and told us he'd be seen immediately and brought us to an exam room.

A short time later, an elderly doctor entered the room and sat across from us. Avery said hello and offered his hand in introduction, which the doctor ignored. Instead he offered in return a look that I would describe as repulsion, as if he didn't want anything to do with Avery. I was offended by his cold demeanor. Any doctor reading Avery's chart would see he had a history of heroin addiction, and I felt as if that was all the doctor could see. He did write a prescription for an antibiotic, though, and, despite his aloofness, I felt we had finally made some progress.

By then, Avery was finally exhausted enough to get some sleep. But at three that afternoon, he woke up and came into my bedroom.

"Mom, look at me. My lip, what the fuck? I belong in a freak show." He was in tears; his entire face was distorted.

His lip was so swollen and heavy that it was tipping forward, exposing his lower gum line. He had to hold a washrag to wipe the drool, as he couldn't feel it or control it with his mouth forced open. The antibiotic wasn't working fast enough. I spoke to Brad, and we decided it would be best to go back to the ER and try and get him admitted into the hospital. At this point, Avery was no longer paranoid or hallucinating, but he'd had so little sleep, in now nearly forty-eight hours, that he wasn't exactly coherent or rational either.

At 4:00 p.m. I returned to the downtown ER, for several hours of waiting for blood and urine tests, an IV with an antibiotic drip, and a staff that treated Avery with suspicion and contempt. A friend who was a nurse later told me that an ER team's worst nightmare is an addict who comes in with erratic behavior. Staff has no idea what they are actually treating because addicts so often lie about their usage.

Avery didn't want to be admitted, but both the attending physician and I felt it would be best, but Avery, as an adult, could choose for himself. In a hospital room, they could watch him and continue IV treatment, which would work much faster that oral meds. Avery confided in me that he felt too claustrophobic in a hospital room; he needed to smoke, and if he had to get out of the room and leave before being discharged that insurance wouldn't pay for the stay, but if that's what I wanted him to do, he comply. He'd just come down off of meds that had him wanting to jump out of his skin.

I was caught in the middle, trying to influence him, but I couldn't force him. I became annoyed that Brad wasn't there helping me figure it out.

And to add to my anxiety, I'd scheduled a visit with Ryder in jail and needed to leave the hospital to get there in time. Latecomers were denied visits. Avery told me to leave to see Ryder; the nurse had said it would be another hour for test results, so I felt I could leave Avery alone for a bit. I went to the parking lot, distraught and emotionally spent. I couldn't find where I'd parked my car.

I called Brad. I was now hysterical.

"I can't find my fucking car. I'll miss the visit if I'm late. Avery's in there upset, and doesn't want to be admitted. But how can he come home?

His lip is still f'd up. They're treating him like he's a gutter addict in there. What the hell am I supposed to do?"

I was crying and running around the parking lot that was mostly dark, my sobs bouncing off of the concrete pavement and walls of the five-story parking ramp.

Brad was calm.

"What do you want me to do? Should I come down to the ER?"

"No, forget it." I hung up and continued to frantically look for my car. I finally found it and drove away crying, knowing I could never get to the jail in time. Brad called back.

"Ryder just called; I told him what was going on; he said it's okay if you miss the visit. Go back to the ER. If you need me to come down there, I will."

An hour later, Avery was admitted to the hospital, and he and I moved to a private room. I planned on staying with him overnight while he continued to have antibiotic IVs every four hours. He wanted me to stay with him. His lip was finally going down, and other than sleep deprivation, he was doing much better.

The admitting nurse came to our room with her cart of medical equipment to take his blood pressure, temperature, and other vitals. She then took a filled syringe and asked Avery to expose his thigh for a shot. As I asked what she was giving him, the needle punctured his skin, and as she emptied the fluid into his bloodstream she said, "Benadryl."

"*No!* What the fuck! He's allergic; he just came off twenty-four hours of paranoia and hallucinating. Didn't you check his records? Oh my God, you've got to be kidding me!?" I was livid. But it was too late.

With that, Avery's descent into psychotic hell was relaunched, and for the next four hours I was in a hospital room with a paranoid, obsessive-compulsive maniac. It was like trying to keep a hyper toddler safe in a room full of exposed razor blades. He wanted a cigarette; he wanted to go home; he pulled at the tubes on his arms, and picked at his lip. "Where's Ryder? Where's my phone? I need a cigarette, let me go home, mom, take me home now ... I gotta get out of here, give me the keys; I can't breathe in here ..." picking his bleeding lip with his fingernails, a pop tab, fingernail clippers ... tearing at his IV and on and on and on for hours.

I began to weep. At midnight, a nurse returned to begin the next antibiotic drip. She walked into a scene from a Hitchcock psycho episode. Avery was bouncing off the walls trying to get out of the room. He'd ripped off his IV, and I was crying and exhausted and still trying to contain him.

He settled down long enough for the next round of antibiotics to get hooked up to a fresh IV and to enter his system. I asked to talk to a doctor. A half an hour later, one arrived.

"What seems to be problem here?" he asked.

"We need to be discharged please." I brought him up to speed and made my case. "Avery has had three rounds of antibiotics now, and his lip is much better. Because of the mistake by the admitting nurse, I'm dealing with a paranoid maniac, and I cannot continue to contain this hysteria within the walls of this hospital room. We need to go home now, and he'll continue the antibiotics orally."

"I would agree the best thing, given your situation, would be to discharge you at this point. But I'm not the physician in charge. I'll need to go speak with him in the ER. If he's not too busy, I'm sure he'll sign off on this, but they just admitted several patients, so I'm not sure if he'll be available."

We never saw him again. By three that morning, I didn't care if I had to pay $20,000 right there. I was taking my kid home, and I'd deal with the consequences later. I couldn't take another minute of the torture.

When I told the nurse at the desk on our floor, she told me that we would have to be discharged by a doctor or sign a disclaimer form.

"Show me where to sign."

With that, we left for home.

That medical disaster seemed to make Avery push away from me. I think he'd felt over mothered and humiliated and helpless. The experience took its toll on him in every possible way. He missed his brother; he was a felon. He was going to federal prison, but he didn't know when, where, or for how long. No job, and no friends left, his life was empty, his future grim. And to add to the pile of misery, he was an addict trying to abstain. Those seventy-two hours of hellish medical trauma pushed him off an already crumbling eroded ledge.

I too was distraught for days, not only for all I'd been through with Avery, but now too the emotional distance he was creating. What happened to my intuition that we were attracting a higher frequency of events? It was the first time I'd questioned if there truly was a God. After all we'd been through, why would a random episode of terror and heartache, unrelated to addiction, have to happen to us? Just an extra added kick in the face for shits and giggles? What kind of malicious and twisted plot was playing out in our lives? Would it ever end? How would it end? That was the most terrifying demon I was trying not to dance with.

41

I N THE WEEKS THAT FOLLOWED the trauma with Avery's lip, the physical wounds healed, but the toll on his morale and self-esteem was devastating. He spent most of his time in his bedroom, Ryder's bedroom, actually, where he had been sleeping since his brother's return to Cass County Jail. When I asked how his day was, or how he was feeling, his replies were terse, usually one or two words. I knew he was pulling away from me, and that was concerning. I believed both of my sons pulled back when they were using or sliding in that direction. I felt, theorized anyway, that with less of an emotional connection to me, they were relieved of some of their addict's guilt.

Avery still picked up shifts bagging birdseed whenever he could, but it seemed the only ones available were overnighters. He still attended NA meetings and spent time at his sponsor's house some evenings. On March 10, Brad found some foil in his truck, which Avery had been driving. It was the sort of stark evidence we'd seen too many times before, and we sat Avery down to find out what was going on.

"I found this in the truck," Brad said, holding the piece of foil. "Tell me what you used it for."

Avery initially denied knowing how it got there but went on to confess.

"There's this break room at work, kind of a warming house where guys take smoke breaks. I found some pot in there and took one hit, not even enough to get high or show up on a drug test."

"You remember what we said at Thanksgiving, no more chances; if you use, you're out of here," Brad reminded him.

I could see the grief in Avery's face as the tears began to fall.

"I'm so sorry. It was stupid. But I've been doin' so good." He looked us in the eyes; his remorse was genuine. "Sometimes I feel like you lump me in with Ryder and all the times he's relapsed. I'm trying and doing mostly good."

I stayed out of the conversation except to nod and observe. My heart was breaking for him. We'd just barely moved past the lip debacle, and my son was at such a low point. My compassion for my sons was unrelenting.

"It's just tough to watch you take yourself down. What if you'd gotten pulled over, and the cops found this? With your legal status, the last thing you need is another violation." Brad was direct without shaming.

"I'm sorry," Avery replied. "I don't want to go to prison, and I know I've fucked it up so bad. But I'd never use heroin again. I'm scared of that shit. I never want to be dope sick again. Detoxing in jail was horrible. I'm not gonna let that happen again."

"We want so badly to help you get on track, but we're running out of patience. You've got to help yourself; we can only do so much," Brad said.

"I don't know how I got into this mess after watching Ryder go down. It's so fucked up. Heroin is the devil drug. If you have to kick me out, I understand."

Brad and I excused Avery so we had time to think and talk about our next move.

"Avery's been close to his sponsor and going to NA meetings. He's trying, more than Ryder ever has," I told Brad. "But I'll go along with your decision."

The truth was that neither Brad nor I wanted to kick him out. He had so little time left at home. We agreed to let it go. Avery was so vulnerable, and tough love seemed a sharp arrow to the heart, not the approach we felt was best.

We called him back and let him know.

"We're on your team, honey. Come to us when you feel at risk of using. Please trust us and let us help you," I told him.

"Thanks. I'll stay clean. The truth is nobody would sell to me anyway at this point. You don't have to worry about it, really," Avery said.

Later that night I said to Brad, "If our life was a movie, the audience would boo, throw popcorn at the screen, stand up and walk out. It'd be too depressing and far-fetched. No family has that much shit go down."

A couple of days later, I texted Avery while he was working an overnight shift and asked that he take care of Murphy the next day while I was at work. I didn't hear back, which was unusual. So in the morning before I went to work, I checked on him. His bedroom door was locked, but I got in through the adjacent bathroom door.

I found Avery lying on his back, his arms outstretched from his sides so his body was in the shape of a cross; his palms were facing up. There was a needle near his arm, having fallen out of a vein that was still bloodied. There was a spoon with some debris on his nightstand. I found his pulse. He was alive. I tried to coax him up, but he just curled up and moaned. I tried to ask him what he'd done, what he'd used. He said he wanted to kill himself.

I called Brad; he'd just gotten to Kellogg for his on-call weekend.

"You need to come home. Avery's incoherent, there's a used needle next to his arm. I don't know what he used." Panic was not an option; my rational self kicked in.

"Get him into the ER anyway you can ... call an ambulance if you have to; I'm leaving now. I'll meet you there in an hour."

All I could get out of Avery was that he'd shot up heroin residue. I calmly continued to coax him out of bed, then downstairs, and then finally into the car. He kept making me promise not to put him in the hospital again. The last place I wanted to go was back there after all the hell we'd been through with them just weeks ago. But I had no choice because that's where we had insurance coverage.

The ER physician, Dr. Dawson, was immensely empathetic and didn't judge him. His gentle kindness made me cry. I had to explain our situation; my God, what an admission. Our story kept getting more perilous and complicated.

Afraid that Brad would be angry with him, Avery initially didn't want him to come to the ER, but finally agreed. He also didn't want to submit to a urine test. Avery was aware that using was a violation of his pretrial probation and that it could send him right back to jail until his court date. Brad arrived, and I'd just sent him a text: "we have to contact Avery's attorney asap." I didn't want Avery to hear me. I didn't want him getting upset for any reason. I said I was going to the bathroom and called Gavin

Campbell, now Avery's private attorney. He agreed to meet me at the law firm at three thirty.

We spoke with a social worker, and she assured Avery that his situation was confidential. No law enforcement would be called, she said, which was his right to privacy. Once Avery's condition was stable, the social worker recommended that we admit him to the Heartland psych ward a few miles away. Avery agreed, and we committed to arrive by 1:00 p.m. Before we went to the psych ward, we brought Avery home to shower. Brad and I assumed that once we dropped him off that he'd be going to jail from there, then his court date, then prison. So we wanted just a little more time with him.

We learned that the night before, standing outside of an NA meeting, Avery had been chased and roughed up by some drive-by druggies. The threatening consequences he encountered seemed never-ending.

Once we got him to the facility, he had to have a cigarette first, then once in the building he had to use the bathroom. He was stalling. Avery took forever in the bathroom, and Brad finally went in to make sure he wasn't harming himself or using. I waited in the hall by the gift store, where I noticed a plaque on display with the words: "A mother's love is the glue that holds the family together." In the background, "Strength" was etched. I didn't feel like I was holding anything together at this point except my composure. That was somehow on autopilot.

What was left to happen to our family in this unrelenting painful saga? Suicide attempt, yet another trip to the ER, and now the psych ward. It was almost becoming impossible for me to believe it anymore or to process it logically or intuitively. As we approached the entrance to the psych department, Brad's eyes were glossy, pooling tears. We hugged Avery and turned to leave. I was devastated, but I didn't feel like I could let down yet. I still needed to go to the attorney's office.

At Anderson Law firm, while waiting to see Gavin, I noticed the newspaper headlines in *the River Bend Forum*.

On the front page: TODAY WAS A BAD DAY, then the story of a police officer that had committed suicide.

On the front page of the variety section: TWIN TASTES, about two chefs at a high end hotel.

Sports front page: UNCERTAIN FUTURE, I don't recall the story.

242

And on the final section, the headline was: DANCE MACHINE.

Whenever I allowed myself to picture better days, I'd imagine the four of us at a celebration, such as a wedding dance. I'd picture dancing with each of them; Avery, Ryder, and Brad taking turns leading me in a lively jitterbug or another flawless ballroom dance. At some point in time, we would have something to celebrate; I had to keep believing that.

Those four headlines seemed in sync with our journey so far, and I hoped that somehow in some way that the last headline was an omen.

I met with Gavin and learned that any Cass County Jail time Avery served would count toward his ultimate sentencing, even though he was being held by the federal government. At that point, Gavin wanted to know if we would continue to allow Avery to stay in our home if he didn't get arrested for this latest violation. If so, he told me, there was a possibility he wouldn't have to go to jail until his sentencing.

My phone kept ringing during our conversation. When I finally went to turn it off, I saw it was Avery calling to tell me they were discharging him. What??? He'd been in for less than three hours, but they'd deemed that he was fine and was no threat to himself. I called Brad, and we decided to allow him home. Things were happening so fast that we were simply reacting and trying to maintain emotional stability.

When I went to pick him up, Avery was loopy, still high on heroin, I assumed. I didn't understand why the medical staff felt it was fine to discharge him. I had lost faith in the hospital system weeks ago. We got into the car, and Ryder called my cell phone. He was relieved we were allowing Avery home because he felt jail was the worst place for Avery, that as low as he was, jail would only isolate and depress him further.

While sitting in the car, still in the parking lot with Avery in the passenger seat and Ryder on my phone, I said to both of them, "You two have got to find God. There's nothing left Brad and I can do for you. You need to find God's grace and lean into it. That's your only hope of surviving addiction."

Avery and I stopped to eat at the Main Avenue Diner restaurant on the way home. I could tell he was high in subtle ways. He'd put a disgusting amount of ketchup on his hash browns, and was entirely amused by it. The lag and tone of his voice, the heavy eyelids, subtle details that would be easy to dismiss if I hadn't absolutely known he was high—mannerisms he and Ryder had explained away as being overtired from working nights all those years. I realized how easy it had been to hide their use from me all this time.

I got Avery home, and texted Brad that he was still high, then I took a nap. I was totally exhausted in every regard.

Avery's attorney was required to tell the prosecution what happened. Drug use under any circumstances was a violation of his pretrial probation. We assumed they would remove him and put him into jail or a halfway house until his hearing, but the prosecution allowed him to remain in our custody. Avery was somewhat resentful that I'd told his attorney about the suicide attempt.

"I could have just been in and out of the psych ward, and they would have never known," he told us.

Brad reminded him that the biggest mistake we could make was to keep secrets from his attorney.

Later I watched tennis, staying up to see Sloane Stevens play Anna Ivanovic at a tournament in Indian Wells, California. Somehow just listening to a long rally, the rhythm of a bouncing tennis ball, the graceful movements, and the powerful strokes of those beautiful athletes was soothing to me.

The next day at work, I was fighting tears all day. Shelia asked if I wanted to talk, but I said I was afraid to, knowing I'd start crying. At eleven, I went into her office and let it all out. I also told Scott what was going on, as I'd probably need some time off. When I told him about the suicide attempt, all he could say was, "I'm speechless." His eyes conveyed his concern and kindness.

"I'm grateful for a job where people care about me, and I enjoy coming to work. I need the distraction; it's good for me. I'm strong; I'll be okay," I told him.

That evening, Brad and I discussed Avery's situation.

"I think one of us has to be home all the time for a while," I said. "Avery's so vulnerable. It's critical that we make the right choices now, or we'll have to live with horrible regret."

"We can't stop working. We've just accumulated thousands of dollars in medical bills in a matter of weeks," Brad said.

"We're not going to die broke, Brad. We've got more important things to worry about. Avery's tried to kill himself. We have to make sure he's not alone for a while."

"You're right. I'll get online and drop my next trip."

Ryder qualified for a work-release program through jail. He was working at a business assembling screen windows. Work-release inmates were also allowed to attend programming at Holy Savior Church in south River Bend. They bused the eligible inmates over three times a week: two evenings weekly for Bible study and a life skills class. Then on Sundays they could come and join the general assembly at the church service, and loved ones could join them.

Ryder called home that night while riding the bus back to jail after attending church service.

"Hi, Mom. How's Avery doing?" Ryder had been so scared knowing he'd almost lost his brother. He felt so helpless not being able to come home and see him.

"He's doing pretty well. Brad and I are going to take time off from work so one of us is always home for a while."

"That's good, Mom; I'm relieved to hear that. I can't talk long, but I've got something else to tell you." There was a slight pause. "I gave my life over to Christ tonight."

I immediately began to cry and continued to listen.

"I'm scared. What's gonna happen when I'm out of here, and I don't have to answer to anyone about drugs? How am I gonna quit? So I prayed with Pastor William, and we told God I was ready to change my life."

I continued to cry, unable to speak.

"And, Mom, I really want you to meet Pastor William. I told him you're spiritual, and all the shit our family's been through. He wants to meet you."

We made plans to meet at Holy Savior Church the following Sunday so I could meet the blessed soul that led my son to God.

That unexpected good news from Ryder felt like a heated blanket had been wrapped around me. The encroaching despair that was taking over my soul and suffocating my hopes began to soften.

Avery had been quiet, sleeping a lot. He'd woken up at three that afternoon, and later he went to a meeting. I watched tennis, more of the

Indian Wells tournament, most of the evening. It was getting late, and I was starting to wonder where Avery was, so I texted him: "Where r u?"

He replied: "At Taylor's's getting my head on straight. Using never got anyone anywhere but the hospital or jail or the graveyard. Our family's been to the hospital and jail I can promise you those are the only two places we will have to go. If I wasn't meant to stay sober and do great things that attempt would've been successful but it wasn't and by God that's a sign to me that I'm destined for much better things than drugs or prison."

I wrote back: "Thank God ur alive and have those awareness's so soon after u were in such a dark place. I agree with everything u wrote."

He continued the string: "Like I'm so much better than all that shit so is Ryder. I can't let something like drugs hold me back I can do so much better than what I have done already mom."

Me back: "100% true. I'm so grateful Tayor is there for you. Tell him so plz Ur so much better for sure and ur so young. So much of a great life ahead for you and Ryder ... Our family"

We never heard back from Cahill Hedland Productions regarding their interest to feature Avery in an episode of *Stylist Next Door*. Maybe they thought Avery didn't have enough drama in his life, or maybe our family life just wasn't colorful enough.

Yeah, that's it—too dull, not enough going on. Lord have mercy.

42

NEVER ONCE DOUBTED MY PARENTS were on the other side guiding and protecting us. I'd had moments of disillusion about my beliefs in God, prayer, feng shui, and intuition, but my terrified heart remained quietly, humbly, and at times distantly connected to the pulse of God's grace.

Beneath the human anguish, my soul whispered that God had a master plan, and every detail of our unfolding nightmare happened by design. Whatever occurred, I kept finding a way to handle it. Were we being dealt a hand of excessive pain? Or were we heading toward a destiny that would bring magnificent blessings? Time would tell. Aligning with my soul's perspective was the key to transcending the pain.

Essentially that meant letting go.

I believed my soul was eternal, connected to God, and seeking to align with my human self to manifest my life purpose. I believe the same is true for everyone. So in the darkest hours, I was able to calm my fear and connect with that truth. I also believe that death is a passage to the afterlife, and the worst suffering that can happen is finite and could be survived.

I tried to focus on the future, and in reflection I realize my commute to work had been an opportunity to visualize my hopes and desires. I'd spend 90 percent of my driving time listening to my iTune playlists. I chose music that lifted me, the majority of it country, and I'd envision our future. My fantasies were grandiose. I would imagine that my book was published and that a screenplay had been adapted from it. I'd picture a cast party for the actors and the filming crew that were shooting scenes for it in Detroit Lakes. I'd imagine an exclusive cast party that included Oscar-winning actors at the Detroit Lakes Pavilion toasting with family and friends. Brad, Ryder, Avery, and I would arrive in a limo for a grand entrance. Lots of dancing—"Dance Machine" just like the *River Bend Forum* headline I'd seen at Anderson Law. Most importantly, I saw my sons' addiction in permanent remission, and both Ryder and Avery as healthy, thriving men, inspiring others who suffered with addiction. That was just one of the many scenes I'd play in my head to attract providence and transcend emotional pain.

Managing despair, dealing with crisis, and coping is a personal journey. I happen to be someone who isolates from others, though I did not feel a separation. Even though I didn't keep loved ones informed on the ever-changing details of our struggle, I felt their love and support. I never chose to search out a support group such as Alanon, but that wasn't because I don't believe that it could be of profound benefit to others. My choice to isolate, and battle my demons individually, privately, is not necessarily what I'd recommend to anyone, but it's what worked for me. And I had Brad. Being true to oneself, connecting with intuition, and healthy self-care, would be the best advice I could give to anyone, and I was most certainly abiding by that creed.

I continued to pray, and my family and friends prayed for us too. My intuition was as much a part of me as the golden hue blended into my hazel eyes. I believed intuition to be the voice of my soul and my connection to divine guidance. It required tremendous courage to stay the course but I truly believed that living in alignment with my soul was my destiny and the best choice I could make for everyone concerned.

The next full moon was approaching on March 16, the day before St. Patrick's Day. I felt it would be an especially auspicious occasion to perform a full moon blessing in my home on the eve of a holiday honoring an Irish saint. My mother's side of the family, the Cronin's, were of Irish descent.

Feng shui was not separate from my belief in God. Rather it was one of the tools from the Divine to help me influence destiny, manifest my intentions, and live with hope. Who knew how much worse it could be if not for my eclectic beliefs and faith? Yes, our current situation was horrendous, but my children were still alive, and given their choices, that was nothing short of a miracle.

Feng shui was not just about performing a blessing in my home each full moon. It was also about creating an environment in my home where

I felt comfortable and supported—building a sanctuary to recharge and live joyfully. I chose décor that was uplifting and resonated with my vision of the life I aspired to live. I avoided décor elements that depicted scarcity, sorrow, or any other portrayal contrary to what I was looking to attract into my life presently and in the future.

When I was pregnant with my sons, I took up cross-stitch until pregnancy-induced carpel tunnel set in. I framed one of my completed projects—a nursery pattern in yellow, peach, lavender, and pastel blues with teddy bears, ducks, balloons, and rocking horses. It featured the boys' names, weight, and birth date. This remained on display in our master bathroom for the seven years we'd lived in our home in Timber Crest.

It occurred to me that twenty-two years later, perhaps this was energetically and subconsciously retaining them in the past, as helpless infants. I realized the symbolism for the first time, and, clearly, replacing it was long past due. In its place I hung a framed piece I had, a collage of blooming sunflowers. I set the intention that each time I saw the sun (son) flowers, I'd think of Avery and Ryder, no longer helpless to addiction and dependent on us, but instead as bright, blooming, and flourishing in the beautiful life that was possible for them. That's part of how feng shui worked. I knew what the décor represented to me, and the intention it was meant to influence. So each time I saw it, my intention was activated, even though it was predominantly a subconscious process. When your entire home is designed intentionally, to activate your desires, then you reap the benefits of feng shui continuously.

I was implementing feng shui to live in alignment with my soul's aspirations. Clearly that plan, that path, had not been sheltered, predictable, or enviable, but I believed I was on the journey that I'd come into this life to experience, and hopefully contribute to others as a result.

One week after Avery's suicide attempt, one of Ryder and Avery's closest friends overdosed on heroin and was in a coma. His family kept vigil, praying they'd not have to pull the plug and end his life. Lucas was a couple years younger than our boys. He'd been at our homes hundreds of times. His grandmother and I had spoken on several occasions about our common struggles, comparing our notes on treatment options, strategy, and heartache. My sons were beating enormous odds, and there were far more life-threatening situations they'd encountered that I didn't even know about. Lucas's critical status was shockingly close to home. I could hear fear taunting from the shadows. How much longer would my sons be spared a similar or worse fate?

The day after we'd learned of Lucas's threatening circumstances, Avery was pulled over and given a DUI at eleven in the morning. He passed the breathalyzer, but the cop brought him to Cass County Jail anyway. Avery claimed he was completely sober, and nothing proved otherwise. He was let go after several hours. Bottom line: every cop in the area knew him, the car he drove, and that he'd been busted. They wanted him off the streets, now.

I was excited to visit Ryder for the first time since he'd shared his experience with Pastor William. I was curious about the church and excited to meet Pastor William. I hoped, of course, that he would lead the way for Avery. Mostly I was grateful they both were alive with hopes of recovery.

Several days after Ryder committed his life to Christ, Avery and I went to visit him in jail. The visits to an inmate in work release status were less involved. We simply walked through security, presented our IDs, and entered a room steps away with four visitation stations. Our side of the glass had two phones, enabling a three-way party line. Ryder entered and sat down. His hair was very short and sticking up in stiff angles. He'd already worked 7:00 a.m. till noon, and he'd been napping just before we arrived.

"How are you?" I was expecting him to be upbeat and pick up on his experience with Pastor William. I wanted to hear more about it.

"I got a bad cold; I feel crappy."

Even though he wasn't feeling good, I could still tell he'd softened. His angry defensiveness was gone.

He and Avery talked about doing time in Cass County Jail, where Avery would be placed if he began serving time prior to his sentencing. Ryder downplayed the experience; the worst of it was boredom and inconvenience.

"It's just that there's so much time to kill. I wish I liked to read—that would help a lot. Dad could do time standing on his head as much as he reads." Ryder smiled.

We laughed.

"Yeah, no shit, that's all he does at home. He never even watches TV," Avery said.

It was true. Brad easily read an average of fifteen books a month. The boys were read to every day when they were younger, beginning in infancy.

"I pick up all the overtime I can get, anything to break up the day. You know it's boring when I'd rather be working overtime assembling screen windows."

A new work-release policy now allowed a sixty-mile radius for travel to jobsites. That would allow Ryder to work with the Lakeland dock installation crew once the ice was out on the lakes. It was a crazy stroke of good luck and timing for him, and for all of us.

"You'll be able to start at Lakeland soon enough. I'm excited to be able to see you every day at work." I smiled

"Me too; that'll be awesome to be outside all day, out of here, out of River Bend. I can't wait."

Avery asked me to leave for the last ten minutes so he could talk to Ryder alone. I didn't mind at all; I understood.

On the ride home, Avery said, "It really helps me to see Ryder's doing okay in there. If he can do it, so can I."

"I was thinking about everything, Avery, and I want you to consider something."

"What's that?"

"Gavin told me that any time you spend in county jail will count toward the total time you get sentenced to federal prison."

I paused, knowing he wouldn't like what was coming. "It's been rough for you on the outside, the DUI, the job situation isn't going anywhere, and you're just killing time until your sentencing. That's not a good situation when you're trying not to use."

Avery mostly just left the house to get cigarettes or to attend NA meetings or to spend time with Taylor, his sponsor. He still seemed unstable, though much better than the previous week.

"Mom, I know what you're gonna say. Just go in now. Right?" He wasn't angry.

"I think it makes a lot of sense. At least that way you're moving forward. Getting some of your time served behind you is actually progressing toward a goal."

I stayed quiet so he could let my idea settle in. I didn't want to be pushy; that approach would surely backfire. Brad and I couldn't trust Avery to stay clean or to be safe, and we couldn't stay home all day every day. Something had to give. We were still one month away from his hearing and two months from his sentencing.

"Next time you talk to Ryder, tell him how much it means to me that he's doing well in there. Okay? I don't want to tell him, but I want him to know."

"Will do."

I knew the change of topic was Avery's way of taking time to think. He also seemed kind of loopy, as though he was high or sleep deprived. I asked him about it on the way home, and he said he was just tired. He slept for five hours when we got home.

I so badly wanted him to begin serving time. It made so much sense. But, of course, if a person has a choice, why wouldn't he or she choose freedom? I'd come to know that the best way to influence them, and Brad too, was a gentle push, then let go, another gentle push, then let go. Allow them to lean into a change of heart slowly without pressure or nagging. For me, it always came back to trust, letting go, and detachment from outcome, strategy that was contrary to serving ego.

I spent the rest of the day and evening cleaning my entire house, much neglected from working and my commitment to writing. I also replaced the baby pictures of the boys on the brick fireplace mantel with some of my books. That area of our home represents the knowledge sector of the Bagua, so it was a great place to display books. At midnight, I did a space clearing and blessing. I prayed nine Hail Marys in each life area.

The next morning, Avery and I left to join Ryder for Sunday services at Holy Savior Church. On the way, Avery spoke confidently that it was a good choice for him to start serving time, to "self-surrender," as we referred to it. He agreed that we should get in touch with Elle, his newly assigned federal probation officer, and Gavin Campbell, his attorney, and find out what we needed to do to set it up.

Once we entered the large lobby and commons area in the church, Janet, a greeter for the newcomers, approached us. I assumed she was a lifelong church-going woman with a sane and blessed life. I was wrong. She had marched through hell. She'd been a desperate alcoholic over twenty years; one of her daughters was a recovering meth addict, and another daughter survived a brain injury. I met Pastor William. If ever someone personified Christ to me, it was Pastor William. He was about seventy years old, gentle, kind, and so endearing. I hugged him and thanked him for being there for Ryder. I felt the same unconditional loving paternal energy I'd felt from my dad.

We entered the large sanctuary, an amphitheater floor plan, and heard loud Christian rock music coming from what looked like a combined altar/ stage area. There were at least twelve musicians, vocals, drums, and guitars, harmonizing in praise of God. Large white paper globes, like Chinese lanterns, were suspended from the ceiling and gave the illusion that they were floating. EXPERIENCE GOD LIVE LIFE was illuminated by a projector onto a massive area on the wall, with lighted neon blue rings in the background. The area where we sat was dim, but the altar area was illuminated. There were no depictions of suffering in the design or décor. There weren't any stations of the cross or crucifixion images, which I'd seen in every Catholic Church I'd ever been in. It was so welcoming and elevating.

My sons were in front of me as the three of us walked toward the pews in the back of the church where the inmates mostly sat. I was overcome with a profound sense of peace, and I began to cry. I tapped my sons on their shoulders, and they turned around. I said, "We made it."

In that moment was the first time in five years I was confident that we'd rise out of the terrifying abyss. My aversion of church all those years was so narrow-minded and presumptuous, but I trust that everything had happened according to God's plan for us and that it wasn't supposed to happen until now, in this way.

"Oh, Mama, don't cry, or I'll cry too." Ryder hugged me.

Once we sat down Ryder said, "Remember when you asked me if I was getting anything out of the Sunday services?"

I nodded yes.

"Well, I lied when I said yes. But ever since I've been listening, and, Mom, I'm hearing stuff that you've been telling me." He smiled

"Really, like what?" I asked.

"Like how watching drug shows on TV can affect your choices. You know, how you've always said, 'What you think about, you bring about'? Too much of that shit, and your brain goes to mush."

He had his arm around me most of the service.

We listened as Pastor Brian spoke about how 2.2 billion people have heard Billy Graham's voice and how it was because one person told Graham about God. It just takes one person touching your life, and we're all called to spread the word. Avery enjoyed the experience too. He said it wasn't a stuffy church; he was referring to the way people acted. He wanted to come back.

Several of the other inmates thought Avery was Ryder. One inmate joked that Avery should wear Ryder's ankle GPS tracker and give Ryder a day off.

I would need the loving, uplifting energy to carry me further. We'd not quite escaped from the abyss.

43

A VERY WAS SERIOUSLY CONSIDERING OUR discussion about turning himself in early. The official term was "voluntarily detaining" himself. It was easier for me to think of it as "self-surrender."

The idea was for Avery to willingly place himself into custody before his sentencing. The time he spent in Cass County Jail before the federal sentencing would count as time served. Ultimately it would mean a shorter stint in a federal prison.

He just wanted to have a conversation with Elle, his federal probation officer, about it before he committed to it. Avery scheduled the appointment with her for the upcoming Friday and asked me to go with him. For Avery, the most difficult aspects of his situation were the unknowns. How long he'd be in prison and which prison he'd be going to were concerns he couldn't turn off in his brain.

Avery had been increasingly elusive, gone for longer periods without saying where. It was getting harder for me to keep track of him, and I was concerned he would use now that he was close to being incarcerated. I'd seen that pattern in the past with Ryder, one more binge before getting locked up. It had been two weeks since Avery's suicide attempt. Heroin was obviously available to him and was back in his system. Brad was scheduled to be gone for nine days, with a couple of overnights in Minneapolis between Asia trips. I dreaded being the solo parent for that many days given what we'd just been through. I tried to talk to Brad about it. "You're going to be gone for nine days, and I don't know what to expect. This whole thing is so unsettling. I feel like he is using. None of what he claims seems to add up."

Brad got defensive. "I can't afford to drop another trip. I don't know what you want me to do."

"I'm not trying to pick a fight," I said calmly. "I have no one else to talk to about this, and I don't know what to think, what to believe."

An unexpected thud startled me. A bird had flown into the window behind me. Murphy started barking. The bird lay still, stunned by the impact. I felt despondency spreading throughout my body; the previous weeks of chaos, the years of assaulting consequences, were locking me up. There had been too much at stake for far too long.

"Avery claims he's with his sponsors all night watching movies. Really? That seems so strange to me. And when I do see him, he's off somehow."

"What do you mean, 'he's off'?"

Brad was growing impatient.

"His mannerisms are like when he was wacked on Benadryl. Spacey, spastic almost, not near as bad though. He's either overtired, high, or the drugs have taken their toll on his brain function."

I could see Brad's frustration begin to boil. "I don't know what you expect me to do. I have to work. Christ, I've got three grand in medical bills sitting on my desk. Somebody's got to pay 'em."

I let it go at that. I'd said my piece. I would just have to deal with whatever unfolded. I wasn't mad or resentful, but I felt myself feeling more anxious, like I'd had no sleep and too much caffeine on an empty stomach. I didn't trust Avery, and I was giving up. It was possible Avery was spending all that time with his sponsors. Either he was committed to working the NA program or more f'd up than ever. I was either totally paranoid or completely on the mark. I noticed the dazed bird that banged into the window had flown away.

When I woke up Thursday, I could tell Avery hadn't slept at home. I sent him a text: "u need to stay in touch with me u have not slept at home in several days I will call the attorney if u don't come home today and talk to me am concerned you're playing me"

Three hours later, no word from Avery, so I sent another text: "call me now or I assume ur using and will do what I have to do to save your life"

He finally called, then came home about three that afternoon. He looked great, coherent and put together, and I was fairly certain he wasn't high. We had an entirely sane conversation, and I told him, "You can't keep disappearing on me. If you go missing again, I'll assume you're in trouble. I'm scared, and I'm running out of courage and strength."

He was reassuring. "Okay, Mom, I'm sorry; I don't want you to worry. I love you."

"I will wake you in the morning so we're on time for the appointment with Elle," I said

"Good idea. Thanks, Mom."

Thursday night when I went to bed, he was at a meeting. I fell asleep at eleven.

In the morning he wasn't home, and his bed had not been slept in. I was scared Avery was hurt or worse. It made no sense given his awareness of how I felt about his elusive behavior, his genuine remorse about causing me worry, and his commitment to be accountable. I could only assume that if he was not answering his phone, it was because he couldn't.

I went to see Elle alone. Her office was in the federal courthouse building in downtown River Bend, another destination inside of a mile radius from the Anderson and Woodland Law Firms, Prairieview, Island Park, and the county courthouse—our tidy, efficient circle of damage control. I was denied entrance the first time because cell phones weren't allowed in the building, and I left to bring it to my car. I returned and passed through the metal detector and took the elevator and was shown to her office.

I waited for fifteen minutes. No cell phone to check if Avery was getting in touch with me. My emotions were bouncing around like a Whack a Mole game at the carnival. I kept trying to pound my anxieties into submission, but they all kept taking turns popping up. Fear, guilt, shame, remorse, and despair persisted the more I tried to subdue them.

Elle was in her thirties, I guessed. She was pretty, professional, and intelligent. She welcomed me, and I asked her if she'd heard from Avery.

"No. I'm surprised he's not here. He's been very reliable."

I felt a visceral response not unlike drinking black coffee to sober up. The alcohol and caffeine collide, and you're not sure what you need worse, a bed to pass out on or a toilet to be sick into. My remaining shattered fragments of courage were now loose and dangling.

She continued, "I think I have a solution that you'll all feel good about." She smiled and explained the option to assign Avery to a halfway house until his sentencing.

"We've talked about that, actually. Avery tells us drugs are easily available there. We need him in jail, where he'll be safe there, and sober," I said.

She acknowledged there was truth to that.

I explained to Elle that Brad and I couldn't handle him anymore. His suicide attempt had been less than two weeks before, and I was afraid he was going to use. Avery had no job, a DUI, and nothing good for him on the outside. Brad and I were missing work, and the emotional toll was debilitating.

Then I said, "If he's still alive, Avery feels self-surrender is the best choice now."

She agreed and said if Avery was willing, it was simply a matter of paperwork that would move quickly once Avery showed up.

I got to my car and checked my phone, but still had no word from Avery. I drove to Anderson Law Firm to update Gavin. He explained that a hearing was required to revoke his pretrial probation, so it wouldn't happen overnight—it would take several days at least. I would miss another day of work. It had started to snow, heavy wet snow blown sideways by strong gusts of wind. It would have been a bad day to travel to work anyway.

When I got home, I put some essential oil on my wrists, a blend called Valor, which claims to stimulate courage. I'd fallen asleep many nights inhaling it with my wrists next to my face, my palms together in prayer. I lay in bed with my rosary in hand, inhaling Valor.

"Please bring him home safe, God. I love him so dearly."

All I could do was lean into the pain and attempt to surrender it. Just like a yoga pose: stretch into the pain, then breathe and release, sink deeper, stretch farther, manage the pain by releasing it, breathe. My mantra was in rhythm with my breath; inhale … "God's" … exhale "hands." God's Hands.

Finally, at 11:46, Avery called. He'd accepted an invitation to spend the night with a girl; he'd overslept, his phone died, and he forgot his charger at home. Oh, well, yes … yes, just as I'd suspected. God in heaven, did this child have any idea what he's putting me through?

He was home an hour later, and we talked about self-surrender. He was struggling with the decision. But later that afternoon, he'd talked to Ryder and made peace with it. I helped him write a letter to the judge explaining his reasons.

3/21/14

Dear Judge Stevens,

Thank you for taking time to read my letter. I want you to know why I made the decision to voluntarily detain myself and begin my incarceration as soon as possible.

Firstly, I know and believe that I have made serious mistakes and that I owe a debt to society for my illegal actions. It is not possible for me to express how deeply sorry I am for my choices that led to my arrest in August 2013. I am making the choice to self-surrender so that I may begin my new life as a healthy, productive, contributing member of society. The first step to my new direction in life is to serve the time I will owe post sentencing. I recognize incarceration is a necessary step for me and that's why I do not want to delay it any longer.

Every day I'm incarcerated is one day closer to my freedom and my future. I'm taking responsibility, and making what I believe to be a pro-active decision. I'm maturing into a responsible man that is seeking to put his past behind him and find a way to serve others with what I've learned from my mistakes.

I aspire to complete an education and move on to the life and the person my parents raised me to be. I now recognize how blessed I've been to have had such a solid foundation beneath me, and the love and support of two remarkable people, my parents. They have done everything possible to help me rise above my mistakes, man up to the consequences and move on to a positive and healthy lifestyle. All of those plans begin with putting my incarceration behind me one day at a time. That is why I willingly and respectfully choose to self-surrender.

I e-mailed a copy of the letter to Elle and to Gavin. I requested that Gavin forward it to Judge Stevens.

The next morning, Saturday, I got in my car to leave for work. The cord I needed to play my iTunes through the car stereo was missing. I got out and opened Avery's car door to look for it. I saw syringes and a paper cup with water in it. Once I'd gone to bed, he'd apparently found his way to using.

I tried to wake him up. He'd stir and moan, but I couldn't get him awake. Brad was in Minneapolis between Asia trips. I phoned him and told him what I'd found and that Avery was asleep. Brad wanted me to get him back into Heartland ER, but I said that's the last place I wanted to go. We agreed that I'd take him to Praireview and try to get him admitted until he was taken into custody. I couldn't handle him anymore, not alone. I was collapsing emotionally.

"What if he won't cooperate?" I asked.

"Call the cops."

Brad wanted to know if he should come home. I wanted to say, "Are you fucking kidding me? Does it get any more crisis than this? Do you really have to ask? Yes, take the next flight; I can't do this; I'm wasted; I'm afraid; I'm breaking down; please come home now. How can you expect me to handle this alone?"

What I said instead was, "Take the trip. I'll handle it." I knew that's what he wanted to hear.

I resent that he didn't come home, but I didn't resent him.

I called Prairieview, and they agreed to do an evaluation. I was able to get Avery in the car by telling him Ryder was there, and we had to go see him. When he realized I'd duped him, he was furious.

Avery was angry, acting like a caged lion, but with the counselor at Prairieview, he became rational, sincere, and agreeable. He knew how to play the game and said what they wanted to hear. They deemed him ineligible to be admitted. I looked like an overbearing mother trying to dump off my perfectly reasonable son. I'd told him that he needs to be admitted or I will call the cops. He wasn't admitted, and I didn't want to call the cops. On the way home, Avery told me that he'd planned to give his life to Christ on Sunday with Ryder.

Really? I didn't believe a word he said at that point.

When we returned to the house, I told him he had to stay home, that I couldn't trust him anymore. At that, he switched back into whiney, victim mode. "I don't want you to visit me in jail; no letters, no talking. I will call you when I get out, but I know I'll never live with you again."

He went upstairs to his room.

The rest of the afternoon he sent me texts from his bedroom.

"r relationship will never be the same … I will never be the same kid again. This harsh of punishment for not using is hard for me to take that's all I'll say about it … Just glad ur happy for once in the past 21yrs … a son can't not love his mother but it'll be different in 4 years when I get out."

"I'm nowhere near happy not even in the same galaxy of happy I'm in hell right now," I responded.

"we all lose then I guess"

"yes that's true"

I stayed frozen in the living room, watching whatever was on TV.

More texting from Avery: "i know u care an love me mom but this stuck at home thing makes me hate everything. I do it for u but makes me hate being here. I hate this mom I'm sorry for everything."

I responded: "I should have kept you safer years ago."

"Ur my mother a bear cub always loves his mom an I always will but I hate everything else I am an inmate at Acorn Drive county jail I feel like. But I can't stop loving my own mother but I can hate everything else I love u hate everything else about my life all I wanna do is find someone to hangout with like a girl or a friend but I can't so I hate everything."

"got it"

"after I get to see Ryder 2mrrw I could care less how long I sit in jail/prison cuz if this is what its gonna be like as a free man then send me away I hate it … I don't blame you at all I just hate everything bcuz nothin good ever happens to me there is nothing up there nobody would screw me over this bad if there was an upper power they'd know I didn't use an wldnt of punished me like this. … sorry ill quit bugging u, ur only one I hav left talk to since I told everyone else I can never hang again they don't talk to me but ill just shut up an go back to bed"

"come talk to me," I said.

Avery stayed in his room.

Who was going to help me now? I had to keep him stable and safe until he self-surrendered. I put calls in to both Elle and Gavin, letting them know we were in full-blown crisis and needed this to go as quickly as possible. I heard back from Gavin very quickly.

"Don't call the cops. Gut it out until next week."

He was getting the process moving as quickly as possible

Avery's texting was tearing at my heart, and to know that he'd be going away in a matter of days, and to God knows where, and for how long. Federal prison, my God, how can this be my precious son's fate? And there I was hoping to get him there as quickly as possible. It had come to that. I bottomed out facing a lose/lose of epic proportion.

It was early afternoon. I didn't want to call anyone because so much had gone on, and I didn't know where to begin to explain what I was facing. The back-story alone would have taken a half hour of conversation. I felt alone in a way I'd never known before. I prayed for help from someone who loved me. Out of nowhere, as though she'd picked up my radar, my dear friend, a healer, Christeen, stopped by unannounced. One of her specialties was zoneology, a precise and deep foot massage. She rubbed my feet and later called Silent Unity, and they prayed for my family.

I mostly cried. She left after an hour.

Avery finally came downstairs because he needed cigarettes and wanted to walk somewhere to buy some. He was edgy and needed nicotine badly, he said. I told him the only way he could leave was if I drove.

"Why would you do that. I'm your no-good loser of a son."

I drove one mile to a convenience store and bought him a carton, some Nero Sleep and Bliss drinks, muffins, cookies, and lemonade. I spent $64 on smokes and junk food at a gas station, a first for me. Avery waited in the car, not wanting to run into anyone he knew. Once we got home, he fell asleep before having the cigarette for which he was so desperate. Murphy puked up both her meals that day. She felt the stress level in the house.

Avery napped, and I dozed intermittently on the sofa watching tennis on TV so I would hear if he tried to leave. Avery woke up about 5:00 p.m.

in the same angry, self-pitying mood, trying to pick a fight with me. He wanted to leave, felt I was being unfair—that he should be able to have freedom and enjoy the weekend before surrendering.

I wanted only to keep him alive and out of trouble before he surrendered.

I offered to take a drive so he could get out of the house. We headed to Island Park as he whined at me the entire way. He seemed to think I was happy about spending my weekend as his warden.

"My job is to keep you alive," I told him. "Lucas is hooked up to life support right now. Do you really want to condemn my decisions?"

Avery heard nothing I said.

"You can feel sorry for yourself all weekend, pick fights with me, resent me, or you can appreciate your home, Murphy, and me. Once this weekend passes, at some point in time you're going to feel awful for treating me the way you are."

He left the car at Island Park and smoked a cigarette in the cold, damp air, standing next to the tennis courts. Then we drove back home.

I was reminded of a cold but bright and sunny November day when I had offered to take my mom for a ride. She was frail, homebound mostly, and less than a week away from death. Her skeletal body fit on the seat of her walker, and I got her into the car. She was so delighted, like a little kid on her way to play on the swings at the park. We drove around the older, beautiful homes in the Eighth Street South neighborhood, just beyond downtown. The sun was warm on her face; she smiled, so content to be out of the house with sunshine on her cheeks. She so appreciated looking around, getting out and about. She was born and raised in River Bend, and every neighborhood we passed provoked a memory. It was such a simple pleasure, her gratitude so humble and true.

It was nothing like the mother-son drive that day with Avery.

Our texts back and forth all night were sad, difficult. He told me at one point that Clay County has a warrant out for his arrest. I called and left that message for his attorney.

Avery made a list of his requests once he was gone.

"Don't write me or visit or call or send anything or be in contact in any way whatsoever."

I slept on the sofa in the living room so I could hear if Avery tried to leave in the night. I skipped my amitriptytline; I had to be ready for anything. But, thankfully, nothing happened.

We went to church the next morning. Avery was still angry at me. As we waited for Ryder, I stood up and walked over to Pastor William. I could feel his compassion across the room. I confessed how awful the week had been. He offered me strength in such a delicate manner.

Ryder told me that Avery felt we were being unfair, that we'd let Ryder get away with more over the years.

"I took the door off and the hinges, pulled everything off on you and Dad. Avery just wants some freedom before he goes away for so long," Ryder said.

"Yes, I get all that, but I'm trying to keep him alive. He's lied about using all week, all month. I've spent at least eight hours, over several days, wondering if he was dead. Lucas's in a coma. Shit happens, and I don't want to lose him. I told Brad I would keep him safe."

I was fried.

We went into the church service and took our seats in the back. Avery and Ryder talked, but I couldn't hear what they were saying. Finally I asked Ryder to step out so I could talk to him. Out in the hall, I sobbed into his chest. I explained again how afraid I was for his brother's safety, and all the lies Avery told me that week. Ryder held me close.

A kind older man came over and gave me a Christian music CD. He told me that God would protect us. It was so caring of him. I went out to the car for a while. Ryder went back into church with Avery. I returned and sat with my eyes closed, holding Ryder's hand, with my head on his shoulder the rest of the service. I inhaled "God's" and exhaled "hands" over and over again.

I got an e-mail from Brad on my phone.

"Hope you all got a chance to go to church together today. Hang in there."

"Yes, it was nice," I responded. Why bother telling him what was actually going on with me? He was on the other side of the earth.

Once we returned home, Avery started back in on me to leave the house.

"Where do you want to go?"

"I have no idea; thought I'd start with the cemetery maybe." He often went to visit my parents' gravesites about three miles from our house.

"I'll take you to the cemetery."

"I'm going to walk there, then hang with someone or be alone. I'm just tired of being in the house. I love you so much, Mom. You can call Gavin, Elle, or Dad; whoever, but I need space."

I finally caved, telling him he did not have permission to leave, but if he did leave I would forgive him and welcome him home. I held his hand to my chest, over my heart, looked him straight in the eyes, and made him swear that he would not take off or use and that he would text every hour that he is safe and sober and that he'd be home before dark. He promised and left about two.

Avery kept true to his word and was texting me at least every half hour. Then at 5:02, I got a text from my sister Ann.

"Are you OK? Paige saw a Facebook post from Avery call if you need me."

I texted back: "No actually I'm horrible have been for over a week. Too tired to discuss."

Moments later, the most intense sense of panic jolted through me. I was certain that he was at the cemetery posting on Facebook before he killed himself. Cortisol was on fire inside my body, exploding every cell. I was completely horror-stricken. After all the atrocious episodes of the last four years, this was oddly the first time I felt that absolutely the worst had happened. I tried to get on Facebook to his page, but it wouldn't allow me.

My legs were melting, as I imagined he'd blocked me so I didn't see his suicidal post. I tried to call him; his phone went to voice mail. I was sure he was at the cemetery attempting suicide for the second time. God in heaven how, why did I let him leave? This is all on me. I'm so weak, so stupid. It felt like a tidal wave of blackness was pulling me under, grief filling my lungs. I sat on the sofa looking at the floor, my hands holding my head. What news was I about to face?

Five minutes later, Avery called me. He could hear the terror in my trembling voice. He felt awful; his phone had been charging. His Facebook post mentioned "voluntarily detaining" himself, which sounded sinister unless you knew his situation and legal terms. He offered to come home from Zach and Laura's, but I said it was okay.

Later I picked him up, and we went out to Applebee's for dinner, just like normal people with manageable lives do.

Jackie sent me a text sending love. Ann had let her know I was in crisis. I'd completely forgotten that Jackie and her family would be in Breckinridge, Minnesota, only thirty miles south of River Bend, the following weekend for her mother-in-law's memorial service. We'd made plans to get together. Thank God; I was desperate to be with my sister.

I did not sleep on the couch that night to make sure Avery didn't leave. And he stayed put.

When the boys were in elementary school, I looked forward to the teacher conferences to hear of their progress. Teachers had similar praise throughout those years, for both boys. "He's so creative, a great imagination, he's kind to everyone, and never spins off in a clique leaving others out. He's got a great vocabulary, very well spoken for his age."

None of them ever said, "I suspect your son has ADD."

They were well behaved, cautious, sweet little boys.

I recall thinking back then, what were the words I most wanted to hear someone use to describe my children? *Kind*? Absolutely. *Creative*? Yes! Yet, all these years later the one word I wanted to hear that described my sons was *alive*.

44

THERE IS NOTHING SUDDEN ABOUT the arrival of spring in North Dakota. It's not like a missing person suddenly entering a room, where one moment they're absent and the next they're standing in front of you. In North Dakota, spring arrives one text at a time, the first to express its plans to arrive at some point, then a parade of quick pokes to indicate that it's making its way. The sun feels warmer, the clocks spring forward, and March winds make a valiant effort to blast winter as far north as possible.

March 2014 rang true to my description as "the teaser" phase of winter. There were only a few days sunny and warm enough to create melting, sloppy, dripping snow. Puddles were everywhere, splashing cars, making them filthy all the way up the windows. March allowed me brief interludes outdoors with temperatures no longer in the life-threatening range.

The last of the autumn leaves were soggy and thawing in corners along the foundation of the house. The smell of wood burning as it trailed from chimneys mixed with the chilly, moist air and reminded me of the winter I'd lived in Eugene, Oregon, when I'd followed a boyfriend out there at twenty-two years old. The lingering promise of winter's tedious exit hung in the atmosphere. It was still cold and wet, but there was anticipation building—a knowing that with the warmth ahead, life would soon break loose. Spring always arrives.

On Monday the twenty-fourth, I got an e-mail from Brad in Tokyo.

"I can put my trip for Tuesday on the board, possibly get rid of it. Actually, probably a pretty good chance it will get dropped. Let me know how things are going and if you think that's necessary."

I responded:

"I'll leave it up to you. The last thirty-six hours have been as difficult emotionally as any I've faced. I don't know if the paperwork for Avery's surrender will be processed tomorrow or not. If it were me there is no amount of money that's worth missing the opportunity to hug my son for the last time in possibly years. Though it may be wrapped by the time you get to River Bend. I have no idea."

I was exhausted, resigned, and waiting to hear how and when Avery would be leaving our home for Cass County Jail. The magnitude of the last six weeks had left me numb from emotional anguish and physical exhaustion. Soon both of our sons would be on the same jail roster. The last time they were on the same roster was their sophomore year: River Bend High boys' tennis team. A lifetime ago, it seemed.

On Tuesday, Jackie called during my commute home to check in about her arrival that weekend. For nearly an hour, I gave her a recap, sobbing through most of it. She'd had no idea what had been going on. I'd only given out occasional bullet points. It had all been too grim to inform others. Once home I went to bed and slept until ten that night, got up and ate, then slept through until morning. My body was trying desperately to recover.

Brad dropped his final trip of the nine-day stretch and arrived home Monday night. He was stressed anyway, and lost wages only added to it. He came home to the piles of bills on his desk and a leaking roof. He knew it would have to be replaced to the tune of $25,000. I avoided him, and I'd wished he'd just stayed on his trip.

Avery remained tame and kept mostly to his bedroom, waiting. We had no idea when he'd be taken away. When I left for work Wednesday morning, I got a few houses away and realized I'd forgotten my phone. I went back into the house and decided to go up to Avery's room to hug him.

"I love you."

"Love you too, Mama."

An hour later, they came to our home and arrested him.

Gavin, his attorney, was livid.

Avery was supposed to have been allowed surrender at the Anderson Law Firm. But why should that step fall into place when everything else had been a mounting pile of mayhem?

The next day was Avery's hearing at the federal courthouse. I was the only one there other than Avery and the cast of professionals required. I was seated when Avery was escorted into the chambers, wearing navy blue scrubs with his wrists handcuffed in front of him. Muscular security officers were on both sides of him, and took a seat behind him. Avery looked at me briefly; he affirmed I was there, then looked down.

The judge, a woman, filling in for Judge Stevens, arrived at last, and we all rose when she entered. Several court reporters, the custody officers, Gavin, and the prosecuting attorney were on one side of the courtroom. I was alone in the otherwise empty row of wooden pews in the "audience" section. Brad had picked up an extra shift at the hospital to try and make up for the trip he'd dropped.

The hearing was meant to ensure that Avery was aware of his rights and that he was willing and mentally stable enough to make the decision to voluntarily detain himself. It is still very hard for me to describe the feelings racing within me: conflicting layers of relief, despair, defeat, and hope for a new beginning. Avery answered appropriately and politely to everything he was asked.

I noticed the prosecuting attorney seemed smug, so I avoided looking in his direction the entire hour that court was in session. Toward the end, the judge looked at me and asked, "Are you Avery's mother?"

I nodded and said yes.

"Is there anything you'd like to say on Avery's behalf?"

I had no idea I might be called on to speak. What flashed through my head was to say as little as possible because I didn't want to say the wrong thing—whatever that might be. So I simply asked her, "Did you read Avery's letter?"

She hadn't seen it yet, so Gavin walked a copy up to her. She asked him if he had a copy for the prosecutor, and he gave him one as well. They both took pause to read it. There were a few more exchanges, and court was adjourned.

As I began to walk to the elevator, I heard my name called; I turned around, and it was Gavin, who was alongside the prosecutor. Gavin asked me if it was okay for the prosecutor to speak to me. I obliged as I felt my stomach shrivel.

I had the feeling he was about to say, "There's no way in hell that punk ass druggy kid of yours wrote that letter," although I didn't actually expect him to use that phrasing. I was prepared to confirm that, yes I'd helped him, a great deal; in fact, I pretty much wrote it, and Avery approved it. But the letter represented his thoughts and feelings 100 percent.

What the prosecutor said left me stunned.

"Your son is very well-spoken. I've found him to be an articulate young man when I've met him on a couple of occasions." He paused and shifted his posture then continued.

"I just have to say, I've been doing this for over thirty years, a very long time. I've seen a great deal over the years, been in this situation many, many times."

My knees began to tremble; I needed to leave. I wanted to be alone; I'd been through enough already.

But I remained still and listened.

"In all those years, I've never read a letter like this. It's excellent, so well-written; well done. As I said, I've been an attorney a long time; I've seen a lot of letters in these situations, and very few have been this well written."

I instantly broke down crying, my quiet way, with shoulders heaving, one hand covering my mouth, the other on my tummy, chin down, tears falling. I was so surprised and grateful to hear his validation of my writing; the power of the words I'd written on Avery's behalf.

The prosecutor felt bad when I started to cry. He made a motion toward me, to hug me, but caught himself and the absurdity of it. Instead he placed his hand on the top of my head, like you see the pope blessing one of his flock. He wanted to console me, but etiquette prevailed. He felt awful and kept apologizing.

I finally gathered myself and said, "Thanks. You cannot imagine how much that means to me. I helped Avery write it."

I took a deep breath.

"All this that happened in our family … it makes no sense. I'm touched by what you said because I'm writing our story. I'm hoping to get it published and that it helps others. I so badly want to put a purpose to our pain."

The prosecutor looked relieved.

Then I concluded, "I hope that when Avery's out of prison, he will join me traveling and speaking to inspire others. To hear you validate my writing, well, it overwhelms me. Thank you; I'm so grateful."

I offered my hand, and we concluded with a handshake.

I left the courthouse and drove to work to put in at least half a day. Brad's shift at the hospital was nine to five, so he was home when I got back from Detroit Lakes. We were officially empty-nesters, and we definitely got there the hard way. We talked for a while. One of Brad's biggest regrets was that we didn't discover their ADD sooner. Once diagnosed, they'd tried Stratera, and they said it didn't work, so we never pursued it further. At that time, they were flunking out of high school, and already doing street drugs. Too little, too late.

Brad had read quite a bit more about the signs and symptoms of ADD, and it described our twins perfectly. All those years before their diagnosis, he'd judged their lack of interest in school as lazy. I'd always related to them; I thought it was normal to hate homework and feel overwhelmed just trying to get Cs on a report card. Would an early diagnosis and treatment have made the difference? We'll never know; there's a lot we'll never know; that's life. I was choosing to trust; it was the only choice that made sense to me. We'd certainly done our best as parents, which is all you can do.

Brad left the next day to fly again, and my sister Jackie, her three children, and their spouses filled our home and my heart with love. Being with them was a jump-start to the healing process I so needed to begin. My sister Kelly and her husband also came for the evening. It was amazing to have them all there on the heels of so much chaos. It calmed my internal raging storm.

I asked them if they'd humor me and allow me to read a chapter from my book. I read only a few of the early chapters, and their faces showed the astonishment of the secrets I'd kept and what I'd been through. They loved it and kept asking for more, another stroke of validation that softly ignited embers of hope.

It was the last day of March. The next day my niece Hailey, in Houston, gave birth to her first baby! New life, a new month, a change of season, a fresh start, and I was ready to turn the page.

45

WITH A SINGLE FLIP OF the calendar page, the first warm spring day arrived in River Bend on April 6, 2014. The earth had been thawing frugally for weeks between March snowstorms. Was the snow melting or the earth emerging? Life was all about perspective. The only remaining snowbanks were peppered with dirt in secluded north-facing corners of buildings. Winter had been a stubborn, annoying leech of a guest, loitering until 4:00 a.m. when the party had ended at midnight.

Spring was the season of emergence, rebirth. No matter how long, dark, barren, and severe winter is, spring will always arrive. The seasons will change, possibilities will emerge, and new life will bloom. I'd learned from a lifetime of spring arrivals to hold on with steadfast hope because nothing lasts forever.

It had been one of the harshest winters in the entire nation. North Dakota had one of its coldest, but it was an underachiever in terms of snow. There would be no sandbagging, nor a single flood headline in the *River Bend Forum*. The stretch of Elm Street along the golf course was never submerged. There had been years that that section of road was closed for over two months because of flooding.

Before I left in the morning to visit Ryder, I stepped out onto our deck and gazed out at the river. All the ice was out except random chunks floating north. Geese had been arriving for weeks back to their summer home. A lone bald eagle, with a majestic wingspan, glided along the treetops that lined the river bank. The landscape was inching out of slumber; the smell of wet thawing earth hung in the damp air. A small fishing boat, with a 9.9-horsepower engine I'm guessing, was trolling along with two fishermen in it. The fishing opener was one month away. The forecast had predicted the first sixty-degree day of the year. Spring was officially here, and my tactile connection with nature could resume!

Ryder and I sat in the last pew among the other inmates attending service at Holy Savior Church. The service began with twenty minutes of contemporary Christian music welcoming the steady flow of people. This week the ushers passed round silver trays specifically designed to hold communion hosts and thimble-sized votives holding a sip's worth of wine. I took communion and passed the tray along. I sat next to Ryder with his arm around me. He looked happier and healthier with each passing Sunday.

"I read from the Bible every night before I go to sleep," he leaned over to tell me. "I like the book of Mark."

"What is it that speaks to you?"

Twelve years of Catholic school, and the only thing I knew about the Bible was how to spell it.

"I guess it's just mostly about that we're all worthy of forgiveness. The past is the past. Jesus forgives us, and we can move on."

"Yes, it's true." I nodded.

"Take the lessons your past has taught you and leave the rest behind," I said.

"I don't know how I'll be able to say no every time I'm tempted to use. It scares me; I'm not gonna lie. I worry how it's all gonna work out."

"That's honest, Ryder, I appreciate that. It's when you start lying to yourself, and to others that you know you're in trouble."

"Yeah, I'm just gonna come straight to you and Dad and tell you what's going on if I ever think I'm at risk of using. I know you'll be there for me."

"Always have been, always will be."

I smiled and leaned my head on his shoulder.

This huge church was filled with worship and hope. I was grateful beyond expression that they welcomed inmates to their house.

"There are a lot of situations in life when the question is how," I whispered to Ryder.

"How will I do it? How will I get through it? How can I survive? I've faced those questions countless times these past years."

I motioned him to look at the notebook I'd brought with me. I knew if he read my words he would remember them better. I had written: "When the question begins with How? the answer is … allow."

He read it, and then looked at me, with those beautiful, clear, gray-blue eyes.

I continued.

"Allow God to guide you, to bring you strength and direction. Listen to the whispers of your intuition. Allow grace by getting your doubts and fears out of the way. We only need to figure out life one moment at a time."

"Thanks, Mom; I love you. I wouldn't be here, anywhere, if it wasn't for you."

"Love you too."

Neither of us could have imagined that our time together would be spent in church. But here we were, looking forward to the remaining Sundays throughout spring and summer until his release. Holy Savior Church had brought the light of Christ into Ryder's heart and Pastor William into our lives.

I left church and drove five miles north to the Cass County Jail for my thirty-minute visit with Avery. My sons would share that roof for most likely three months, sleeping beneath it with no means of saying good night to one another. The night before I'd spoken to Avery; he was excited to see me. Now that he had a solid idea of what lay ahead, he sounded more stable, less emotional about everything, more acclimated to incarceration.

He sat down and picked up the phone on the other side of the glass. There was no animation in his demeanor. I knew he was grateful I was there, but no expression of happiness was evident. I never expected it; an improvement in morale still fell short of it being a good day in his world.

He calculated how much time he was facing based on a federal point system and several potential scenarios. The prosecution was asking for forty months, our team twelve months. Avery speculated the difference would be split. There was a possibility that twelve months would be dropped, assuming he'd be able to complete a federal rehabilitation program within the system. His equation had him out in one year, four seasons. That was manageable, we both felt.

I left the jail on that perfect spring day. It was all the forecast had promised, sunny, calm, sixty-two degrees. Our future was emerging; hope had breath, a pulse, moving parts. I sensed that one day I would look back to this time when my twin sons lived at Cass County Jail, and it would be a part of our journey that made sense on a divine scale. In time both of our sons would complete their sentences, and new chapters from a different genre would be written.

On the drive home, I passed Elephant Park. The March snowbanks that'd been scattered throughout the open soccer fields were now small ponds of water evaporating into the clear spring air. As I drove closer to Elm Street, I could see that the nets had just been put up on the tennis courts since I'd left for church that morning. I caught my breath as joy escaped my heart; outdoor tennis season had officially begun!

I looked into the rearview mirror. I saw a young girl with almond-shaped hazel eyes, long brunette pigtails, and a wooden tennis racquet in her hand. She had dreams for the future, love in her heart, and strength in her spirit. She was brave. I knew she was going to be okay. *Gimme the ball*, I heard her whisper.

I will never know what the future holds for our family. However, I can say for certain that by the grace of God, whatever happens, I will find a way to handle it.

42399069R00169

Made in the USA
Middletown, DE
11 April 2017